STM32 PRACTICAL COOKBOOK WITH DUMMY

The Ultimate Guide to STM32 Development a
Tasty Collection of Recipes for Success

By

Aharen-san

TABLE OF CONTENTS

PWM INPUT DMA

In the STM 32 timer series, and today we will see how to use the PWM input mode. I covered the PWM output in my previous project about the timers. And that's why I decided to go with the PWM input today, we will see how to measure the input frequency and the duty cycle using the PWM input mode. So let's start by creating the project in cube IDE. I am using STM 32 F 446 R E, give some name to the project and click Finish. So first of all, I am selecting the external crystal for the clock. Let's see the clock configuration. Type in the crystal frequency of your controller. Choose this as per your board. Don't just use what I am using my board have eight megahertz crystal, choose the H S E for external crystal choose PCL K for PLL clock, type the frequency you want to run the controller at and hit enter.

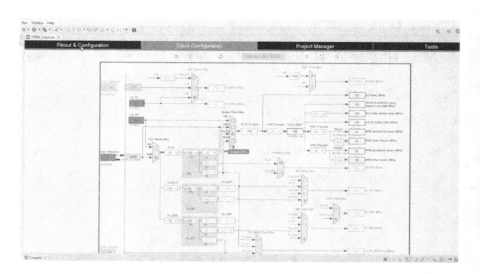

That's all about the clock configuration. Now let's configure the timer. I am choosing timer one to provide the PWM signal PWM output has already been covered on the top right corner timer one is connected to a PV two clock which is running at 180 megahertz, I am choosing the auto reload period of 1800. So the output frequency will be 100 kilohertz This is it for the timer one. Now timer two is going to be used for the PWM input choose the clock sources internal clock and choose the combined channels as PWM input timer to channel one will be our main channel where we will provide the input clock you can see here the pin PA zero got selected. Now comes the parameters. Here I am keeping the prescaler zero. So the timer clock will be same as a PB one and that is 90 megahertz. The auto reload is set to maximum value, this is a 32 bit register. And that's why this value is very high. If you have 16 bit register, this will be 65,535 So leave it to default. Next is the internal clock division. To understand this, we need to check the reference manual. Here in the control register one we have the clock division. This clock division basically sets up the dead time and sampling clock. The DT s clock decides how fast we want to sample the input signal. And here are the settings for the di t s clock. I am keeping it to no division and that means the DTS clock will be same as the internal clock we can skip the rest and come to the channel configuration. Here the input trigger is Ti one F p one which means that the input from Channel One after the filter and polarity selection will be connected to the Capture One next we have is the parameters for channel one. The polarity is set to rising edge which means that this channel is going to measure the rising edges of the signal by sea selection is direct and we will connect the input signal directly to this channel.

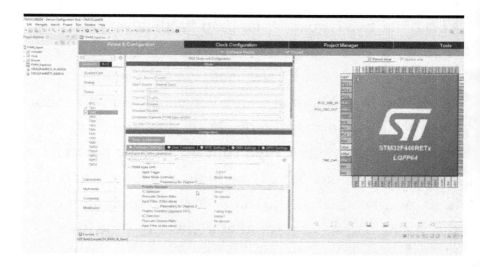

This channel is our main channel and it will measure the frequency. Now for the prescaler division ratio. Let's see the reference manual again. Here we are interested in the capture compare register. We have the input capture prescaler and as you can see, it basically controls the capture frequency. These bits controls how often we want to do the capture. Let me explain In this in detail, let's assume that this is the input clock, and we want to capture the rising edges. A rising edge would be counted as an event. Now suppose we use the prescaler division eight, that would mean that interrupt will trigger after the eight events. And that means here, this will keep happening after every eight events. Remember that if we do the CAPTCHA is of very high frequency, then the interrupts will trigger very often, and this will leave the rest of the code useless. So this is an important parameters, I am going with the highest possible value. And that means the CAPTCHA will be done once every eight events. But the issue is that the cube MX is not letting me choose this one. Don't worry about this, we can set it in the code itself. Next comes the filter. I am not going to use it, but let me explain it anyway. Here we have the input capture filter, the filter configures the frequency at which the input signal will be sampled. It is also used as a low pass filter, but I couldn't find more information on the topic. For now we will keep the filter zero.

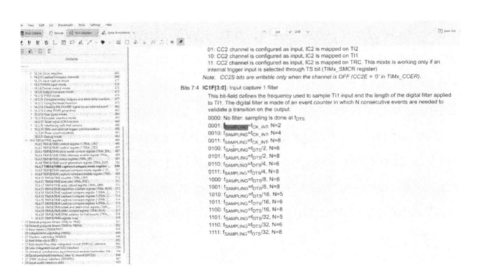

And that means the sampling frequency will be DTS and that is the internal clock. I will update you if I find more information on how to use these filters. Now comes the parameters for channel two, the polarity should be opposite to the first channel, and that's why it's falling edge. The icy selection is indirect and this means we don't need to give the input to this channel. It's internally connected to the channel one and it is used to calculate the duty cycle. All right, let's enable the interrupt for the timer to do this is it for the Setup, click Save to generate the code now. Let's create few variables where we can store the results. Now in the main function, start the timer in input capture mode for channel one. Channel two can be used in the normal mode. Since we only need the interrupt from channel one. After the input capture has been started, we will start the PWM for timer one. And finally set the value of capture compare register for the duty cycle. Everything related to PWM output has been covered in the previous project. So if you don't understand PWM output, Once the input capture actually does the capture and interrupt will be triggered and this input capture callback will be called now we will write the rest of the code inside this callback function. Here we will check if the interrupt was triggered by the channel one that is due to the rising edge of the input signal.

If it is, then we will read the input capture value for the channel one. Then we will read the capture value for the channel two and use it to calculate the duty cycle. I will explain this in a minute. Next calculates the frequency. This 90 megahertz is my time to clock. Now let's understand this calculation. Let's see the PWM input mode in the reference manual. Well we are mainly interested in this figure. Here you can see when the first rising edge is captured, the counter is reset and so do the captures values. When the second rising edge gets captures the capture value read this value is actually this time difference between the first and second edges. So period of the signal. In the callback, we also read the capture value for the falling edge. Using that value, we can determine the pulse height time as a percentage of the total time. This will be the duty cycle for the signal. Similarly, using the clock frequency, we can determine the frequency of the input signal I am just giving this delay in the while loop to test if the control enters the loop or not. All right, let's test this I have added all three variables to the live expression. Okay, you can see the frequency is around 100 kilohertz and the duty is around 50%. Also note that the input capture value is pretty consistent. Let's put a breakpoint in the while loop to check if the control enters the loop. So the loop is also working all right. Since it's working fine for now, let's test the higher frequencies now the auto reload his 450 Making the output frequency 400 kilohertz. And let's change the capture compare to 225 Making the duty cycle 50%. And there we have it around 400 kilohertz frequency and 50% duty cycle. But the wild loop isn't running any more. This is because the interrupts are getting triggered at very high rate making the rest of the code impossible to run this is where the input capture prescaler comes in. Right now it's set to division one, but we will change it to highest and this will make the capture to be performed every eight events let's test this and now you can see the while loop is running pretty well. Let's see how high can we measure with this setup this time the auto reload is 180 Making the frequency equal to one megahertz. Let's change the capture compared to 60. So the duty cycle will be 33%. I would say the result is approximately correct. The frequency is around one megahertz and the duty is 31%. The while loop is still running so we can test even higher range. Now the frequency will be two megahertz and the capture compare is still 60 Making the duty cycle equal to 66%. This is still working all right. Surprisingly, the while loop is still running. Honestly, I wasn't expecting it. But let's go even higher. Now the auto reload is 60 Making the frequency equal to three megahertz and I am keeping the auto reload at 30. So the duty would be 50%. Here we do have approximate to what we need. But the while loop is not running any more. I guess this is the limit for the while loop with the current setup. Even though it was able to measure the two megahertz clocks, I would suggest that you keep the measurement below one megahertz. For those frequencies, the rest of the code can run pretty well too. If you want to measure high frequencies well Lynnae won't be able to run the rest of the code, you can play with some other settings to improve the accuracy of the frequency measure. Before finishing this project, I want to share one more thing. It's quite possible to measure the high frequencies also. In fact, I did some tests and you can see the result in the picture. The accuracy even at 10 megahertz frequency is quite phenomenal. This is a different method by the way, I was able to measure up to 18 megahertz input frequencies, and even then the while loop was still able to run.

ENCODER MODE F103C8

Which covered the encoder STM 32. Using the simple GPIO pins, it was working fine, but as few users pointed out that it would have been better to use the timer feature. So this project covers the STM 32 timer in encoder mode basically, and I will use the same encoder here also, So let's start with the encoder first.

I have this encoder here, and it's rotary as you can rotate the shaft the shaft is free to rotate in either direction, as there is no limit on the rotation have five pins, but we are interested in the bottom two pins. The pin names do not justify their functions. So we will call the clock pin is pin A and D T pin is pin B. The middle one is the switch and it represents the push button on the shaft. That's it about the encoder. Now let's see how it works. I got this gift from the Wikipedia and it shows exactly what happens. Think of the black region as ground and white region as VCC. So it starts with both the pins in contact with the white region. So both of the pins are high. Now let's say we move the shaft clockwise, so the outer pin goes low, while the inner one is still high. Now the inner pin goes low and both the pins are low. And now they are going back to high again. If we move it counterclockwise, the inner pin goes low first, then the outer one. And then they both goes back to high. This is the entire working. Basically, we just have to check which pin goes live first, and based on that we can figure out whether the shaft moved clockwise or counterclockwise. Let's see one more time with the logic analyzer. Here I have connected the channels to the pin A and pin V supply is five volts. Let's start this pay attention I am rotating the shaft counterclockwise.

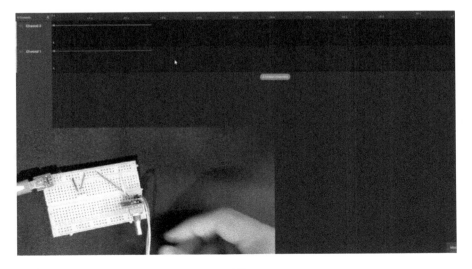

Here we got the signal on both pins. Let's zoom in. We have some unwanted signals here, but we will take care of them in the code itself. Let's focus on the main part. As you can see here, the first pin goes low and after some time, the second one goes low now I am rotating it in the other direction. This time the second one goes to low first and after some time, the first one goes low. This is exactly what's shown in this animation. This is the entire working of this encoder and we will use these pins to identify the direction of rotation. Now let's see the timer part. Here is the reference manual for f 103 controller and I am choosing the general purpose timers for this function. Here we have the encoder mode. You can go through this explanation. I'll just get to the point and that is this particular figure. Here you can see we have signal on the two different channels as we have two outputs from the encoder. Notice that if the T one goes too high first and then T two the counter will start counting upward. As long as both the signals have rise and fall, the counter will keep updating. But in case of a jitter, only one of the signals will change and in that case the counter will not update. And if the T two goes too high before T one, the counter will start counting down. This will indicate that the movement is in opposite direction.

Figure 134. Example of counter operation in encoder interface mode

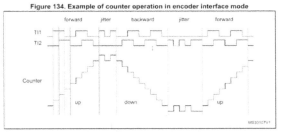

Figure 135 gives an example of counter behavior when TI1FP1 polarity is inverted (same configuration as above except CC1P=1).

Figure 135. Example of encoder interface mode with TI1FP1 polarity inverted

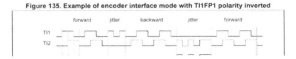

Again in case of jitters, the counter will not update at all. This is pretty convenient considering what we did in the last project to get rid of these jitters. Let's keep this in mind and create a new project I will be using the same f 103 controller enable the external crystal for the clock. I have eight megahertz Crystal and I want the system to run at maximum 72 megahertz I am using time a two for the encoder. Here we will use the combined channels and select encoder mode. You see the pins P A zero and P A one got selected. Keep in mind that do not use any prescaler value here or else it won't work. Let's keep the auto reload to maximum value which is 65,535. Encoder mode will be both T one and T two as we will be using two inputs. Let's change this to falling edge polarity as you saw in the first half. That's how this encoder sends the signal. I tested it with rising edge also and somehow it was working all right. Enable the timer interrupt as we will perform this entire operation in the interrupt service routine. That's it. Now click Save to generate the project. Here I have the encoder connected with the pins pa zero and Pa one and it is powered by 3.3 volts. Let's start the encoder in the I T mode. Here we have the channel parameter. Let's see what we need to input in this. As mentioned here, for two channels, we must use channel all. Now once the encoder sends the signals, the interrupt will be called and we will use the input capture callback for the ISR. The encode mode is the input capture in a way. Here we will go one step at a time. Let's start with reading the counter value only. Some people have confusion with this htm. Actually, since we are calling this function inside the ISR, so whatever time I have called ISR, the same time a handler will be used here. That's why I prefer to keep it this way. Let's test this much part first and see what counter values do we get. By M rotating the encoder in clockwise direction, one click at a time the counter increased by four second click and it is eight now. Now there are totally five clicks and the counter is 20. This means the counter is increasing four counts per click on average. Now I am rotating in counterclockwise direction. And again one click at a time. You see the counter is decreasing in counterclockwise direction, just like it's mentioned in the manual. Also the four counts per click is quite persistent. I can't say for sure. But maybe that's why it's shown four counts here also. Anyway, if you try this and find that the counter is not increasing by four counts,

18

let me know in the comments. I tried with other MC use that I have and it was always fun accounts, this is fine. But there is one more thing if the counter goes below zero, it will underflow and start from the auto reload value again, we need to tackle this situation and to do so, I am defining a sign 16 bit integer now, we will typecast the counter and store the value in this variable let's check the result now the things are working fine, you can have the negative values if you want them still, we are getting four counts per click, and I would prefer the number of clicks over the count let's create another variable position and this will just be count divided by four. This way for every four counts the position variable will be updated notice the movement is clockwise and the position is increasing. Also, the position is around 1/4 of the count value. And now a counter clockwise movement will decrease the position. This is very easy to deal with. And the results are very accurate to I just want to add one more thing here. And that's the speed. I haven't tested this path properly. So I can't say that it will work for sure. But it seems pretty okay to me and you can see how I am approaching it. In this case, we will do the calculations in the interrupt file the position is defined in the main file bold position is off course the old position data speed is also defined in the main file and index is to keep track of milliseconds.

```
179
180      /* USER CODE END PendSV_IRQn 0 */
181      /* USER CODE BEGIN PendSV_IRQn 1 */
182
183      /* USER CODE END PendSV_IRQn 1 */
184  }
185
186 /**
187   * @brief This function handles System tick timer.
188   */
189 void SysTick_Handler(void)
190 {
191      /* USER CODE BEGIN SysTick_IRQn 0 */
192
193      /* USER CODE END SysTick_IRQn 0 */
194      HAL_IncTick();
195      /* USER CODE BEGIN SysTick_IRQn 1 */
196
197      /* USER CODE END SysTick_IRQn 1 */
198  }
199
200 /******************************************************************************/
201 /* STM32F1xx Peripheral Interrupt Handlers                                    */
202 /* Add here the Interrupt Handlers for the used peripherals.                  */
203 /* For the available peripheral interrupt handler names,                      */
204 /* please refer to the startup file (startup_stm32f1xx.s).                    */
205 /******************************************************************************/
206
207 /**
208   * @brief This function handles TIM2 global interrupt.
```

The SysTick handler is called every one millisecond and inside it we will update the index variable. Once the 500 milliseconds have passed, we will calculate the speed you can reduce this time if you want more frequent updates on speed. Speed is basically be how much difference is there in the old and new positions in one second. I am multiplying by two because this code will be executed every 500 milliseconds, and therefore it will give speed every 500 milliseconds. But we want it every second. So the speed into to this will give us the speed in clicks like how many clicks per second, we will then update the old position and reset the index. You can convert these clicks to rpm or something based on how your encoder works. For me, I have found out that it takes 20 clicks per revolution this should be 16 bit integer here. That's how it's defined in the main file let's see the working now. Let's start it slow. The speed is around 20 clicks per second. And now I am going faster and the speed is around 70 clicks per second. We have speed in the negative direction also. I would say this is pretty good. Like I said one revolution takes around 20 clicks and I think I'm making around three and a half revolutions per second. As I mentioned earlier, I am not sure if this is correct.

EXAMPLE DUMMY CODE

```
#include "stm32f4xx_hal.h"

void pwm_input_dma(void) {
    // Initialize the timer and DMA.
    TIM_HandleTypeDef htim;
    DMA_HandleTypeDef hdma;

    // Configure the timer for PWM input mode.
    htim.Instance = TIM1;
    htim.Init.Prescaler = 84; // 84 MHz / 84 = 1 kHz
    htim.Init.CounterMode =
TIM_COUNTERMODE_UP;
    htim.Init.Period = 1000; // 1 kHz / 1000 = 1 ms
    htim.Init.ClockDivision =
TIM_CLOCKDIVISION_DIV1;
    HAL_TIM_Base_Init(&htim);
```

```c
  // Configure the DMA to transfer the timer's
capture value to a buffer.
  hdma.Instance = DMA1_Channel1;
  hdma.Init.Direction =
DMA_PERIPH_TO_MEMORY;
  hdma.Init.SourceAddress =
(uint32_t)&htim.Instance->CCR1;
  hdma.Init.BufferSize = 1;
  hdma.Init.Mode = DMA_CIRCULAR;
  HAL_DMA_Init(&hdma);

  // Start the timer and DMA.
  HAL_TIM_Base_Start(&htim);
  HAL_DMA_Start(&hdma,
(uint32_t)&htim.Instance->CCR1,
(uint32_t)buffer, 1);

  // Wait for the DMA to complete.
  while (HAL_DMA_GetState(&hdma) !=
HAL_DMA_STATE_TRANSFER_COMPLETE) {
  }

  // Print the captured value.
  printf("Captured value: %d\n", *buffer);
}

int main(void) {
```

```c
// Initialize the HAL library.
HAL_Init();

// Call the PWM input DMA function.
pwm_input_dma();

// Infinite loop.
while (1) {
}
}
```

This code will first initialize the timer and DMA. Then, it will configure the timer for PWM input mode and the DMA to transfer the timer's capture value to a buffer. Finally, it will start the timer and DMA, and wait for the DMA to complete. Once the DMA is complete, the code will print the captured value.

To run this code, you will need to have a development board with an STM32F4 microcontroller. You can also use an emulator, such as STM32CubeIDE. Once you have the code compiled and loaded onto the board, you can run it by pressing the reset button.

INPUT CAPTURE FREQUENCY AND WIDTH

And we will create a new project in cube ID. I am using STM 32 F 446 r e controller give some name to the project and click Finish. Here is our cube MX The first thing we will do is select the external high speed crystal for the clock. I have eight megahertz crystal on the board and I want the controller to run at maximum 180 megahertz frequency. Make sure you input the correct crystal frequency as for your board now I am going to use the timer one for the PWM output which I will then measure with the timer to using the input capture.

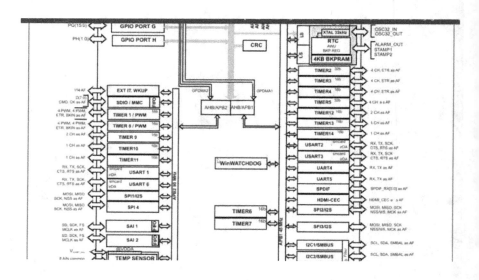

Enable the PWM generation with timer one. If we check the datasheet of the controller here, it's shown that the timer one is connected to the APB two clock as per our clock set up, the AP v two timer clock is running at 180 megahertz. Also the timer two is connected to the APB one clock, which is running at the 90 megahertz. Just keep this in mind while we set up the parameters for the timers. Let's start with the timer one. Right now the timer clock is running at 180 megahertz. And if we use the prescaler of 180, this clock will come down to one megahertz. I am further using the auto reload of 100 which would bring the PWM frequency to 10 kilohertz. This is already explained in the PWM output project. And if you don't understand it, That's it for the PWM output. Now we will configure the timer to select the clock sources internal clock, enable the input capture direct mode. If you remember the APB one clock is running at 90 megahertz. So using a prescaler of 90 will bring it down to one megahertz. This will be our timer clock frequency. I am leaving everything else to default here. If you want to know more about these parameters, watch the PWM input project. I have explained everything in that one. Note here that the polarity selection is set to a rising edge by default. Also I am not using any prescaler division. Now the last thing we need to do is enable the timer to interrupt. This is it for the setup. Click Save to generate the project. Here is our main file. Timer one will be responsible for producing the PWM signal and we have the auto reload period of 100. Here I am using the CAPTCHA compare value of 50. So the duty will be 50%.

Let's start the timer one in PWM mode. Now we will start the input capture in the interrupt mode for timer to. Once the rising edge is detected, the interrupt will be triggered and the input capture callback will be called Let's define few variables that we are going to use in this tutorial. First I am going to measure the frequency this is the code for the same let's go through it first we will check if the interrupt is triggered by the channel one if the first reading hasn't been captured, we will capture the first value and this is basically the counter reading for the first rising edge. Now we will set the first capture to one when the second rising edge comes the interrupt will be triggered and this time it will capture the reading for the second rising edge. Now we will calculate the difference between the two readings if there is overflow, we will get the difference backwards. The timer to in my case is 32 Big timer and that's why I am using 32 bit value here. Next step is to calculate the reference clock. This is something you need to define yourself Timer Clock is the frequency of the timer to which in my case is 90 megahertz, we also need to define the prescaler I have set it to 90 during the setup process you can check it here so it will calculate the reference clock based on the parameters and finally the frequency will be referenced clock divided by the difference value.

In the end we will reset the counter let's build it wants to check for any errors all right we are good to go the timer one is producing the PWM signal at a frequency of 10 kilohertz and here we got the result of 10 kilohertz from the input capture the while loop also runs pretty well I am going to add some delay here to test the while loop a little better let's modify the timer one prescaler and now the output frequency will be 100 kilohertz let's see if the input capture is able to measure it all right here you can see the 100 kilohertz and the while loop is still running pretty well all right we will go a little more higher and this time the output frequency will be 200 kilohertz you can see it's able to measure it pretty well. our while loop is still operational fine, we will increase it a bit more. Now the output frequencies 300 kilohertz now it have started showing errors. So this particular method is good for measuring frequencies up to few 100 kilohertz. If you want to measure higher frequencies, I will release another project using the DMA. So we were able to measure the input frequency using the rising edge triggers. Now we will see how to measure the width of the signal I will comment out this frequency code and we will write another one for measuring the width most of it will be similar to the frequency one. So, I am just using the same code and I will edit it in a while. To measure the width of the signal, we have to measure the time between the rising edge and the falling edge. So, here we want the interrupts to trigger in both cases. To do so, we will change the polarity to both edges when the rising edge will trigger the interrupt the counter value will be stored in the IC value one and similarly, I see value two will store the counter value for the falling edge, then we will measure the time difference between the two values. This difference in time will depend on the input capture timer configuration. This is why we need to add a little code here to change it to microseconds irrespective of the time or configuration you are using. Now, this microsecond width will always show the width of the signal in microseconds. Next test it if you notice here, our PWM timer is running at one megahertz clock. This means each count of the counter will take one microsecond if we are using the capture compare value of 20 the signal should be high for 20 microseconds. Here you can see we got the 20 microseconds whipped for it let's modify the timer prescaler and now it's running a 10 megahertz clock. Now each count in the counter takes 0.1 microsecond and we still have the capture compare value of 20. So the signal high time should be two microseconds. As you can see it here. That's exactly what we got. So the input capture works for measuring the frequency and the signal with you should use it to measure lower frequencies only up to few 100 kilohertz.

EXAMPLE DUMMY CODE

Implementing Input Capture Frequency and Width measurement typically involves using hardware timers and interrupts, which might vary based on the microcontroller or platform you are using. Below is an example of how you can measure the frequency and pulse width using Arduino's Timer1 on an Arduino board:

```
const int inputPin = 2;  // Input pin for the signal
you want to measure

volatile unsigned long pulseStart;  // Stores the
timestamp of pulse start
volatile unsigned long pulseEnd;    // Stores the
timestamp of pulse end
volatile bool pulseDetected = false; // Flag to
```

indicate a pulse has been detected

```
void setup() {
  Serial.begin(9600);
  pinMode(inputPin, INPUT);

  // Configure Timer1
  noInterrupts();  // Disable interrupts during
configuration

  // Set Timer1 to normal mode (no prescaler)
  TCCR1A = 0;
  TCCR1B = 0;
  TCNT1 = 0;

  // Enable input capture interrupt
  TCCR1B |= (1 << ICES1);  // Capture on rising edge
  TIFR1 |= (1 << ICF1);    // Clear Input Capture Flag
  TIMSK1 |= (1 << ICIE1);  // Enable Input Capture
Interrupt

  interrupts();  // Enable interrupts after
configuration
}

void loop() {
  if (pulseDetected) {
    // Calculate pulse width and frequency
```

```cpp
    unsigned long pulseWidth = pulseEnd -
pulseStart;
    unsigned long frequency = 1000000UL /
pulseWidth; // Frequency in Hz

    // Print results
    Serial.print("Pulse Width: ");
    Serial.print(pulseWidth);
    Serial.print(" microseconds, Frequency: ");
    Serial.print(frequency);
    Serial.println(" Hz");

    pulseDetected = false; // Reset the pulse
detection flag
  }
}

// Interrupt service routine for input capture
ISR(TIMER1_CAPT_vect) {
  if (bit_is_set(TCCR1B, ICES1)) {
    // Capture on rising edge, store the timestamp
    pulseStart = ICR1;
    TCCR1B &= ~(1 << ICES1); // Switch to capture
on falling edge
  } else {
    // Capture on falling edge, store the timestamp
and set the flag
    pulseEnd = ICR1;
```

```
    TCCR1B |= (1 << ICES1);  // Switch to capture on
rising edge
    pulseDetected = true;    // Set the pulse
detection flag
  }
}
```

In this example, Timer1's Input Capture feature is used to measure the frequency and width of the signal connected to pin 2. When a rising edge is detected, the ISR (Interrupt Service Routine) stores the timestamp in pulseStart. When the falling edge is detected, it stores the timestamp in pulseEnd and sets the pulseDetected flag to true. The main loop then calculates the pulse width and frequency and prints the results to the Serial Monitor.

Please note that this example is specifically for Arduino boards using Timer1. If you are using a different microcontroller or platform, the timer configurations and interrupt handling might be different. Always refer to the datasheet and documentation of your specific microcontroller for accurate information and implementation details.

TIMER SYNCHRONIZATION 3 PHASE PWM

Today we will continue with another application of the timer synchronization. We saw how the master timer can control the start of the counter of the slave Timer by using the slave mode along with the trigger mode. There was however, a restriction the slave counter could start only when the master counter overflows. Today we will see how the master timer can issue a trigger signal when it reaches a predefined value. And by making use of this feature, we will generate a three phase PWM signal. Basically the signal will be generated when the counter reaches 33% of its value. This is the point where the timer two will start counting and it will also generate a signal when it reaches 33% of its value. Then the timer three will start counting. Since all the timers will have the same frequency and duty we will be able to generate three PWM signals which will be 120 degrees out of phase with each other. Here you can see the internal trigger connection which you can find in the reference manual of your controller. This is the table for f 446 r e controller.

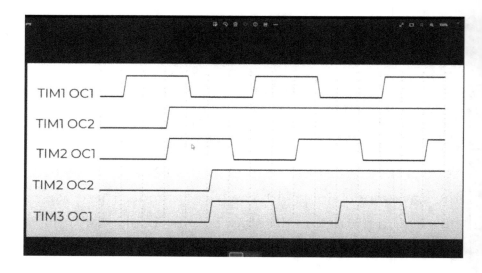

You can see the timer two can be controlled by timer one by using the ITR zero signal. Similarly, the timer three can be controlled by the timer two by using the ITR one signal. This table might be different for your controller, so you must look in the reference manual of your controller. This is the picture I took from one of the STS projects. Here you can see how this whole system will work. Basically, the timer one will generate a PWM signal and when the counter reaches the 33% of its value, its output compare signal will go Hi, this is where the ITR zero signal will be issued, and the timer two will start counting from this point. When the timer two's counter reaches 33% of its value, its output compare signal will also go high. And this is the point where the timer two will generate the ITR one signal and the timer three will start counting from this point. Let's start the cube ID and create a new project. I am using the nucleo F 446 r e controller give some name

to the project and click Finish. Let's set up the clocks. First.
I am selecting the external crystal to provide the clock.
The board has eight megahertz crystal on it and I want to
run the system at 90 megahertz frequency. I am choosing
90 Because that's the maximum clock at which the APB
one time a clock and run it. And I want both the APB
buses to run at the same frequency so that we could use
the same configuration for all three timers. Let's configure
the timers. Now.

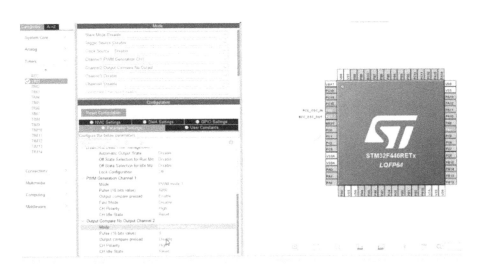

Timer one is going to be the master for timer two. Here
we will generate the PWM signal on channel one. Also
output compare with no output on channel two as this
will be used for the internal trigger. Let's configure the
PWM frequency and duty cycle the timer is running at 90
megahertz. So a prescaler of 90 will bring down the
frequency to one megahertz, then the auto reload of

10,000 will further reduce the frequency to 100 Hertz. Now for the trigger event selection we will go with the output compare for channel two. This OC two ref is used as the trigger signal and it will trigger the timer to hear I am setting the PWM signal duty cycle at 40%. For the output compare, change the mode to active level on match. This will basically activate the signal once the counter value matches the compare value. And this compare value we will set it at 33% of the auto reload value. This is it for the timer one let's configure the timer two now. Timer two will act as a slave for timer one and master for timer three. We will use the trigger mode so that the counter starts counting once the ITR zero signal is received by the timer. The rest of the configuration is exactly the same as the timer one. So basically the timer to counter will start upon receiving the signal from the timer one. Once the counter reaches 33% of the auto reload value, the output compare signal will go high, which will generate the I T r one event. And now we will configure the timer three, which is a slave to the timer to and can be controlled by using the ITR one trigger, we don't need to generate the output compare for timer three and the rest of the configuration is the same as that of the other timers. Here these three PWM output pins are connected to the logic analyzer. Let's save the project to generate the code there is not much in the coding part, we just have to start the PWM for channel one and output compare for channel two. We will only enable the

PWM for timer three as we have not set the output compare for this.

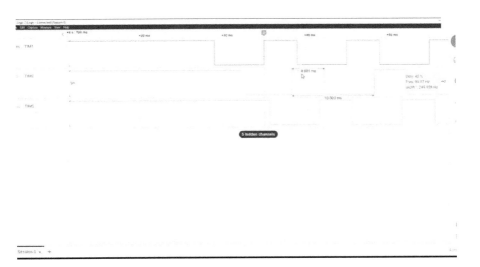

That's it for the code part, let's build and flash it to the board. I am using the logic analyzer to see the output of the PWM let me reset the board once we will start at the first rising edge of the timer one output. I am setting two more markers for the timer two and three. Now in the measurement, set the first marker as the t zero you can see the timestamps of the other markers compared to the first one. Note that all three PWM have the same frequency of 100 hertz, so the period is 10 milliseconds. Now you can see the second PWM starts at 3.3 milliseconds, and the third one starts at 6.6 milliseconds. If you convert this time to angles, you could observe the 120 degrees phase difference between these waves this phase difference will remain constant. So if you had more markers anywhere on the waves, you could still see the same time difference between them. So we saw how to generate a three phase PWM signal using the timer synchronization technique. I hope you understood the process.

CASCADING TIMERS EXTERNAL CLOCK MODE RESET MODE

And today we will continue with another application of the timer synchronization. We will see how to cascade the timers in series and by doing this we can combine 3 16 bit timers into a 48 bit timer. Basically in cascade, the frequency of one timer will be used as the clock for another timer. This can be achieved by using the update event as the master timer output signal along with external clock mode for the slave timer. The project was going to be very long, so I have decided to split them into two parts. This project will basically cover the slave timer in the external clock mode. Also, we will see the reset mode towards the end of the project. And in the next project, we will make a 48 bit counter using three timers and we will also see its application. So let's start the cube ID and create a new project. I am using the STM 32 F 446 R II give some name to the project and click Finish. First of all, I am selecting the external crystal to provide the clock to the MCU the board has eight megahertz Crystal and I want to run the controller at 90 megahertz. I am choosing 90 megahertz because I want all the timers to have the same clock speed and APB to timer clock can run at a maximum of 90 megahertz. The clock setup is done. So let's start setting the timers. Now. Timer one is going to be the master timer. Here I am enabling the PWM on channel one, so that we can see the output of timer one. Right now the timer clock is at 90 megahertz. So the prescaler of 90 would bring the clock down to one megahertz. The auto reload of 100 would further reduce the timer frequency to 10 kilohertz. The trigger event should be selected as the update event. Basically when the counter will reach the auto reload value of 100. This update event will get triggered and if we use the Update event in combination with the external clock mode or gated mode, the output frequency of this timer can be used as the clock for the slave timer. Since the auto reload is 100 If I keep the pulse at 40, there will be the PWM signal with 40% duty cycle. Let's quickly see what we have configured so far. The timer one output frequency will be APB Timer Clock divided by the prescaler times the auto reload value and this will be equal to 10 kilohertz. Now we will configure the timer to let's see the internal trigger connection diagram you can find it in the reference manual of your controller. Here you can see the timer two can be a slave to timer one, and it will be triggered by the

ITR zero. Similarly the timer three can be triggered by the timer to via the ITR one signal. Let's configure the timer to now.

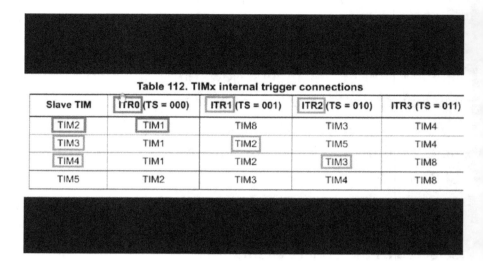

Table 112. TIMx internal trigger connections

Slave TIM	ITR0 (TS = 000)	ITR1 (TS = 001)	ITR2 (TS = 010)	ITR3 (TS = 011)
TIM2	TIM1	TIM8	TIM3	TIM4
TIM3	TIM1	TIM2	TIM5	TIM4
TIM4	TIM1	TIM2	TIM3	TIM8
TIM5	TIM2	TIM3	TIM4	TIM8

The slave mode will be the external clock mode and the trigger source will be ITR zero. I am selecting the PWM on channel one so that we can see the output of this timer. Now as I mentioned, when the update event is used with a combination of the external clock mode, the timer ones output frequency will act as the input clock for the timer to timer two's frequency will be equal to input clock divided by the prescaler times the auto reload. The timer one frequency is 10 kilohertz and if we use the prescaler one an auto reload of 100 the timer TOS frequency will be 100 hertz so let's configure the prescaler as one and the auto reload is 100 I am keeping the pulse at 40. So the PWM duty cycle will be 40%. This timer to is a slave to timer one and master to timer three. So we also need to enable the trigger event selection as the update event. Now the timer three will also have the similar configuration accepted the trigger sources from timer two. So I try one timer three frequency will be calculated in the similar manner.

$$\text{Tim 1 Freq} = \frac{90 \times 10^6}{90 \times 100} = 10000 \, Hz$$

$$\text{Tim2 Freq} = \frac{\text{Tim1 Freq}}{PR \times ARR}$$

$$= \frac{10000}{1 \times 100} = 100 \, Hz$$

$$\text{Tim3 Freq} = \frac{\text{Tim2 Freq}}{PR \times ARR}$$

$$= \frac{100}{1 \times 10} = 10 \, Hz$$

And if I use the auto reload of 10 the frequency will be 10 hertz Now since the auto reload is set to 10, I am keeping the pulse at four so that we could get the duty cycle of 40%. Now all three timers are set with timer one running at 10 kilohertz timer to at 100 hertz and timer three at 10 Hertz. Click Save to generate the code there is not much to do in the programming part, we will just start the PWM for all three timers. All right, let's build and flash the code to the board. I have connected the PWM pins to the logic analyzer. Here we are getting the output from each timer.

Let's analyze it now. Here you can see the timer one with 10 kilohertz frequency and 40% duty cycle the timer two is running at 100 hertz with 40% duty and timer three is a 10 hertz with 40% duty. This is as per the calculations we did earlier. So we saw how the frequency of one timer can be used as the clock for the second timer. Using this we will cascade three timers and make a 48 bit counter so that we can read a wide range of frequencies. This will be covered in the next project. Let's take a look at the reset mode. Now. Here I have already configured the timers I have disabled timer one and timer two is now in the Master Mode with PWM enabled on channel one, it is being clocked by the APB clock. So the base frequency is at 90 megahertz. The auto reload value of 10,000 will reduce the clock to nine kilohertz also I am keeping the duty at 40. So with the auto reload value being 10,000 This is equivalent to 0.4%. Here is the calculation for the timer to output frequency. Also the trigger event is set to update event. Now the timer three is the slave to timer two and is being used in the reset mode. In reset mode, whenever the update event is triggered, it will reset the counter of the slave timer. The trigger signal is coming from timer two so it is set to ITR one. As I mentioned, when the update event is used with the reset mode or trigger mode, all the timers will be clocked by the APB clock. Unlike the previous case, where the frequency of the master timer served as the clock for the slave timer. Here I have set the auto reload of 1234. The timer clock was 90 megahertz and now it is around 73 kilohertz, the pulse is set to 300 which is approximately 24% of the auto reload value. This is it for the Setup, click Save to generate the code, the code will remain the same just comment out the timer one as it is not being used. Let's build and flash the code. Here we are getting the PWM output for both the timers you can see the timer two has the frequency of nine kilohertz and duty is around 0.4%. Timer three has the frequency of around 73 kilohertz with the duty around 24%. Let's zoom in to understand what's happening. If you check the width of the timer three signal it is around three or 3.5 microseconds. The data is a little bit inconsistent because I can't use higher sampling rate with this logic analyzer. But this is enough for us to understand how reset mode works. So the width is either three or 3.5 microseconds except at this point.

Here it is five microseconds. So what happens here, if you have seen my PWM project, you would know that this is the point where the overflow occurs in the timer to when this happens, an update event gets triggered and the counter of timer three resets at this point. Basically here the counter of timer three overflowed and then it started counting up while doing so another RESET signal came and the counter resets back to zero and again starts counting up. If you measure the time from here till the signal goes slow, it will be approximately the same as the others. This 3.5 microseconds is the actual width of this PWM signal, we can calculate the similar thing at any other point, and it will give us the time equal to the width of the signal. So, you saw how the reset mode is used to reset the counter of the slave timer. In this case, the trigger source was used as the ITR one. So, the timer two was responsible for this reset, but you can also use some external signal to do this reset. We will see that in the upcoming projects. One more thing you noticed that when using the trigger mode, the APB clock was used as the timer clock.

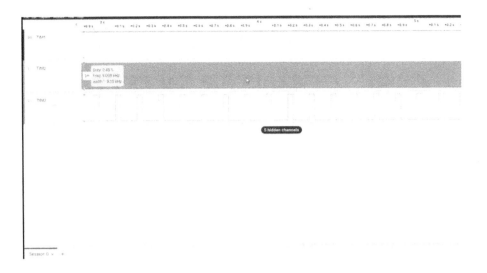

But if I switch it to the external clock mode, now the timer TOS frequency will be used as the clock for timer three. Let's quickly see the output of this here you can see the frequency has been reduced significantly. This is because now nine kilohertz is being used as the input clock rather than 90 megahertz in the reset mode. So I hope this project was able to explain the difference between the external clock mode and the reset mode.

CASCADING TIMERS MAKE 48BIT COUNTER EXTERNAL CLOCK MODE

This is the continuation of the STM 32 timer series, and we will continue with the timer synchronization. we will discuss how to cascade the timers together and make a bigger counter than the default 16 bit. The project title says making a 48 bit counter, but actually you can make the counter however big you want. Depending on the number of timers you have, you must watch the previous project to understand how the cascading works for these timers. The project is in the top right corner, we will first see what is the need for such a big counter. Let's assume our APB Timer Clock is at 90 megahertz and we use the prescaler of nine to bring it down to 10 megahertz, this 10 megahertz is counter frequency basically the counter will be counting at this rate.

40 MHz $\qquad$ PSC = 9

$$\text{Counter freq} = \frac{40MHz}{9} = 10 MHz \longrightarrow \boxed{\text{lowest freq}}$$

$$\text{Each count takes} = \frac{1}{10MHz} = 0.1 uS \boxed{\text{*Highest}}$$

16 bit counter , ARR = 65535

$$\text{Counter Period} = 65535 \times 0.1 us = 6.5 mS$$

$$\text{Highest freq} = \frac{1}{6.5mS} = 150 Hz$$

This means each count in the counter will take 0.1 microseconds. Now most of the time has an STM 32 or 16 bit in size. So the maximum auto reload value we can set is 65,535 this is the maximum number of counts the counter can count. This makes the period of the counter equal to 6.5 milliseconds. And the lowest frequency we can measure with this counter will be 150 hertz. So ideally, the counter can measure the highest frequency of 10 megahertz and lowest of 150 Hertz. Obviously it cannot measure 10 megahertz due to the limitations like interrupt processing time, but let's assume for now that it is possible. Now the problem is how do we measure even lower frequencies like 100 hertz or 50 hertz or even lower ones like one hertz. Of course, you can reduce time a clock by increasing prescaler but then it will also reduce the highest frequency you can measure. The issue can be resolved by using a larger counter. Say for example, if we had a 48 bit counter, we could get the auto reload value of 65,535 cube. The counter is still running at 10 megahertz, but the maximum number of counts have been increased now and so it can measure even the very low frequencies. We will achieve this by cascading the timer's together. So depending on how many times you can cascade you can make the counter as big as you want. Let's start the cube ID and create a new project. I am using STM 32 F 446 R E, give some name to the project and click Finish. First of all I am selecting an external crystal to provide the clock. The board has eight megahertz crystal on it, and I want the system to run at 180 megahertz. Let's configure the timer's now, I am configuring the timer one in the input capture mode so that we can measure the input signal. The pin P a TT will be used as the input pin for the signal. Actually, since I gave you the example with a PB clock, the 90 megahertz let's change the system clock to 90 megahertz. The APB two timer clock is at 90 megahertz now and the timer one is connected to it. So the timer one is also running at 90 megahertz. Let's use the prescaler of nine This will bring the clock down to 10 megahertz also I am using the auto reload value of 10,000. I will show the calculation in a while the timer one is the master timer. So we will enable the trigger event selection to update event. Here is the configuration for the input capture and I am leaving it as it is let's understand the calculation now. The counter one frequency is 10 megahertz right now.

$$\text{CNT1 Freq} = \frac{90\text{MHz}}{9} = 10\text{MHz}$$

$$\text{Each Count takes} \frac{1}{10\text{MHz}} = 0.1\text{uS}$$

CNT1 has Period of 10000x0.1uS = 1mS

$$\text{TIM1 Output Freq} = \frac{90\text{MHz}}{9 \times 10000} = 1\text{KHz}$$

This means that each count in the counter one takes 0.1 microseconds, I have set the auto reload value to 10,000. So the counter one will have a period of one millisecond. This means the counter one can measure the signal whose period is between 0.1 microseconds to one millisecond. Of course 0.1 microsecond is an ideal case, and it's not possible for this microcontroller to measure it. Now for the signals with a period more than one millisecond. We will cascade another timer with this one I am configuring the timer three for this purpose. Timer three will be configured in the slave mode, and that two in the external clock mode one, the trigger source will be from the timer one, so we will set it to ITR zero. Now the timer one output frequency will be equal to APB Timer Clock divided by the prescaler times the auto reload value. This will be equal to one kilohertz timer three will be clocked by this frequency band if we keep the prescaler at one, the counter three will be running at one kilohertz to this means each count in the counter three will take one millisecond. If we set the auto reloads to maximum 65,535, the counter three will have a period of 65 seconds. Basically, the counter three can measure frequencies between one kilohertz and 0.015 Hertz. Now think of these two counters as the single counter and we have ourselves the frequency bandwidth of 10 megahertz to 0.015 Hertz. This is a huge bandwidths considering we were only able to achieve up to 150 hertz with the single counter, we will use the Input Capture mode with the interrupt So enable the respective interrupt for the timer one. That's it for the cube MX Configuration, click Save to generate the project. Inside the main function, we will start the timer one channel one in the input capture interrupt mode. Also, we will simply start the timer three so that it's counter can also count when the rising edge will be captured by the timer one and interrupt will be triggered and the input capture complete callback will be called we will write the rest of the code inside this callback function. Here first of all I am defining some variables which we will need later. Counter one and three will hold the values of the respective counters. His first captured will be used to reset these counters. Now first, we will check if the callback is called by the timer one channel one, then we will check if the first edge is captured or not.

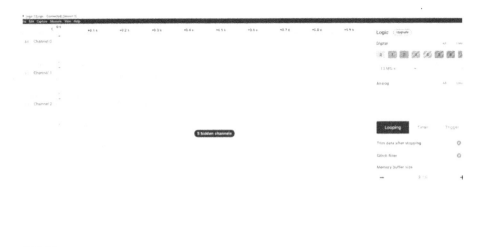

If this is the first edge, then reset the counters and set the first captured to one indicating the first edge has been captured. Now when the interrupt is triggered by the second edge, we will first read the respective counters. And now calculate the frequency. To calculate the frequency, we will convert the counter threes value in terms of the counter ones value. Basically every tick in counter three is equivalent to having 10,000 ticks in counter one. So to make them equal, we will multiply counter three with 10,000. Since the overall counter value is now in terms of the counter one to calculate the frequency, we will simply divide the counter ones clock by the counter value. After the frequency has been calculated, we will reset the first captured so that the whole process can start from the beginning. Let me revise this one more time. When the first edge arrives, we will reset the counters. Now when the second edge arrives, we will read the counter values then convert all the counter values in terms of the counter one and finally use the counter one clock to calculate the frequency. If you are confused about this part, you can think of this as the simple formula counter is equal to counter one plus counter two times the counter ones reload value plus counter three times the counter twos reload value times the counter ones reload value and so on. Of course this is considering the three timers are in cascade mode, with timer one clocking the timer to which is clocking the timer three. This is it for the coding part. Let's build and debug the code now. I am using the any triple five module which basically outputs square waves of different frequencies. I have connected its output to the logic analyzer and also to the input capture pin of the STM 32.

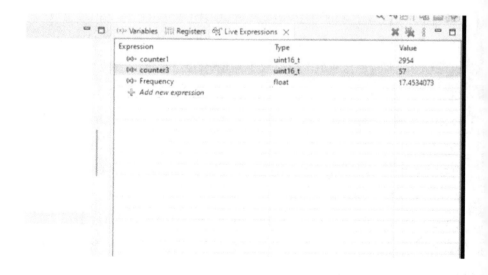

Let's add the counters and frequency to the live expression for some reason it's not working. All right, I have found the issue here instead of time at channel one. It should have been helped him active channel one on, let's build and debug the code again. Now it's working all right, you can see the frequencies 200,000. If we check the logic analyzer, it also gives similar values. Now I am going to reduce the frequency values you can see the frequency is decreasing, and now it's around 97 kilohertz. Let's check the analyzer. Here we have a similar frequency. Now the reading is around 13.9 kilohertz, and you can see the similar reading in the logic analyzer. Let's reduce it further. Notice that so far, the counter three is always zero. This is as we discussed, the counter one is capable of reading up to one kilohertz. And if the signal period is less than one millisecond, the counter three cannot count up. So as long as our frequency is higher than one kilohertz, the counter three will remain zero. But if we go lower than one kilohertz, now the counter three also starts contributing to the frequency measurement. Right now, the frequency is around 558 Hertz. And this is exactly what the analyzer is also showing, let's keep going lower.

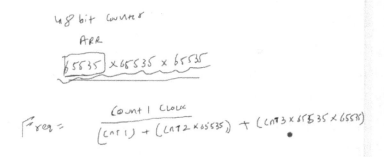

48 bit counter

ARR

$$\boxed{65535} \times 65535 \times 65535$$

$$Freq = \frac{Count\ 1\ Clock}{(cnt\ 1) + (cnt\ 2 \times 65535) + (cnt\ 3 \times 65535 \times 65535)}$$

Now the frequency is around 17.5 Hertz. As we discussed in the beginning, this is way lower than the limit we set for a single 16 bit counter. Let's keep reducing. This 0.57 Hertz is the minimum frequency achievable using this module I have. And if we measure it in the analyzer, it is exactly the same. I cannot show lower values than this. But with my current setup, I can go as low as 0.015 hertz. So this is how cascading the timers can be used to increase the counter size to whatever resolution you want. This wasn't exactly a 48 bit counter, but if you do use that, you can achieve an extremely high frequency bandwidth. As I mentioned earlier, to calculate the frequency while using the 48 bit counter, you can use the counter one clock divided by the counter one plus the counter two times the 65,535 plus the counter three times the 65,535 squared. Basically, we have to convert every other counters value in terms of the counter one value and then divide the counter one clock by the overall counter value. So I hope you understood the concept the need and the process of implementing the 48 bit counter. We will continue with the timer series and more projects will be coming out soon, which will cover some other timer modes.

ONE PULSE MODE

Today we will cover the one pulse mode. One pulse mode is used to generate a pulse of a programmable length in response to an external event. The pulse can start as soon as the input trigger arrives, or after a programmable delay. I have here a PDF explaining the different modes have STM 32 timers, and here is the one pulse mode. As mentioned here, the capture compare registers value defines the pulse start time, and the auto reload value defines the end of the pulse.

One-pulse mode is used to generate a pulse of a programmable length in response to an external event. The pulse can start as soon as the input trigger arrives or after a programmable delay. The compare 1 register (CCR1) value defines the pulse start time, while the auto-reload register (ARR) value defines the end of pulse. The effective pulse width is then defined as the difference between the ARR and CCR1 register values. The waveform can be programmed to have a single pulse generated by the trigger, or to have a continuous pulse train started by a single trigger.

One-pulse mode also offers a retriggerable option. In this case, a new trigger arriving before the end of the pulse will cause the counter to be reset and the pulse width to be extended accordingly.

So basically, the effective pulse width is the difference between the auto reload and a CCR values. We can also program the output to be a single pulse or a continuous pulse train started by a single trigger. There is also a re triggerable option where the pulse width will simply extend if a new trigger arrives before the output pulse goes low. We will cover everything shown here in this project. Let's see this in working and we will start by creating a new project in the cube ID. I am using STM 32 F 446 R E, give some name to the project and click Finish. First of all, I am selecting the external crystal for the clock. The board has eight megahertz crystal on it, and let's run the system at 90 megahertz clock. This will keep both the APB clocks at the same 90 megahertz frequency and we don't have to worry about which timer is connected to which APB bus. Let's configure the timer now I am using timer one for this application. Select the slave mode as the trigger mode. In trigger mode, the counter starts at a rising edge of the trigger but it does not reset the trigger source is set to TI to F P two that is the channel two of the timer. I am selecting channel two for the trigger because I am going to use channel one for the output. You can see the pin PA nine has been selected as the channel two pin and this pin will be used as the input signal. Set channel one in the output compare mode. The pin P eight will be used as the output pin for the timer and here we will measure the one pulse generated by the timer make sure to enable the one pulse mode. Now we will configure the timers parameters. Since the APB Timer Clock is at 90 megahertz, a prescaler of 90 will bring the clock down to one megahertz. Now the counter is counting at one megahertz. So each count will take one microsecond, I am setting the auto reload to 50,000. So the counter period will be 50 milliseconds. This is also going to be the maximum pulse width. If we keep the capture compare register at minimum, the trigger polarity for the input signal is set to a rising edge, we will change the mode of the output compare later in the code. The pulse is basically the stop time for the generated pulse and I am keeping it at 10,000. That means 10 milliseconds, I have set the auto reload value to 50,000 which represents 50 milliseconds. This makes the effective pulse width of 40 milliseconds for the output signal. That's all we need to set up in the cube MX click Save to generate the project. Let's see the connection first. Here the black wire is connected to the pin PA nine which is the input pin and is connected to the button. The other end of the button is connected to the 3.3 volt pin on the board. So if I press the button, the pin PA nine will be pulled high to 3.3 volt and the timer will recognize this as the trigger signal. The blue wire is connected to the pin PA eight which is the output pin on channel one and is connected to the logic analyzer where we will monitor the output signal. Go to the timer initialization function. Here in the output compare mode. Open the declaration of the predefined mode. Out of the listed modes.

```
#define TIM_SLAVEMODE_RESET             TIM_SMCR_SMS_2
#define TIM_SLAVEMODE_GATED             (TIM_SMCR_SMS_2 | TIM_SMCR_SMS_0)
#define TIM_SLAVEMODE_TRIGGER           (TIM_SMCR_SMS_2 | TIM_SMCR_SMS_1)
#define TIM_SLAVEMODE_EXTERNAL1         (TIM_SMCR_SMS_2 | TIM_SMCR_SMS_1 | TIM_SMCR_SMS_

/** @defgroup TIM_Output_Compare_and_PWM_modes TIM Output Compare and PWM Modes

#define TIM_OCMODE_TIMING               0x00000000U
#define TIM_OCMODE_ACTIVE               TIM_CCMR1_OC1M_0
#define TIM_OCMODE_INACTIVE             TIM_CCMR1_OC1M_1
#define TIM_OCMODE_TOGGLE               (TIM_CCMR1_OC1M_1 | TIM_CCMR1_OC1M_0)
#define TIM_OCMODE_PWM1                 (TIM_CCMR1_OC1M_2 | TIM_CCMR1_OC1M_1)
#define TIM_OCMODE_PWM2                 (TIM_CCMR1_OC1M_2 | TIM_CCMR1_OC1M_1 | TIM_CCMR1_
#define TIM_OCMODE_FORCED_ACTIVE        (TIM_CCMR1_OC1M_2 | TIM_CCMR1_OC1M_0)
#define TIM_OCMODE_FORCED_INACTIVE      TIM_CCMR1_OC1M_2

/** @defgroup TIM_Trigger_Selection TIM Trigger Selection

#define TIM_TS_ITR0                     0x00000000U
#define TIM_TS_ITR1                     TIM_SMCR_TS_0
#define TIM_TS_ITR2                     TIM_SMCR_TS_1
#define TIM_TS_ITR3                     (TIM_SMCR_TS_0 | TIM_SMCR_TS_1)
#define TIM_TS_TI1F_ED                  TIM_SMCR_TS_2
#define TIM_TS_TI1FP1                   (TIM_SMCR_TS_0 | TIM_SMCR_TS_2)
#define TIM_TS_TI2FP2                   (TIM_SMCR_TS_1 | TIM_SMCR_TS_2)
#define TIM_TS_ETRF                     (TIM_SMCR_TS_0 | TIM_SMCR_TS_1 | TIM_SMCR_TS_2)
#define TIM_TS_NONE                     0x0000FFFFU
```

Choose the PWM to mode this configuration is not available in cube MX So we need to manually do it here. Now in the main function, start the timer in the one pulse mode. I am using timer one channel one. Let's build and run the code now.

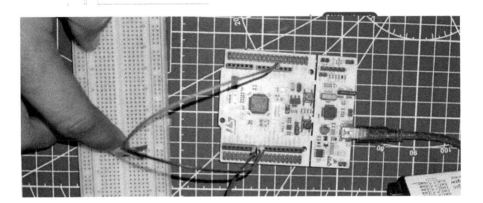

We will see the result in the logic analyzer you can see whenever I am pressing the button, there is a pulse being generated in the output. If you see the pulse width, it is approximately 40 milliseconds. This is as for the setup we did for the timer, we set the false stop to 10 milliseconds and auto reload to 50 milliseconds, and the width is the difference between them. That is 14 milliseconds. Now, let's see how to generate multiple pulses with a single trigger. Here in the timer configuration, the repetition counter was zero, and this would generate only one pulse. Now let's assume that I want to generate eight pulses. To do that, I need to update the value seven here. Let's see how this is working. You can see when I am pressing the button, multiple pulses are being generated. There are a total of eight pulses, each having the width of 40 milliseconds. Let's say if we want to generate the pulse with a software trigger instead of an external signal. For this purpose, we will use the internal trigger mechanism between the timers in STM 30 to open the reference manual of your controller and search for the internal trigger connection. Here you can see the timer one can be the slave to all these timers. And if I want to use the timer two as the Master I have to use the ITR one signal to trigger the timer one. Let's configure the timer two now. Here I am selecting the clock source as the internal clock. The timer to is also running at 90 megahertz, and using the prescaler of 90 will bring down its clock to one megahertz. Since the pulse width is set to 40 milliseconds in timer one, I am going to choose the trigger period higher than that the auto reload value of 60,000 will generate the trigger every 60 milliseconds, set the trigger event selection to update event. Now in the timer one, we will set the trigger source to ITR one you can see the channel to pin PA nine has been disabled since the trigger has been changed to internal now the rest of the configuration is unchanged. Let's generate the project now. Here the repetition counter has been changed back to zero. And let's change this to the PWM to mode we also need to start the timer to so that it can generate the trigger Let's build and run the project now. Here you can see the pulse is high for 14 milliseconds and then low for 20 milliseconds. The timer two is generating the trigger every 60 milliseconds, and therefore we see the pulse being low for 20 milliseconds. So we saw how to use the one pulse mode with single and multiple pulses and also how to use the software trigger to generate the pulse. Now, we will see the RE triggerable one pulse mode. In order to use the RE triggerable mode the timer must be set in the reset and trigger mode combined. But this option is not available in the F 446 r e actually the RE triggerable mode is not available in many controllers and therefore I am going to use the F 750 Discovery Board for this purpose I am going to use the same clock here so that the configuration would remain the same. I am using timer three. Here you see the combined reset trigger mode it is available. The trigger source is selected as channel to the channel one is being used as the output compare mode, enable the one pulse mode. Here you can see the two pins for timer three. I am going to use another pin for channel two that is the pin PC seven. This is because I have this pin available for connection. Here PC seven is going to be the input pin for channel two and PB four is going to be the output pin. Since the clock is the same, I am keeping the same configuration makes sure to keep the pulse zero for a triggerable mode to work. For the output compare, select the mode as re triggerable one pulse mode two. That's it for the configuration. Click Save to generate the project. I forgot to select an output pin. So let's select the pin PA zero. The trigger signal will be provided by this pin PA zero. Let's see the connection I made for this board. The black wire is connected between the pin PA zero and the timer input pin PCE seven.

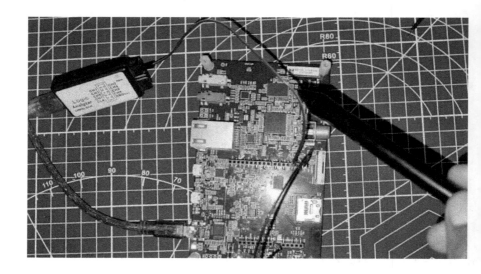

The blue wire is connected to the timer output pin PB four and to the logic analyzer. In the main function, start the timer in one pulse mode. Now in the while loop, we will toggle the pin PA zero the total time before the pin goes high again is 40 milliseconds. Also keep in mind that the pulse width is set to 50 milliseconds, so the trigger will happen before the pulse goes low. And if the RE triggerable mode works, the pulse width will be extended. Let's build and run this. Here you can see the pulse remain high and never goes back to low. This means the RE triggerable mode is indeed working. Let's change this delay so that the trigger will take place every 60 milliseconds. Our pulse width is 50 milliseconds. So now we should see the pulse going low. Here you can see the pulses high for 50 milliseconds and low for 12 milliseconds. The extra two milliseconds could be due to whole processing time. Let's change this to a total of 45 milliseconds delay. Now the pulse is again being extended because the trigger is happening before the pulse goes low. If we try something similar without the RE triggerable option being selected, this won't work. The pulse extends only when the RE triggerable option is enabled. This is it for the project. I hope you understood the different configuration is the one pulse mode.

EXAMPLE DUMMY CODE

To use the ONE PULSE MODE on STM32 microcontrollers, you typically need to configure the timer and set it up to generate a single pulse on an external pin. Below is an example code using HAL (Hardware Abstraction Layer) for STM32 microcontrollers, specifically the STM32CubeHAL library, to configure the TIM (Timer) in One Pulse Mode to generate a single pulse with a specific period and pulse width. The example assumes you are using TIM1, but you can adapt it to other timers like TIM2, TIM3, etc., based on your MCU.

Ensure you have the STM32CubeHAL library installed and your IDE set up for STM32 development before proceeding.

```c
#include "stm32f4xx_hal.h"

// Timer handler
TIM_HandleTypeDef htim1;

void SystemClock_Config(void);
static void MX_GPIO_Init(void);
static void MX_TIM1_Init(uint32_t period,
uint32_t pulseWidth);

int main(void) {
  HAL_Init();
  SystemClock_Config();
  MX_GPIO_Init();
  MX_TIM1_Init(1000, 500); // Set period to 1000
and pulse width to 500 (change as needed)

  // Start the timer in one-pulse mode
  HAL_TIM_OnePulse_Start(&htim1,
TIM_CHANNEL_1);

  // Infinite loop
  while (1) {
   // Your application code here
  }
}
```

```c
// System Clock Configuration
void SystemClock_Config(void) {
  RCC_OscInitTypeDef RCC_OscInitStruct = {0};
  RCC_ClkInitTypeDef RCC_ClkInitStruct = {0};

  __HAL_RCC_PWR_CLK_ENABLE();

  __HAL_PWR_VOLTAGESCALING_CONFIG(PWR_RE
GULATOR_VOLTAGE_SCALE1);

  RCC_OscInitStruct.OscillatorType =
RCC_OSCILLATORTYPE_HSI;
  RCC_OscInitStruct.HSIState = RCC_HSI_ON;
  RCC_OscInitStruct.HSICalibrationValue =
RCC_HSICALIBRATION_DEFAULT;
  RCC_OscInitStruct.PLL.PLLState = RCC_PLL_ON;
  RCC_OscInitStruct.PLL.PLLSource =
RCC_PLLSOURCE_HSI;
  RCC_OscInitStruct.PLL.PLLM = 8;
  RCC_OscInitStruct.PLL.PLLN = 168;
  RCC_OscInitStruct.PLL.PLLP = RCC_PLLP_DIV2;
  RCC_OscInitStruct.PLL.PLLQ = 4;
  if (HAL_RCC_OscConfig(&RCC_OscInitStruct) !=
HAL_OK) {
    Error_Handler();
  }

  RCC_ClkInitStruct.ClockType =
```

```
RCC_CLOCKTYPE_HCLK | RCC_CLOCKTYPE_SYSCLK
|
                RCC_CLOCKTYPE_PCLK1 |
RCC_CLOCKTYPE_PCLK2;
  RCC_ClkInitStruct.SYSCLKSource =
RCC_SYSCLKSOURCE_PLLCLK;
  RCC_ClkInitStruct.AHBCLKDivider =
RCC_SYSCLK_DIV1;
  RCC_ClkInitStruct.APB1CLKDivider =
RCC_HCLK_DIV4;
  RCC_ClkInitStruct.APB2CLKDivider =
RCC_HCLK_DIV2;
  if (HAL_RCC_ClockConfig(&RCC_ClkInitStruct,
FLASH_LATENCY_5) != HAL_OK) {
    Error_Handler();
  }
}

// GPIO Initialization
void MX_GPIO_Init(void) {
  // Enable GPIO Clocks
  __HAL_RCC_GPIOA_CLK_ENABLE();

  // Configure GPIO pin : PA8
  GPIO_InitTypeDef GPIO_InitStruct = {0};
  GPIO_InitStruct.Pin = GPIO_PIN_8;
  GPIO_InitStruct.Mode = GPIO_MODE_AF_PP;
  GPIO_InitStruct.Speed =
```

```c
GPIO_SPEED_FREQ_LOW;
  HAL_GPIO_Init(GPIOA, &GPIO_InitStruct);
}

// TIM1 Initialization
void MX_TIM1_Init(uint32_t period, uint32_t
pulseWidth) {
  // Enable TIM1 Clock
  __HAL_RCC_TIM1_CLK_ENABLE();

  // Configure TIM1
  htim1.Instance = TIM1;
  htim1.Init.Prescaler = 0;
  htim1.Init.CounterMode =
TIM_COUNTERMODE_UP;
  htim1.Init.Period = period - 1;
  htim1.Init.ClockDivision =
TIM_CLOCKDIVISION_DIV1;
  htim1.Init.RepetitionCounter = 0;
  htim1.Init.AutoReloadPreload =
TIM_AUTORELOAD_PRELOAD_DISABLE;
  if (HAL_TIM_OnePulse_Init(&htim1,
TIM_OPMODE_SINGLE) != HAL_OK) {
    Error_Handler();
  }

  // Configure TIM1 Channel 1 in PWM1 mode
  TIM_OC_InitTypeDef sConfigOC = {0};
```

```
  sConfigOC.OCMode = TIM_OCMODE_PWM1;
  sConfigOC.Pulse = pulseWidth - 1;
  sConfigOC.OCPolarity = TIM_OCPOLARITY_HIGH;
  sConfigOC.OCFastMode =
TIM_OCFAST_DISABLE;
 if (HAL_TIM_PWM_ConfigChannel(&htim1,
&sConfigOC, TIM_CHANNEL_1) != HAL_OK) {
  Error_Handler();
 }

 // Start TIM1 PWM generation
 if (HAL_TIM_PWM_Start(&htim1,
TIM_CHANNEL_1) != HAL_OK) {
  Error_Handler();
 }
}

// Handle any errors
void Error_Handler(void) {
 while (1) {
  // Error occurred, do something or just hang
here
 }
}
```

In this example, we use TIM1 and configure it to generate a single pulse with a specific period and pulse width on pin PA8. The MX_TIM1_Init function sets up the timer in one-pulse mode and configures the pulse width. The main loop starts the timer in one-pulse mode, and the timer will generate the specified pulse. After the pulse is generated, the timer will stop automatically. Adjust the period and pulseWidth values in the MX_TIM1_Init function to control the output pulse characteristics.

SLAVE GATED MODE

The STM 32 timer series and today we will see another application of the timer in slave mode. We will see how to use the timer in the gated mode, you can use this application note A n 4013 to see the timer applications. We have already covered other slave modes which includes reset mode, trigger mode and combined reset and trigger mode. So, today we will finally see the gated mode. As mentioned here, in gated mode, the counter clock can be controlled by the trigger signal. Also both the start and stop of the counter can be controlled. Basically I am going to use a button to control the trigger signal and the timer will output a PWM wave. When the button is pressed, the trigger will go low. This should enable the counter and the timer will output a PWM signal. When the button is released, the trigger goes high, the counter clock will be disabled and so does the PWM output of the timer. I will also cover how to automate this process where a fixed PWM signal will be generated at a fixed rate. We will see the connection diagram in a while let's start the cube ID and create a new project. I am using STM 32 F 446 r e nucleo board give some name to the project and click Finish. We will start with the clock first I am selecting the external crystal to provide the clock for the controller. The board has eight megahertz Crystal and I want to run the system at maximum 180 megahertz now let's configure the timer one in the slave mode. Select the gated mode under the slave mode. Since I want to use the button for the trigger, the trigger source is set to T i one. This will enable channel one for the trigger. And here you can see the pin PA has been enabled where we will connect the button to I am setting the trigger polarity to the falling edge. Now let's configure channel two for the PWM timer one is connected to a PB two bus which is running at 180 megahertz right now, using a prescaler of 180 will bring down the clock to one megahertz, the counter value of 1000 will further reduce the clock to one kilohertz and this will be the output frequency of the PWM signal. I am using the PWM mode to and I am setting the pulse at 500 which is 50% of the auto reload value. Therefore the PWM duty cycle will be 50%. If you don't understand the PWM configuration, watch the PWM project in the timer's playlist. So this is it, click Save to generate the project. Let's see connection. Now. I have connected the button between the ground pin and the PA eight. The pin P A nine is connected to the logic analyzer where we will see the PWM output.

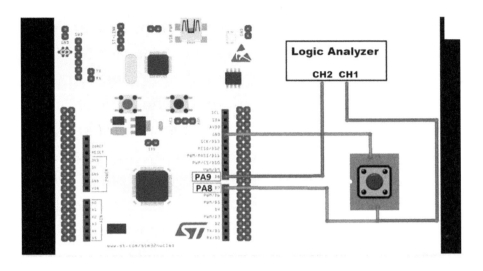

Let's write the code now. In the main function, we will simply start the timer in the PWM mode. I am using timer one and channel two. Let's build and run the code now. We will see the output in the logic analyzer. I have connected the output of the button to channel one and the PWM output to channel two. Here you can see whenever the button is pressed, the output on Channel One goes low, and along with it we see the wave being generated on channel two. The PWM signal continues as long as the button is pressed, and when it is released. The signal also stops. If you zoom in here, you can see the PWM signal has a frequency of one kilohertz and the duty cycle is 50%. This is as per the setup we did for the timer.

So this is working well with the PWM signal being controlled by the button trigger. Now let's say we want to automate this process where we want to generate the PWM signal of the same one kilohertz frequency at some fixed rate. Before we use another timer for this, let's see the MCU reference map manual here he looked for the internal trigger connection, you will find a table like this. I have already explained this in the previous time of projects. Here you can see that the timer one is a slave to the timer two and it can be controlled via the signal ITR one. So, we will change the trigger source from T i One to the I T r one the channel one pin has been disabled since we are using the internal trigger now, we will use the timer to to generate the trigger signal at some fixed rate. Here we will generate the PWM signal with no output. This is because the output will be used for the trigger signal. Timer two is connected to the APB one bus which is running at 90 megahertz right now. Using the prescaler of 90 will bring down the clock to one megahertz, the auto reload value of 100,000 will further reduce the clock to 10 Hertz. This is the rate at which the PWM will be generated. The trigger event is set to output compare of channel one, I am using the pulse value of 50,000 which is half the auto reload value and this will make the duty cycle 50%. This will keep the trigger signal high and low for an equal amount of time. This is it for the setup. Let's generate the code now. Here in the main function, we will start the timer in PWM mode. We are using channel one of the timer to let's build and flash the code to the board. Here you can see the PWM being generated at fixed intervals. The time difference between two signals is 100 milliseconds, which corresponds to a 10 hertz frequency. The PWM signal is still one kilohertz that we set in the timer one. So we finally have a PWM signal of one kilohertz being generated at a rate of 10 Hertz.

STM32 ETHERNET HARDWARE CONFIGURATION

we are going to start the Ethernet series where we will cover all sorts of protocols. This project will cover the initialization of the Ethernet port and in the end we will do the PING Test. Before I start the project, I want to share some important information. So first listen to the information and then decide for you after I saw some different MC use, I found out that there are four major things with the Ethernet some of the boards of media independent interface, EMI while the others have reduced EMI. Other than this some MC use let us configure the memory in the cube MX while others don't. These four things are mixed up with each other so your board could have AMI with memory config, or without it or the RMI with memory config or without it. I am going to make two projects for the initialization of the hardware itself.

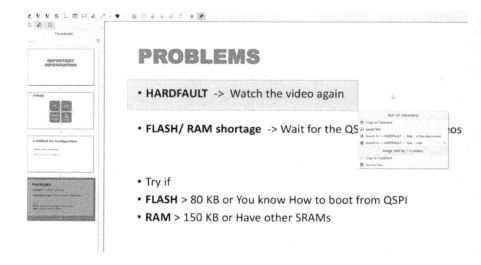

One of the boards I have support semi with memory configuration, while the other half are mi without memory configuration. But again, since we don't know what you could have watched both the projects carefully. Let's assume for now that I don't know which one do I have. We will find out eventually as we progress in the project. Now let's see the problems you are going to face most of you are going to face hard fall tissues. I know this I have seen the watch time in my projects and there are very few who actually watched till the end. Let me be clear here the half fault you are going to get is because of the memory issue. And I am not going to address any comment regarding hard fault errors. Probably I will delete them too. So if you don't want the heart fault, The next problem is the memory issue. Same goes for the RAM. Last but not least, watch the previous projects about memory configuration and MPU configurations

First, don't comment about not understanding the flesh script or MPU part. So if you are okay with everything, I am using H 745 Discovery Board and here is the Ethernet port on it let's give some name to the project and click Finish.

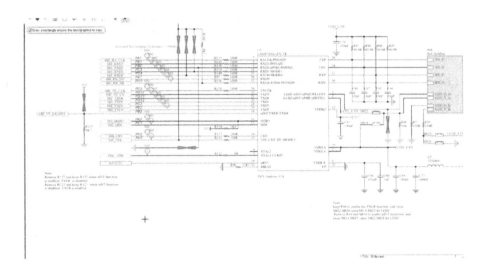

By the time it configures the cube let's take a look at the schematics here is the Ethernet module. And as you can see it have the Mi connection type. Remember that the MCU can support both types but what is connected with your hardware that matters all right let's keep it open and go back to our cube MX First things first let's configure the clocks I am selecting external high speed crystal to provide the clock make sure you use the correct crystal frequency at the input. Let's configure for the maximum frequency for her 100 megahertz is enough the clocks are fine now. Notice that the cache are disabled by default and I am leaving it like this. Let's go to the Ethernet tab. Enable the module I have MI type connection on this board. So I am going to choose mi we will configure the parameters in a while but first take a look at the GP i o the cube MX mostly configures the wrong pins by default, so make sure that you choose the right ones. Match every pin with The schematics. In this case, they are all configured correctly, so it's fine. If any pin is incorrect, you can click on the correct PIN and choose the function, the incorrect one will disable automatically. Now comes the very important part memory configuration. Here we have some buffer lengths and their addresses to configure these RX and TX or the DMA descriptors. And if you remember the DMA is used with cash, I think you got an idea about the part MPU is going to play here. Notice that here the cube MX is letting me configure the memory locations. So this is the memory config type. I can leave everything to default here. But just for the sake of explanation, I am going to choose another memory location. Let's see the reference manual First, go to the memory organization to find more about memory distribution. Here I have a lot of s rams, the main code is organized in the FCS RAM.

Table 6. Memory map and default device memory area attributes (continued)

Region	Boundary address	Arm® Cortex®-M7	Arm® Cortex®-M4	Type	Attributes	Execute never
	0x3B801000 - 0x3FFFFFFF	Reserved				
	0x3B800000 - 0x3B800FFF	Backup SRAM				
	0x38010000 - 0x387FFFFF	Reserved				
	0x38000000 - 0x3800FFFF	SRAM4				
	0x3C048000 - 0x37FFFFFF	Reserved				
RAM	0x30040000 - 0x3004FFFF	SRAM3		Normal	Write-Back Write Allocate	N
	0x30020000 - 0x3003FFFF	SRAM2				
	0x30000000 - 0x3001FFFF	SRAM1				
	0x24080000 - 0x2FFFFFFF	Reserved				
	0x24000000 - 0x2407FFFF	AXI SRAM				
	0x20020000 - 0x23FFFFFF	Reserved				
	0x20000000 - 0x2001FFFF	DTCM	Reserved			

And let's say I don't want to touch it. I have few more options to choose from and I am going with s ram one. This is 130 kilobytes in size and it's perfect for the job as RAM one started the address of 3 million and that's where I am going to put the RX descriptor. Now the length of descriptors is set to four by default, so let's leave it like that. But I don't know how many bytes does one DMA descriptor takes. If it's 24 bytes, then the total size for RX descriptor would be 96 bytes. But if it's 32 bytes, then the size will be 128 bytes. Let's go with the higher range and I am assuming that the each DMA descriptors is going to occupy 32 bytes. So the memory occupied by each descriptor will be 128 bytes. Now we need to put the address of TX descriptor have an offset of 128 bytes and therefore the address for TX descriptor will become 3,000,008 Zero. Now comes the RX buffer. The total space occupied by both the descriptors is 256 bytes, so we will keep the RX buffer at that offset. So the RX buffer address will be 3,000,100. The length of the RX buffer is 1524.

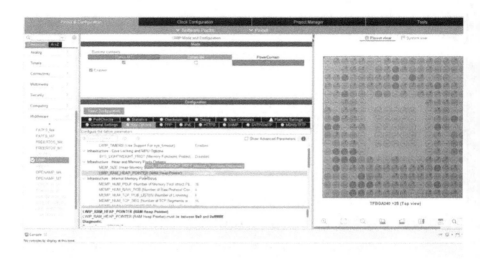

And I will explain this in a while. So everything is set for the Ethernet. Now let's enable the lightweight IP. Okay, it's not letting me enable this. This is because the cache are disabled. So let's go and enable the cache first. Now we can enable it. Let's configure this first option is if we want to enable the DHCP enabling Dynamic Host we'll assign the dynamic IP address to our module. But we will disable it and assign the IP ourselves. This will be a static IP address and it's easier for us to test with right now. So let's assign some IP address Netmask and the gateway. Leave everything to default here and we will go to the second option. Here this option is for free RT O S and since we are not using it, it's disabled. Next we need to set the memory pool size. Let's keep it 10 kilobytes for now, it's enough for our current application. Now comes another memory assignment. Let's see our memory distribution by far. The memory starts at 3 million and here we have the DMA RX descriptor, then at an offset of 120 ti eight bytes, we have DMA TX descriptor. Again, it's another offset of 128 bytes, we have RX buffer I forgot the size of RX buffer, the length was 1524. The size will be our X buffer length multiplied by our x descriptor length, the RX buffer is 6096 bytes in total, the address here will be 80. Here is 100. And the address at the end of our x buffer will be one eight D zero. Totally, they takes 6352 Bytes now we need to assign the address to this 10 kilobytes of heap. So we will assign it here. But not exactly to the very next position, let's round it up a little 2000 seems fine. The address for the heap pointer will be 3,002,000. So this is our entire memory range starting from 3 million and going up to 4800. A total of 18 kilobytes of RAM out of this 10 kilobytes is used by the heap around six kilobytes is used by these buffers. And then there is some space in the middle. So that completes our memory allocation for now. Let's see the rest of the configuration. Leave the rest of them as it is, we don't need to set up any of these. Here make sure the hardware checksum is enabled. And in this platform setting, both are set as Lan 8742. That completes our configuration for the L wi P and now comes the MP you if you haven't watched the MP you configuration projects don't complain about this part. Let's select the MPU privileged access only enable the

MPU region our base address is going to be the address of the SRAM one where everything starts. Enter the base address here.

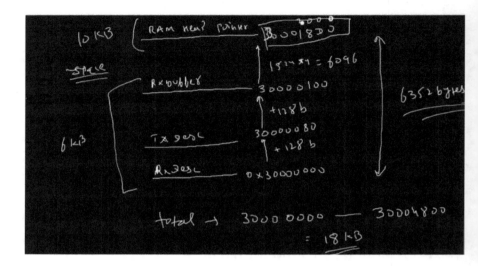

Now the size of the region we are using a total of 18 kilobytes of this RAM. So we need to choose 18 kilobytes after 16 We have 32 So select the 32 kilobits size. Now comes the configuration. I hope you remember this picture from the memory attributes project. As we are using the DMA descriptors in the normal memory region we need to make it non cashable. So I think this one should work. The text value is one and it is non cacheable non buffer level but shareable. All right, let's set the region permit the access set the Texas one and set the rest of the configuration so that's it, we have configured the MPU also click Save to generate the project let's build the code once to see the memory details. If you notice here, the ram D two is still unused even after we have defined the buffers in the RAM. This is because we still need to configure the flash script. Before we do that, open this Ethernet IP dot c file. This is where everything is configured even the pin connections. But here we are only interested in the As definitions, we are using GNU C. So this is our region. Here the sections are already defined, we just need to define them in the flash script. If you haven't watched the memory configuration project yet, we watch it first or else you are on your own. I am going to call it L W IP section. Let's define the memory locations for all those sections individually. Make sure you use the same locations that you have used in the cube MX I hope you remember this from the memory management project all the sections should be same as they are defined in the Ethernet F dot c file. Okay, so I have defined them and now if we build the code, you can see the D to ram have some space occupied we can see the locations in the memory details apparently the DMA descriptors are taking 96 bytes each. But that's all right, since we have given them the space of 128 bytes, so I guess it's fine so this completes the configuration part. Now let's write some code I am disabling the second core related functions.

You don't need to worry about this I write the exact same code that I am writing Ethernet if input handles the incoming data, it determines the type of packet received and calls the appropriate input function. This is just to test the ping let's debug this set a breakpoint here and run it this is to check if there is any heart fault due to memory issue. So we hit the breakpoint and everything is fine. Now we will let it run freely. And we are going to ping to the IP address. Let me reset it once. All right, it's working pretty good. Our static IP addresses responding well. The initialization of the hardware is complete and we can go for some protocols now.

UDP SERVER

Well, most of you know the reason for starting with UDP, I did a poll on the YouTube and here is the result. So I am going to go with UDP first then TCP and later with the HTTP and after covering all of them, we will move to next column with our T O S. Please watch the previous project about the hardware connection as I am not going to explain much about that part. UDP is the simplest of all the protocols. This is because it does not need any connection to be established between the server and the client. You simply connect and start the transfer it have its own advantages and disadvantages. You can read about them somewhere else as I am not explaining that part. create a new project in cube ID I am using F seven board for this tutorial. Give some name to the project and click Finish.

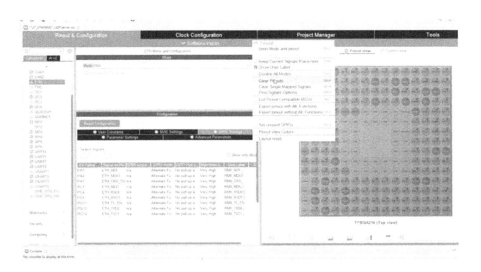

Here is our cube MX and let's enable the Ethernet this entire setup looks too messy so I am clearing the pin outs first and now enable the Ethernet r m i make sure you cross check the pins with the schematics as cube MX sometimes assigns the wrong pins by default all right now let's enable the clocks first I am choosing the external high speed crystal to provide the clock configure the clocks according to your board now let's go back to Ethernet and change this to zero as I am using on board module enable the interrupt also. This is it for the Ethernet setup. Now we will configure the lightweight IP disable the DHCP and here we will provide the static IP for our module leave everything else as it is I am going to use the same memory size just like last time that sets just leave everything else to default. Let me just enable the cache this is it for the setup click Save to generate the project now. Here is our main file. First thing we are going to do is check the connection and to do that we will just do the ping same as the last time I am fast forwarding this as I have already covered this in the previous project let's build and flash it now we will ping to the IP address that we assigned to the module it's not working looks like something is off okay, this should be input not in it let's try again. It's flushed successfully.

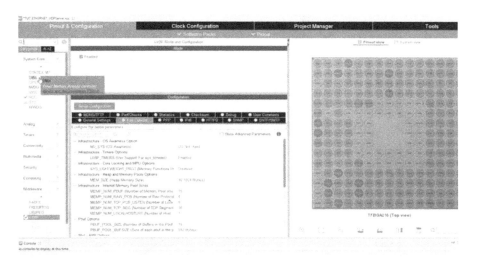

It's working now. So our hardware connections is okay. And now we can go to the UDP part. Let's copy the UDP Server files in our project. I took some functions from the STS examples, and I tried to write a simplified version so that it would be easier to explain it. So let's see what's going on here. Here are the steps to implement a UDP server, and this is the source where I got them, you can check out the website. Anyway, in order to implement the UDP server, we need to create the UDP socket, bind it to the server address wait for the packet to arrive from the client process that packet and repeat this process. Let's see how it is implemented here we have the server init function here we are creating the UDP block first, and then we need to bind this block to the IP address and the local port. First, we need to convert the address to a 32 bit integer format and then bind it to the block we just created using the function UDP bind. Here seven is the local port for the module that is the server port. Next, we need to wait for the packet to arrive from the client. To do this, we can set up a receive callback, which will be called whenever a client sends something. If we check out this function, it takes the control block as the first parameter. And the second parameters is the receive function. This receive function is our received callback, which have been defined here. As I mentioned, this callback will be called when the client sends some data to the server, we can do the processing inside this callback itself.

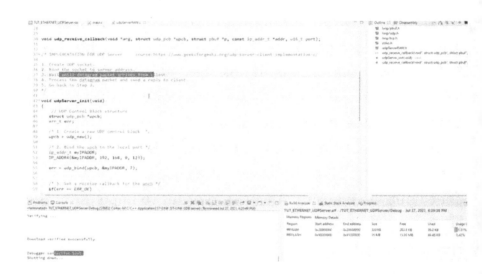

Or you can create another function for that. Hear P buffers the packet buffer structure, and it contains the information related to the packet sent by the client information like the payload, its size etc. We also have the UDP control block, and it contains the information about the client and the server information like the IP address, port, et cetera. Here we will first create a packet buffer that we are going to send then I am mixing the data sent by the client with some additional data. Then we will allocate the memory for this packet buffer and copy the data into it. Next, we will connect to the client the address and port for the client or the parameters of this function itself. And finally send the data to the client in the end, free all the memories that were allocated before. That's it. Now let's build it once. We will call this UDP server in it in our main function. We also need to include the header file here. This is the only function we need to call and as I mentioned before, it will initialize the rest of them. That's it. Let's test it now. I am going to use the Herculis as the UDP client. Enter the server address and the server port And the local port can be anything let's start this client will initiate the transfer. So I am sending test and we got the response from the server. This here is the same string that we sent to the server.

Let's try something else and you can see we are receiving the data just all right here you can see the receive callback does all the job, it allocates the RAM for the buffer, and then copy the data into the buffer and then connects to the client and sends the data let's say we want to get the IP address of the client for some processing the address which is passed here is a 32 bit integer. And we need to convert it into the proper address format we can do that by using this function here IP address in to a let's pass the 32 bit address to this and it will do the conversion and will give us the address as a string let's test this part I am putting a breakpoint right in front of it. This received callback will be called when the server receives some data from the client Okay, let me put a breakpoint in the next line. Now you can see we got the address as the string this is the address of the client. If you want to confirm it, you can just run IP config on your

Windows machine and here is the address the client port is 12 which is exactly what we are listening at.

If you need the IP and port for some data processing, you can get them like this so here we are making use of the payload that we received from the client you can write another function to handle the data. I will show that part in the TCP programming as the things are going to get more complicated there. And by the way, we can still run ping test this Ethernet if input function handles the incoming request and based on what protocol is being used, it can call the necessary functions. So we will pretty much use the same code in TCP also. This is it about the UDP server. I hope you understood it.

EXAMPLE DUMMY CODE

Below is an example code for an Ethernet UDP server using an Arduino board with the Ethernet shield. This example receives UDP packets, reads the data, and sends a response back to the client.

Make sure you have the Ethernet library installed in your Arduino IDE before running the code. Go to "Sketch" -> "Include Library" -> "Ethernet" to add the library if it's not already installed.

```
#include <SPI.h>
#include <Ethernet.h>
#include <EthernetUdp.h>

// Define the UDP port to listen on
#define UDP_PORT 8888

// Create an instance of the Ethernet server
EthernetUDP udp;

void setup() {
  // Start Ethernet connection
  if (Ethernet.begin(mac) == 0) {
    Serial.println("Failed to configure Ethernet
using DHCP");
    while (true) {
```

```
    // If Ethernet initialization fails, hang here
    }
  }

  // Print the local IP address
  Serial.print("Server IP address: ");
  Serial.println(Ethernet.localIP());

  // Start UDP server on the specified port
  udp.begin(UDP_PORT);
}

void loop() {
  // Buffer to store incoming UDP packet
  char packetBuffer[UDP_TX_PACKET_MAX_SIZE];

  // Check if data is available
  int packetSize = udp.parsePacket();
  if (packetSize) {
    // Receive the UDP packet
    int len = udp.read(packetBuffer,
UDP_TX_PACKET_MAX_SIZE);
    if (len > 0) {
      packetBuffer[len] = 0; // Null-terminate the
string

      // Print the received data
      Serial.print("Received: ");
```

```
    Serial.println(packetBuffer);

    // Process the received data (optional)

    // Send a response back to the client
    udp.beginPacket(udp.remoteIP(),
udp.remotePort());
    udp.print("Message received successfully!");
    udp.endPacket();

    // Print a confirmation message
    Serial.println("Response sent!");
  }
 }
}
```

This example sets up an Ethernet UDP server that listens for incoming UDP packets on port 8888. When it receives a packet, it prints the received data to the Serial Monitor and sends a response back to the client with a simple message. You can customize the server behavior and response according to your specific application.

Remember to update the mac variable with your Arduino's MAC address. Additionally, ensure that your Arduino is connected to a network with DHCP enabled or adjust the IP settings according to your network configuration.

Please note that this example is for Arduino boards with the Ethernet shield. If you are using a different Ethernet module or microcontroller, the library and pin configurations might be different. Always refer to the documentation and library references for your specific hardware to ensure compatibility.

UDP CLIENT

I covered how to create UDP server with STM 32 Ethernet. And as I mentioned in that project today we will see the UDP client. In the previous project I used the F seven board which doesn't need any memory configuration and we went with the default setup. I will use the h seven board which is going to need the memory configuration and we will try to keep things as close to default as possible. I am saying this again, you need to watch the first two projects about the hardware connection for

Ethernet module. create a new project in cube IDE. As I mentioned I am using h seven board give some name to the project and click Finish. Here is our cube MX let's enable the Ethernet connection the pins looks too messy.

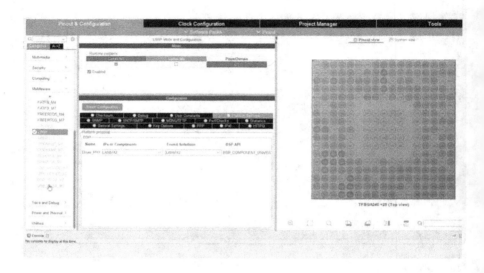

Let me clear the pin out first. Now we will enable the am I or RM I whatever type your board have, make sure the pins are configured properly as per the schematics, we will check the rest of the settings in a while let's configure the clocks. First, I am selecting external high speed crystal for the clock. Configure the clocks as per the crystal available on your board. All right, now let's go back to Ethernet and configure the rest of the setup and enable the global interrupt. In the parameter setting, we do have the option to configure the memory I am leaving everything to default. Take a good look at these addresses as we are going to use them in the flash script. Now let's enable the lightweight IP it's not letting me enable it because I haven't enabled the cache yet. So enable the data and instruction cache. Now I got the option to enable the L W IP I am going to do the same configuration that I usually do. The memory size will be 10 kilobytes leave everything to default here. And now we will disable the DHCP and instead provide a static IP to our module and that's it. Now choose the available solution here. The MPU configuration must be done when we have configured the memory in the Ethernet settings. Enable the background region privileged access enable the MPU region the base address will be the start of the DMA descriptor addresses. The size will be 32 kilobytes text should be one and this way we set the region as non cacheable memory region. Before we go any further, let's enable the timer and we will set this periodic interrupt which when triggered will send the data to the server. I am choosing timer one for this purpose and choose the source as internal clock. If we check the datasheet we can see that in this particular MCU. The timer one is connected to the APB two clock right now the APB two timer clock is running at 240 megahertz.

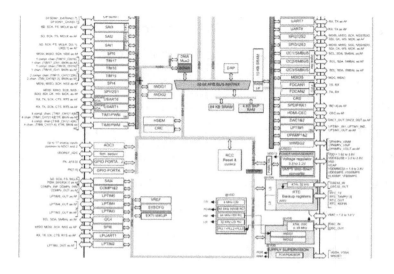

The plan is to use a periodic callback every one second so that the clients can send the data to the server. To bring this 240 megahertz clock to one hertz we will first use the prescaler of 24,000 this will bring the clock down to 10 kilohertz and all To reload value of 10,000 will further divide this clock and bring it down to one hertz. Make sure the update interrupt is enabled. This is it for the configuration. Now click Save to generate the project I am going to use the same code that I did in the previous project. This way we will be able to test the ping first let's build and test this part first. We also need to add the memory details in the flash script. This is necessary in this project. As we did the memory configuration in the cube MX. Everything so far has already been covered in the hardware connection project. So if you didn't understood anything, This is it. Let's try to ping to the module. This is the IP address that has been assigned to the module and here you can see the ping test is a success. All right, let's move on. And now we will see the UDP client copy the UDP client source and header files into the project folder. So here is the UDP client dot c file. Here are the steps to configure the UDP client, you can check out this source website. Here I have defined the timer, you can change it as per your setup. Here is the period elapsed callback function and it will run every one second. Inside the callback, we will send the data to the server. Now let's see the steps to configure the client mode. First of all we will create the UDP block we can do this by calling UDP new then we will bind the client to the local IP address and port. The local IP is the IP of the module and port is just some random port and also connects the client to the server using the server IP and port. You can look for the destination IP by typing IP config in your Windows machine this port seven we will assign to the server when we will create the server now the step two is to send the data to the server I am using this function UDP client Send to send the data to the server then we will wait for the response from the server. To do this, we will set a receive callback which will be called when the server will send some data to this client UDP receive takes the UDP control block as the parameter and the next parameter is the UDP receive function which is the callback in our case let's see the function to send the data now. here first we are creating a packet buffer which we will send later this buffer will contain the information about the data that we

are going to send next we will copy this string into the
data buffer this counter value will keep changing then we
will allocate the memory for the packet buffer next to P
buff take will copy the data into the packet buffer. Finally
UDP send will send the data to the server. And in the end
we will free the memory for the packet buffer. When the
client receives some data from the server, this callback
will be called. Here we will copy the data from the server
into this buffer. This is just in case if you want to utilize
that data. And here we will increment this counter
variable. This counter variable will increment every time
the server sends some data to the client. And the data is
being sent by the timer callback every one second. Now in
the main function, all we need to do is call the UDP client
connect function. Also, don't forget to start the timer let's
build and flash this I am using Hercules to create a UDP
server so that the client can connect to it and I am
opening the port seven, which will be the server port.
Here you can see the same message is being continuously
sent by the client until the server sends some data to the
client.

As soon as the server sends the data, the counter value is increased. It will keep continuously sending the same data again until the server sends some data. The message has been sent every one second just as we programmed it in another timer callback. When the client receives the data from the server, the received callback is called where the value of the counter variable gets updated. So the UDP client is sending the data to the server, the server sends some response to the client and this process keep going on forever.

EXAMPLE DUMMY CODE

Below is an example code for an Ethernet UDP client using an STM32 microcontroller with the STM32CubeHAL library. This example sends a UDP packet to a remote UDP server.

Make sure you have the STM32CubeHAL library installed and your STM32 development environment set up before running the code.

```c
#include "main.h"
#include "lwip.h"

#define UDP_SERVER_IP "192.168.0.100" // Replace with the IP address of your UDP server
#define UDP_SERVER_PORT 8888

void udp_client_task(void *argument);

int main(void) {
  // Initialize the HAL, peripherals, and TCP/IP stack
  HAL_Init();
  SystemClock_Config();
  MX_GPIO_Init();
  MX_LWIP_Init();

  // Create a thread for the UDP client task
  osThreadDef(udp_client_task, udp_client_task, osPriorityNormal, 0, 512);
  osThreadCreate(osThread(udp_client_task), NULL);
```

```c
  // Start the scheduler
  osKernelStart();

  // We should never reach here
  while (1) {
  }
}

void udp_client_task(void *argument) {
  ip_addr_t server_ip;
  struct udp_pcb *udp_client_pcb;
  err_t err;

  // Parse the server IP address
  IP4_ADDR(&server_ip, 192, 168, 0, 100); //
Replace with your server's IP address

  // Create a new UDP PCB (Protocol Control
Block)
  udp_client_pcb = udp_new();
  if (udp_client_pcb == NULL) {
    while (1) {
      // UDP PCB creation failed, handle the error
here
    }
  }

  while (1) {
```

```c
    // Wait a short delay between each UDP packet
(you can adjust this delay as needed)
    osDelay(1000);

    // Buffer to store the data to be sent
    char udp_message[] = "Hello, UDP Server!"; //
Replace with your data

    // Send the UDP packet to the server
    err = udp_sendto(udp_client_pcb, (uint8_t
*)udp_message, strlen(udp_message),
            &server_ip, UDP_SERVER_PORT);

    if (err != ERR_OK) {
    // UDP packet sending failed, handle the error
here
    }
  }
}
```

In this example, we use the lwIP (lightweight IP)
stack to handle the UDP communication. We
create a UDP client task that sends UDP packets
to a remote UDP server with IP address
"192.168.0.100" on port 8888. Replace the server
IP and port with your actual server details.

This code creates a UDP packet containing the

message "Hello, UDP Server!" and sends it to the server every second (you can adjust the delay as needed).

Please note that this example assumes that you have configured lwIP and Ethernet on your STM32 microcontroller correctly. Additionally, the IP address and other network settings need to be adjusted according to your network configuration.

TCP CLIENT RAW API

the Ethernet series and today we will cover the TCP client mode. Here the STM 32 controller will be used as the client and it will communicate with the server which we will create in the computer. So let's start and I will directly go to the main file, you can check the connection part in the first is the main file and I will start with the ping test first, you can see the same code is being used, which we have used in all the projects till now. Ethernet input calls the appropriate function based on the type of the package received. That's why we have been using the same code for all the protocols so far. Let's test the ping now. All right, the flashing is done.

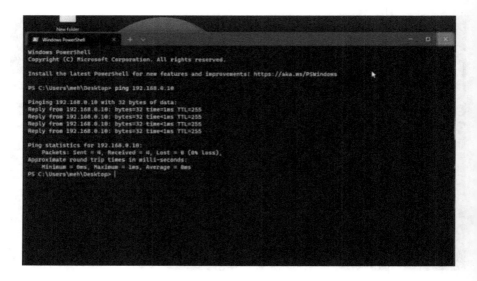

This is the IP that I set up in the cube MX and they passed the ping test, so we are good to go ahead. Now include the TCP client library files let's take a quick look at the source file to see some important functions. I took the example provided by the S T and modified them a little here. If you have watched the TCP server project, you will see a lot of similarities here. These are all the functions that are being used. Most of them are similar to the TCP server functions. I have created a periodic timer callback just like the UDP client project, and this function will be called every second. Here are the steps to implement a TCP client create a TCP block connects to the server and start communicating to create a TCP block we will use the same function TCP new then we will connect to the TCP server. here first we will convert the server IP address in the integer format. This is the IP of the computer and you can check it by typing IP config on Windows command prompt. Finally, we will use TCP connect to to connect to this server. Let's use some random port. Later we will create the server with same port. And once the client is connected to the server, this callback will be called. Just like the TCP server. Here also we will initialize few other callbacks. We are mainly interested in the receive callback, which will be called whenever the server sends some data to the client. We will check it in a while the timeout callback, which will be called every one second. Here we will send some data to the server using the function TCP client send.

```
142
143
144
145
146  /* IMPLEMENTATION FOR TCP CLIENT
147
148  1. create TCP block.
149  2. connect to the server
150  3. start communicating
151  */
152
153  void tcp_client_init(void)
154  {
155      /* 1. create new tcp pcb */
156      struct tcp_pcb *tpcb;
157
158      tpcb = tcp_new();
159
160      /* 2. Connect to the server */
161      ip_addr_t destIPADDR;
162      IP_ADDR4(&destIPADDR, 192, 168, 0, 102);
163      tcp_connect(tpcb, &destIPADDR, 80, tcp_client_connected);
164  }
165
166  /** This callback is called, when the client is connected to the server
167   * Here we will initialize few other callbacks
168   * and in the end, call the client handle function
169   */
170  static err_t tcp_client_connected(void *arg, struct tcp_pcb *newpcb, err_t err)
171  {
172      err_t ret_err;
173      struct tcp_client_struct *es;
174
175      LWIP_UNUSED_ARG(arg);
```

When the server sends some data back, the received callback will be called just like TCP server, this function has some predefined code to handle the errors, but we are interested in this part if the state is switched to connected here, first of all, we must acknowledge the data received TCP receive function is used for the same then we will call the client handle function to handle the received data. And in the end, we will free the buffer. Let's see the client handle function now. While I am not doing anything special here I am getting the IP address of the server just in case if you need the IP and in the end increment the counter. This counter variable is being used in the timer callback function. Here I am sending this message to the server which will send the updated count To value. So whenever the server sends some data, the counter will increment. Otherwise, this call back will keep sending the same counter value every second, we will allocate the memory to the buffer using P buff Alec function, then copy the data into the payload of the P buff. And finally send the data to the server. In the end, we will free the buffer. Let's build it once to check for any errors. We have a few warnings, but that's all right. Let's write the main function now. First, we will start the timer interrupt so that the periodic callback can work then initialize the TCP client we also need to include the header file for the TCP client. All right, let's build and flash it I am going to use the Hercules for the TCP server. Here I have used the port 31. So let's listen to the same port we can check the status here in this window. Let's run the code now. We got the client connection success message. Here you can see the client sending data every one second. The counter is one because we are not sending any data to the client. And this is why the client handle function is not being called and the counter is not incrementing. But as soon as the server sends some data to the client, the counter will increment and you can see the updated data sent by the client and again, we can see the updated data. Let's see the process of execution. Here I am setting a breakpoint inside the clients connected callback one inside the receive callback another one inside the sent callback and one last breakpoint here. Let me clear everything first.

Let's run it now. As soon as the client got connected to the server, we got a hit inside the connected callback another hit in the handle function this is because we are calling the client handle function inside the connected callback. Now after the client sends the message there is another hit inside the sent callback. You can see the messages are being sent to the server. Let me remove this breakpoint. Okay, now we will send some data to this client. Here we got a hit inside To receive callback this function will call the server handle and now the counter value will increment. The connection got disconnected for being idle for some time. But I think you got the idea of how this works.

EXAMPLE DUMMY CODE

example code for a TCP client using the RAW API of lwIP on an STM32 microcontroller with the STM32CubeHAL library. This example demonstrates how to establish a TCP connection to a remote server and send and receive data over the TCP connection.

Please note that this example uses the RAW API of lwIP, which requires you to manually handle TCP packet processing. It provides more control but can be more complex than using the higher-level SOCKET API. If you prefer a simpler approach, you can use the SOCKET API provided by lwIP.

```
#include "main.h"
#include "lwip.h"
#include "tcp_client.h"
```

```c
#define SERVER_IP "192.168.0.100" // Replace
with the IP address of your server
#define SERVER_PORT 5000 // Replace with the
port number your server is listening on

static struct tcp_pcb *tcp_client_pcb;
static struct pbuf *recv_buffer;

// Function prototypes
static err_t tcp_client_recv_callback(void *arg,
struct tcp_pcb *tpcb, struct pbuf *p, err_t err);
static void tcp_client_error_callback(void *arg,
err_t err);
static err_t tcp_client_connected_callback(void
*arg, struct tcp_pcb *tpcb, err_t err);

void tcp_client_init(void) {
  ip_addr_t server_ip;
  err_t err;

  // Parse the server IP address
  IP4_ADDR(&server_ip, 192, 168, 0, 100); //
Replace with your server's IP address

  // Create a new TCP PCB (Protocol Control Block)
  tcp_client_pcb = tcp_new();
  if (tcp_client_pcb == NULL) {
```

```c
    // TCP PCB creation failed, handle the error
here
    return;
  }

  // Connect to the server
  err = tcp_connect(tcp_client_pcb, &server_ip,
SERVER_PORT, tcp_client_connected_callback);
  if (err != ERR_OK) {
    // TCP connection request failed, handle the
error here
  }

  // Set up receive callback
  tcp_recv(tcp_client_pcb,
tcp_client_recv_callback);

  // Set up error callback
  tcp_err(tcp_client_pcb,
tcp_client_error_callback);
}

void tcp_client_send_data(const char *data) {
  if (tcp_client_pcb != NULL) {
    // Send data over the TCP connection
    tcp_write(tcp_client_pcb, data, strlen(data),
TCP_WRITE_FLAG_COPY);
    tcp_output(tcp_client_pcb);
```

```
  }
}

// Callback function when data is received
static err_t tcp_client_recv_callback(void *arg,
struct tcp_pcb *tpcb, struct pbuf *p, err_t err) {
  if (p != NULL) {
    // Copy the received data to a local buffer
    recv_buffer = pbuf_clone(PBUF_RAW,
PBUF_POOL, p);

    // Set up a new receive callback
    tcp_recv(tpcb, tcp_client_recv_callback);

    // Free the original pbuf
    pbuf_free(p);
  } else if (err == ERR_OK) {
    // The remote host has closed the connection
    tcp_client_close();
  } else {
    // Error occurred during reception, handle the
error here
  }

  return ERR_OK;
}

// Callback function for handling TCP connection
```

```
errors
static void tcp_client_error_callback(void *arg,
err_t err) {
  // Handle the TCP connection error here
}

// Callback function when the TCP connection is
established
static err_t tcp_client_connected_callback(void
*arg, struct tcp_pcb *tpcb, err_t err) {
  if (err == ERR_OK) {
    // Connection to the server is successful,
handle accordingly
  } else {
    // Connection to the server failed, handle
accordingly
  }

  return ERR_OK;
}

void tcp_client_close(void) {
  // Close the TCP connection
  if (tcp_client_pcb != NULL) {
    tcp_close(tcp_client_pcb);
    tcp_client_pcb = NULL;
  }
```

```
  // Free the receive buffer
  if (recv_buffer != NULL) {
    pbuf_free(recv_buffer);
    recv_buffer = NULL;
  }
}
```

In this example, we create a TCP client using the RAW API of lwIP. The tcp_client_init function initializes the TCP client and establishes a connection to the server. The tcp_client_send_data function sends data to the server over the established TCP connection. The tcp_client_recv_callback function is called when data is received from the server, and the tcp_client_error_callback function handles any TCP connection errors. The tcp_client_connected_callback function is called when the TCP connection is established.

Please note that this example is a basic framework for a TCP client using the RAW API. You may need to modify it and add error handling or application-specific logic based on your use case. Additionally, make sure to configure the lwIP stack and Ethernet properly for your STM32 microcontroller and network setup.

HTTP SERVER PART 1 SIMPLE WEBPAGE

Ethernet series and today we will see how to create a HTTP server. We will use the HTTP daemon to handle the requests for the server. I am going to make three projects for this. Which is this one will cover the setting up of the HTTP daemon and we will also run a basic server. we will see how to use the SSI server side include feature to update the web page with new data. And finally in the third project, we will use the CGI Common Gateway Interface. So let's start the today's project in which we will simply set the HTTP basic web server I am using STM 32 F 750 Discovery Board give some name to the project and click Finish First things first, let's set up the clock. I am using external high speed crystal to provide the clock and running the MCU at max 216 megahertz frequency now if you are using Cortex M seven processor enable the cache. This MCU I am using have low flash memory and this is why I need to use the external flash. I have already made a project about cue SPI and here I am doing the same processes mentioned in that project.

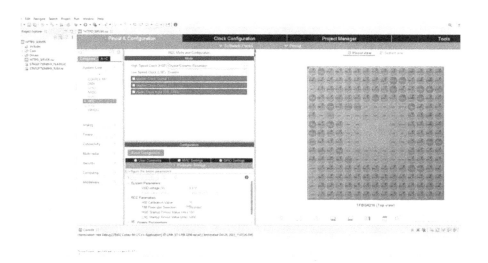

If you have enough flash, you don't need to do this part. All right, now let's enable the Ethernet module I have our M i connection type make su these pins are correctly configured as per the board schematics. P pH y address must be zero as I am using the onboard Ethernet module. This is it for the Ethernet setup. Now let's go to the L w i p here first we will disable the DHCP and manually assign a static IP for our server. Next, assign the memory of 10 kilobytes for the heap. This is the basic setup which has been already covered in the first project of the Ethernet series. Now go to the httpd and enable it if you click on the Advanced Parameters, you can see a lot of additional setup.

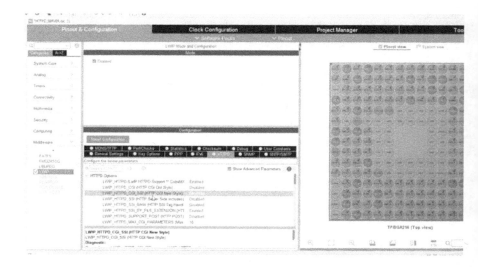

Like I said in the beginning, we will cover the SSI and CGI in the upcoming projects. So keep them disabled for now. That's it for the L Wi Fi setup. Now click Save to generate the project. There will be a lot of errors and we will fix them one by one. So let's build the code once the first arrow we have in the FS data. It is trying to look for the FS data custom dot c file which isn't present in the project. So open this declaration and set it to zero. We still have the error here. But this time it's looking for the FS data dot c file, we need to include this file in the project. Here is the folder make Fs. This is the program to create the FS data file. This folder Fs contains all the resources you are going to use for the server. By default, it has the index page, a 404 error page and image. You can modify these or add new pages here. But for the simplicity, I will go with this basic setup for now. The index page looks something like this. And the 404 page looks like this. Now

Go to middleware, third party I WAP source apps HTTP and open this folder we need to copy these files here after copying, just double click the Make Fs data and it will create a f s data dot c file alright we have created the FS data file So refresh the project and build again we still have errors but they are not about the FS data file not being present the error is due to these functions. So, next we have to do is exclude the FS data dot c file from the build you can see it has been excluded from the build. Let's try building again all right the FS data related errors are gone now, this error is because my flash is overflowing So, I am going to use the external flash I am mentioning this again that this part has been covered in the queue SPI project and all I am doing is booting from the external flash memory and now we have zero errors I still need to relocate the vector table to the external flash All right, let's write the code now.

First of all include the HTTP D header file. Next we will create the net F structure just like we did in the previous projects in the main file, initialize the HTTP daemon. And finally in the while loop we will use our usual setup Ethernet if input and check timeout let's build and debug this now. Since I am using the external flash I need to use the external loader let's put a breakpoint here to check if everything is initialized properly All right we are hitting the breakpoint so everything is fine. Let's go to the IP we assigned to the server and here we got the web page. If we try to access something else, it will show the 404 error so the webpage is working all right. Like I mentioned all the resources you are using must be in this Fs folder. And this is the index page. You can modify this according to your need. But after modifying you need to again create the FS data file. Let me show this I am modifying this index file now.

Create The new Fs data file will decode again and run it and now you see the new data is showing up. All right, what will happen if we don't rebuild the code I am modifying the file again Chris create a new Fs data file. reloading the page doesn't show the new data it doesn't work like this, we must rebuild the code and then upload it again and now you can see the new data showed up. So we can't change the webpage in the run time. And this is where the SSI comes in.

EXAMPLE DUMMY CODE

```c
#include "stm32f4xx_hal.h"
#include "lwip/apps/httpd.h"

static const char *html_page =
```

```c
  "<html>"
  "<head>"
  "<title>STM32 HTTP Server</title>"
  "</head>"
  "<body>"
  "<h1>Hello, world!</h1>"
  "</body>"
  "</html>";

void httpd_init(void) {
  // Initialize the HTTP server.
  httpd_init_server(80);

  // Add a webpage to the server.
  httpd_add_page("/", html_page);
}

int main(void) {
  // Initialize the HAL library.
  HAL_Init();

  // Initialize the HTTP server.
  httpd_init();

  // Infinite loop.
  while (1) {
  }
}
```

This code will first initialize the HTTP server and add a webpage to it. Then, it will enter an infinite loop. When a client connects to the server, the webpage will be served.

To run this code, you will need to have a development board with an STM32F4 microcontroller. You can also use an emulator, such as STM32CubeIDE. Once you have the code compiled and loaded onto the board, you can run it by pressing the reset button.

To access the webpage, you can open a web browser and enter the IP address of the board followed by the port number, for example:

http://192.168.1.100:80

You should see the webpage displayed in the browser.

HTTP WEBSERVER PART 2 SSI (SERVER SIDE INCLUDE)

Today we will see how to use the SSI serve aside include this part will basically cover how to refresh the webpage with the new data. Since this is the continuation from the previous HTTP project, I will also continue where I left things last time, I am not going to cover any setup process again. So please watch the HTTP web server part one and then come back to this project. Let's start the cube ID. And here we have the old project. Let me quickly show you the what we did in the last project.

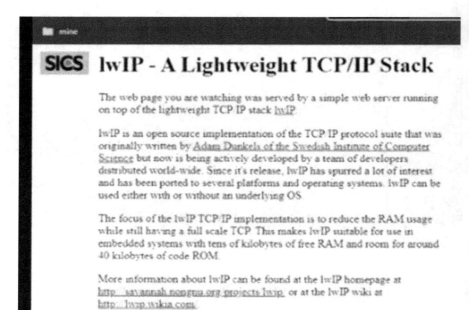

So this is the web page we created. And there was one more page for the 404 error. Let's continue with our project we need to enable the SSI in the cube MX so open the file, go to L w i p and then go to http D here check the Show Advanced Parameters box we got some additional settings. Now enable the LW IP HTTP D S S I. This is it for the Setup, click Save to generate the project. Let's try to build it once we have some errors, and it's the same one we got last time also. So first we will disable the use of the custom Fs data file. And if you build it again, you will get another error but this one is for the FS state of file and it's okay we will deal with it later. Now we need to create a new webpage where we will update the data I am going to use the HTML table for this purpose. Let's see which one is suitable. Not this one. Not this one either. This looks okay, let's continue with this. I am changing the name of the columns this looks fine. I am going to add the head section since we are going to use the meta tag and the title for the webpage now at the meta tag and here we will give the refresh time I am setting it for one second. Let's run it once you can see the page refreshes in one second. It's all okay up to here.

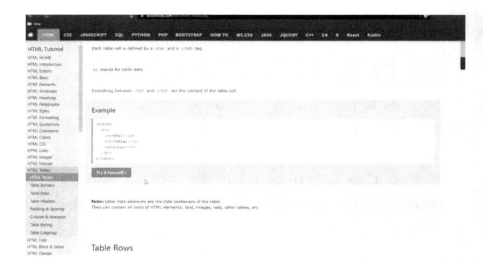

Table Rows

Now since we are going to use the data from the MCU we will use the tags instead of the values. These tags x y and Zed are being used for the first second and third columns. Let me change these headings real quick I forgot to close the head All right, let's copy this and we will create a new file save the file as s HTML. Here you can see the page is refreshing every one second. Now go to the location where we copied our Fs folder last time Inside the FS folder, copy the file you just created. Now double click the Make Fs and the new Fs data file is generated. Let's build the project now all the errors are gone.

Run >

```html
<!DOCTYPE html>
<html>
<head>
<title> SSI TEST </title>
<meta http-equiv="refresh" content ="1">
<style>
table, th, td {
   border:1px solid black;
}
</style>
<body>

<h2>TEST PAGE FOR SSI</h2>

<table style="width:100%">
   <tr>
      <td>V1</td>
      <td>V2</td>
      <td>V3</td>
   </tr>
   <tr>
      <td><!--x--></td>
      <td><!--y--></td>
      <td><!--z--></td>
   </tr>
</table>

<p>This page refreshes every 1 second.</p>
```

And notice this Fs data is still excluded from build, just like how we set up last time. So everything is good so far, I have created these files for the SSI just to ease the process, include them in the project, and I will explain them. The source file we just included will mainly handle the SSI here this index variable will be used for the values that are going to be displayed on the webpage. These are the three tags I am using, just like I created in the HTML file. Next is the function to initialize the HTTP server. This function will first initialize the HTTP D, which we were initializing in the main file earlier, then it will set the SSI handler This function takes three parameters, the SSI handler, the tags, and the number of tags we are using.

I am using three tags here. Let's see the SSI handler now. It takes three parameters. I index basically represents the number of the tag in the tag array. PC insert is the pointer to the data that we want to send to the tag, I insert Len contains the size of the buffer pointed to by the PC insert. If the eye index is zero, that means the first tag is detected, we will increment our variable and save this value to the PC insert, then return the number of characters written to the PC insert. Similarly, we do for the i index one and two.

That means when the tag two and tag three are detected, in each case, our variable is incrementing. So the values will always have a difference of one among them. In case you want to display the ADC data or any other census data, just call the get value function here and then convert the value to the characters and save it in the PC insert. That's it for the SSI related functions. Now in the main file, first include the header file we just copied. In the main function, we will call server in it as it will initialize both HTTP D, and SSI. And that's it. Now build the project and flash it to the board. Let's test it our homepage is fine. Let's go to the SSI page. We need to add the extension. The page is refreshing but the values are not displaying. I might have messed up something in the HTML file. I forgot to put the hashtag here. Okay, let's try it one more time. We need to do the entire process again. First copy the file in the FS folder. Then generate the FS data again, then build the code and run it whoa, hopefully it will work now. It's working. As you can see the values are updating every second Let's see what happens if we go to another page. I left the page when values were 4344 45. After almost 10 seconds, when I reopen the SSI page, the values started where we left them. The page will only refresh if it's opened. And so the values will update. We can leave it open in the background and do other things with our server. So the SSI seems to be working well. But refreshing the entire page is certainly not a good idea, especially if you have a lot of content like images or videos on the web page. Well, there is a solution for it, but we can only implement it if we use the R tos. So we will cover that part later. We covered how to send data to the web server and now remains is receiving data from this web server.

EXAMPLE DUMMY CODE

Implementing Server-Side Includes (SSI) on a microcontroller with limited resources like an STM32 can be quite challenging. SSIs typically involve processing dynamic content on the server-side and embedding it into HTML pages. Due to the resource constraints on microcontrollers, it might be more feasible to use client-side techniques for dynamic content generation.

However, I can provide you with a basic example of how to simulate SSI-like behavior on the server-side using static HTML and placeholder tags that get replaced with dynamic content.

Let's assume you want to include the current time in your HTML page:

```
#include "main.h"
#include "lwip.h"
#include "http_server.h"
#include <stdio.h>
#include <time.h>
```

```c
// Define the HTML template with placeholders for
dynamic content
const char http_template[] =
  "HTTP/1.1 200 OK\r\n"
  "Content-Type: text/html\r\n\r\n"
  "<html><body><h1>Hello, STM32 HTTP
Server!</h1><p>Current time: <!--TIME--
></p></body></html>";

// Function to get the current time
void get_current_time(char *time_str, int buf_size)
{
  time_t now;
  struct tm timeinfo;
  time(&now);
  localtime_r(&now, &timeinfo);
  strftime(time_str, buf_size, "%Y-%m-%d
%H:%M:%S", &timeinfo);
}

// Callback function for handling HTTP GET
requests
static err_t http_server_serve_page(const char
*url, char *buf, size_t buflen, int *content_len) {
  // Check if the URL matches the page where you
want to use SSI
  if (strcmp(url, "/ssi_page") == 0) {
```

```c
    char dynamic_content[50];
    get_current_time(dynamic_content,
sizeof(dynamic_content));

    // Copy the template to the response buffer and
replace the placeholder
    snprintf(buf, buflen, http_template,
dynamic_content);
    *content_len = strlen(buf);
  } else {
    // Return a generic response for other pages
    strcpy(buf, "HTTP/1.1 404 Not
Found\r\nContent-Type: text/html\r\n\r\nPage
not found");
    *content_len = strlen(buf);
  }

  return ERR_OK;
}

void http_server_init(void) {
  // Initialize the HTTP server
  http_set_serve_fn(http_server_serve_page);
  httpd_init();
}
```

In this example, we define an HTML template in
the http_template string with a placeholder <!--

TIME--> where we want to insert the current time. When a client accesses the /ssi_page URL, the http_server_serve_page callback will be called. Inside this callback, we get the current time using the get_current_time function and replace the placeholder in the HTML template with the dynamic content.

Please note that this is a simple simulation of SSI-like behavior and not a complete implementation. In real-world scenarios, you might use client-side JavaScript or more sophisticated server-side techniques like AJAX or server scripts (e.g., CGI or PHP) to achieve dynamic content generation on an STM32-based HTTP server.

HTTP WEBSERVER PART 3 CGI (COMMON GATEWAY INTERFACE)

Ethernet series and this is going to be the last project on the role of API's. After this, we will look into the Ethernet with the RT OS. This project is the continuation from the previous one where we sent the data to the web server using the SSI. In this project, we will see how to receive data from the web server using the CGI Common Gateway Interface. As I mentioned, this is the continuation from the previous project. I will also continue where we left off last time. This here is the project and this is how the web server looks. The SSI page updates every one second, and we display the values from the controller.

Since we are sending the data from the web server to the controller, we need to create a new web page. And for this purpose, I am going to use the HTML form this looks good enough. Let me change the heading real quick. TOS here is the action which will act after the submit button is clicked. Let's keep it unchanged for now. The F name and I name are the parameters. Let me show you. Here F name is the first parameter and John is the first value. Similarly I name is the second parameter and DOE is the second value. We will talk about these later the action for the form I wanted to call form dot CGI. I will declare this later in the code. Let's copy this and we will create an HTML file I am calling it CGI form dot html This works fine, you can see the action then the parameters and their values. All right, we will come back to this but first we need to enable the CGI and to do that we will go to the cube MX go to L W IP HTTP Advanced Parameters and enable the CGI old style that sets click Save to generate the project. If we build it, we will get our usual error about the custom Fs data file. You need to disable the use of custom Fs data again. The next arrow will be about the FS data file.

Let's go to the HTTP folder. Copy the HTML file here in the FS folder, generate the FS data dot c file again. Now all the errors should be gone. All right, we are good to go. I am going to write the functions in the same file that we use for the SSI. Last time we use the function set SSI handler to assign the SSI handler to the tags. We are going to use a similar function for the CGI handler also. Here is the set CGI handler function and it takes two parameters. The first is the pointer to a T CGI structure. And second is the number of CGI handlers we are using. This T CGI structure is defined right above and it have two elements the file name of the CG UI and the handler itself this is the function for the CGI handler. Let's copy this into our file I am calling it CGI form handler. The CGI handler takes three parameters. The first parameter I index provides the index of the CGI in the CGI array. For example, if you are using more than one CGI handlers, this parameter will give the index of the handler being called. The next is the num parameter, and it gives the index of the parameter within the same handler. For example, in this tutorial, I have used the F name and I name. So this num parameter will basically indicate whether it's the F name parameter or the L name parameter that called the handler. Then comes the PC parameter and PC value. They basically are the parameter and its value. For example, here in this case, they will be F name and John or L name and DOE. One last thing about this handler is that it should return

135

the pointer to the HTML page basically the CGI page let's write the rest of the code now. First of all, we will define a structure with the file name and the handler I am calling it form CGI.

```
55  * @ingroup httpd
56  * Function pointer for a CGI script handler.
57  *
58  * This function is called each time the HTTPD server is asked for a file
59  * whose name was previously registered as a CGI function using a call to
60  * http_set_cgi_handlers. The iIndex parameter provides the index of the
61  * CGI within the cgis array passed to http_set_cgi_handlers. Parameters
62  * pcParam and pcValue provide access to the parameters provided along with
63  * the URI. iNumParams provides a count of the entries in the pcParam and
64  * pcValue arrays. Each entry in the pcParam array contains the name of a
65  * parameter with the corresponding entry in the pcValue array containing the
66  * value for that parameter. Note that pcParam may contain multiple elements
67  * with the same name if, for example, a multi-selection list control is used
68  * in the form generating the data.
69  *
70  * The function should return a pointer to a character string which is the
71  * path and filename of the response that is to be sent to the connected
72  * browser, for example "/thanks.htm" or "/response/error.ssi".
73  *
74  * The maximum number of parameters that will be passed to this function via
75  * iNumParams is defined by LWIP_HTTPD_MAX_CGI_PARAMETERS. Any parameters in
76  * the incoming HTTP request above this number will be discarded.
77  *
78  * Requests intended for use by this CGI mechanism must be sent using the GET
79  * method (which encodes all parameters within the URI rather than in a block
80  * later in the request). Attempts to use the POST method will result in the
81  * request being ignored.
82  *
83  */
84  typedef const char *(*tCGIHandler)(int iIndex, int iNumParams, char *pcParam[],
85                                     char *pcValue[]);
86
```

The file name will be same as we declared in the action of the HTML file and handler is the CGI handler. Now we will write the CGI handler since we are only using one handler, the eye index will be zero. And we have to write a for loop for the number of parameters we have in our HTML file. As I mentioned, we have two parameters F name and I name. If the F name parameter is detected, we will copy the value into our name array. And similarly, if the parameters is L name, we will concatenate the value to our initial string. This way, we will get the name as first name space last name. And at the end of this handler, we need to return the pointer to the HTML file. This is the name of the CGI file that we have created. Now we will set the CGI handlers The first parameter is the pointer to the T CGI structure. We will pass the address of the form CGI here. And the number of handlers are one in our case. That's it. Since we already calling the HTTP server in it in our main file, we don't need to do anything else. Let's build and test the code. I have added the name in the live expression. Let's run it now we will go to the CGI form dot HTML type in the first and last name and click Submit. You can see the name has been stored in the array. Let's try something else the data did get stored, but we have the leftover from previous data, we need to clean the buffer before storing the new data. Before copying the first name, we will clear the buffer let's test it now. This time we got the data and there is no leftover from the last time, we can still access the s si page from the previous tutorial. It keeps refreshing in the background. In the meanwhile, we can transfer data from the web server to our buffer now let's say you want to use another section for the data. For example, some buttons to control the LEDs. To do that, we will create another CGI handler. I am calling it CGI led handler. We will create another T CGI structure we need to change the handler also, let's create an array of the CGI structures. Before setting the CGI handler, we need to assign the T CGI structures to the array and now we will pass the structure array to the set handler function. Also we are using two handlers now. Finally, we will write the CGI led handler. Since the LED handler is the second element in the array, the eye index will be one. After this, you do the rest of the processing in the similar way. First check for the parameter and then check for the value based on that control the LEDs.

EXAMPLE DUMMY CODE

Implementing a Common Gateway Interface (CGI) on an STM32 microcontroller can be challenging due to the limited resources and the need for dynamic content generation. CGIs are typically executed on the server-side to generate dynamic content and interact with the HTTP server.

However, I can provide you with a basic example of how to simulate CGI-like behavior on the server-side using static HTML and URL parameters.

Let's assume you want to have a CGI-like functionality that accepts a parameter name in the URL and displays a personalized message on the webpage.

```
#include "main.h"
#include "lwip.h"
#include "http_server.h"
```

```c
#include <stdio.h>
#include <string.h>

// Define the HTML template with placeholders
for dynamic content
const char http_template[] =
  "HTTP/1.1 200 OK\r\n"
  "Content-Type: text/html\r\n\r\n"
  "<html><body><h1>Hello, STM32 HTTP
Server!</h1><p>Personalized message: <!--
MESSAGE--></p></body></html>";

// Callback function for handling HTTP GET
requests
static err_t http_server_serve_page(const char
*url, char *buf, size_t buflen, int *content_len) {
  // Check if the URL matches the CGI endpoint
  if (strstr(url, "/cgi_page?name=") == url) {
    char dynamic_content[100];
    char name[50];
    int name_start = strlen("/cgi_page?name=");

    // Extract the name parameter from the URL
    int i;
    for (i = 0; url[name_start + i] != '&' &&
url[name_start + i] != '\0'; i++) {
      name[i] = url[name_start + i];
    }
```

```c
    name[i] = '\0';

    // Create the personalized message
    snprintf(dynamic_content,
sizeof(dynamic_content), "Hello, %s!", name);

    // Copy the template to the response buffer
and replace the placeholder
    snprintf(buf, buflen, http_template,
dynamic_content);
    *content_len = strlen(buf);
  } else {
    // Return a generic response for other pages
    strcpy(buf, "HTTP/1.1 404 Not
Found\r\nContent-Type: text/html\r\n\r\nPage
not found");
    *content_len = strlen(buf);
  }

  return ERR_OK;
}

void http_server_init(void) {
  // Initialize the HTTP server
  http_set_serve_fn(http_server_serve_page);
  httpd_init();
}
```

In this example, we define an HTML template in the http_template string with a placeholder <!--MESSAGE--> where we want to insert the personalized message. When a client accesses the /cgi_page URL with a name parameter (e.g., /cgi_page?name=John), the http_server_serve_page callback will be called. Inside this callback, we extract the name parameter from the URL and generate a personalized message using the sprintf function.

Please note that this is a simple simulation of CGI-like behavior and not a complete CGI implementation. In a real CGI implementation, you would typically run a script or program on the server-side that generates dynamic content based on the request parameters. On an STM32 microcontroller, this could be challenging due to the limited resources and may require more sophisticated techniques or external solutions for dynamic content generation.

NETCONN UDP SERVER FREERTOS LWIP

I covered the Ethernet in STM 32, which includes UDP, TCP, and HTTP based servers and clients. All the projects we covered so far were based on the raw API. As promised in the last project, today, we will start another series for the Ethernet projects, but this time, we will cover them with RT O S. In order to use the L w i p with the RT O S. STM 32 uses the net con API, which is basically to make the stack easier to use compared to the raw API. You can think of the net con as a layer on top of the raw API that we used so far. For this project, I am going to use the controller with our EMI connection type and no memory configuration. If you are using the MCU, which allows you to configure the memories, as I will use the H 745 controller in the next project. If you don't know what memory configuration means, or what am I even talking about,

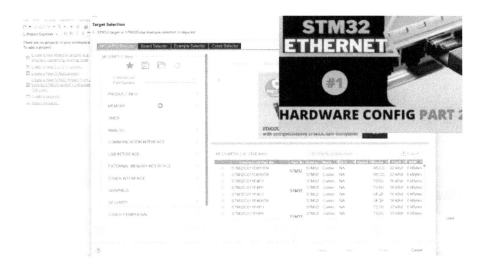

The link for the playlist is in the description. Other than the Ethernet configuration, the things will remain same for all the controller types. And by this I mean the UDP, TCP and HTTP part. Let's stop the project and create a new project with cube ID I am using the STM 32 F 750 Discovery Board give some name to the project and click Finish let me clear the pinouts First we will start with the clock configuration. I have 25 megahertz crystal on board and I am running it as 200 megahertz clock All right now go to the Ethernet and enable the type of connection you have. As I mentioned earlier, this board have our Mi connection type. Let's start with the parameter configuration first, since we are using the onboard connector, the pH y address must be zero.

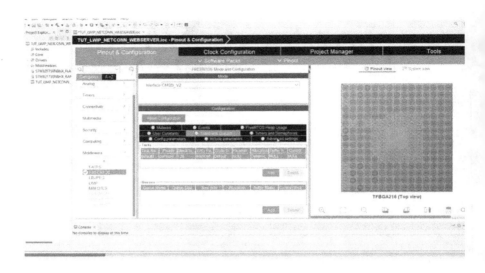

Also change the RX mode to the interrupt mode. When you do this you can see the Ethernet interrupt is enabled. Finally do check the pin outs and match it with the schematics of your board. Also make sure that the speed is set to maximum Next go to the free r t o s I am enabling the version two of the CM sis no changes are needed to be made in the free RT O S Just leave everything to default. You can see there is a default task created and later the L wi P will use this task. So leave this to I am enabling the new library reentrant as it gives the error while generating the code. Now go to the L wi p here first of all we will disable the DHCP and manually enter the IP address subnet mask etc you can see here the RT o s usage is enabled by default as we have enabled it already. Anyway, leave everything else to default in the General Settings. In the key options, the only change we need to make is increase the heap memory size I am setting it to 10 kilobytes This is it for the L WAP configuration. Leave everything else to default for now. Last but not least, since we are using the R to S we have to use the time base as anything other than cystic I am using the timer six for this purpose. All right. If you are not using Cortex M Seven based MCU go ahead and generate the code. As I mentioned, I am using the F 750 Discovery Board and as st recommends, we must enable the instruction and data cache for better processing. Also, this board has less flash memory and it won't be able to store all the variables in the flash. That is why I am going to use the external flash memory and for this purpose, I must use the MPU. Set the MPU to background region privileged access only plus MPU will be disabled during hard fault. Now enable the MPU region. The base address will be the address of the external flash that is the QoS p i which is at 9 million hexa. The size will be 512 megabytes, and we will disable all the access in this region.

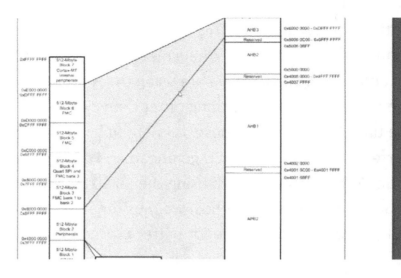

As mentioned here in the memory description, the QS P eyes in the block for which is 512 megabytes. This is why I blocked access to 512 megabytes of memory so as to prevent the speculative access to this region. If you don't understand this part, watch the MPU configuration series in the Cortex M seven playlist. The link is in the description. The region two we'll start again the 9 million hexar and the size will be 16 megabytes. This is the actual size of the QS pi memory available on the board. Here we will permit the access and we will set the region to cashable and buffer bubble. This was actually explained in my project about the memory configuration in Cortex M seven series MCU we are trying to set this region as the normal memory region with the right back attribute.

Prevent Speculative access

- QSPI memory range
- QSPI set as flash
- Disabled instruction access

```
MPU_InitStruct.Number = MPU_REGION_NUMBER1;
MPU_InitStruct.BaseAddress = 0x90000000;
MPU_InitStruct.Size = MPU_REGION_SIZE_16MB;
MPU_InitStruct.AccessPermission = MPU_REGION_FULL_ACCESS;
MPU_InitStruct.DisableExec = MPU_INSTRUCTION_ACCESS_DISABLE;
MPU_InitStruct.IsCacheable = MPU_ACCESS_CACHEABLE;
MPU_InitStruct.IsBufferable = MPU_ACCESS_BUFFERABLE;
MPU_InitStruct.IsShareable = MPU_ACCESS_NOT_SHAREABLE;
```

This is according to the STS recommendation for the Q SP I memory configuration we will create one more memory region at 9 million hexa. But this time we will enable the instruction execution from this region this is it for the MPU configuration for the external flash. Click Save to generate the code you can see there is the default task getting created. And inside the default task, the L WAP gets initialized. Let's build the code once to check for errors. All right, we have four errors. Let's solve them. The first one is about the multiple definitions of IRLO. It is defined in the middleware third party L W IP system OS sis arch file, let's open this file first.

147

This must be where the redefinition is causing error. Let's comment out this line and rebuild the code. We still have some errors, but the error regarding redefinition is gone. Now the issue is related to the flash memory being overflowed. For this reason, we have already set up the MPU so that we can use the external flash memory to store the data. Let's go to the flash script file to do the modification we have to change the origin of the flash to the Q SP I memory the address is 9 million hexa and the size is 16 megabytes save the file and generate the code again and all the errors are gone. Now we have modified the flash script but this is not enough. We still need to make some changes in the system file go to System init function and we will add some code here. First we will reset the configuration register and then we must relocate the vector table to the new flash base. This is all the set up needed for now, we will do the ping test first. And for that we don't need any functions. Let's build the code and debug it. Since I am using external flash, I need to use the external loader in the debugger. So here we will create a new debug configuration. Go to debugger tab, check external loader and click Scan. Now choose the MCU F 750 In my case, and click Apply to save the configuration.

Now click debug download verified successfully. Let's reset the controller and let's put a breakpoint in the error handler to make sure we don't hit it let's run the code let's ping to the board the ping test is successful. And before we go ahead I want to show you the configuration for the Ethernet. This time I have connected the controller directly with the computer without using any router. This is why I want to show the configuration for the Ethernet in the windows. Here I have changed the IP assignment to manual and you can see the rest of the configuration I will upload these images along with the project so you can access them later also. All right the ping test was successful. And now we will go ahead with the UDP server. Here I have created the library files for the UDP server. Let's include them in the project folder.

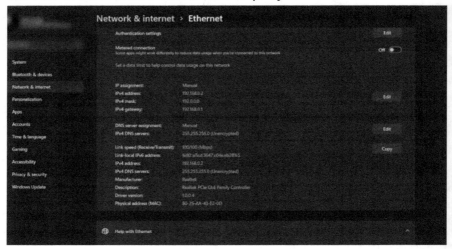

Here is the UDP server source file. Here is the net con structure to handle the connection parameter and the net path structure to handle the message related parameters. The address and port will store the same for the client. First of all the UDP server in it will be called. In this function we will create a new task the name is UDP thread and the entry function is here the argument is null, the stack size will be default one kilobytes, the priority will be normal. Once the UDP thread is called this function will be executed. Here we will create a new net con connection. Net con UDP will be used to create the UDP connection. If the connection is successfully created, we will bind it to any available IP address and the port will be seven. This will be the port for the server. If we don't have any error, we will receive the data from this connection. This function will wait for some data to be received from the client. If the receiver is successful, we will first get the address and port of the client. Then we will copy the payload into the message buffer. So you can make use of this message but here I am going to modify this message and store it in the s message. Next we will allocate the RAM for the P buff. Actually while using NET con. The net buff is used to store all the information related to message and the P buff is just a part of this net buff along with other things like address and port this TX buffer is the pointer to the P buff structure we created in the beginning. P buff take is used to copy the message into the P buff next we will refer the P buff in the net buff to our P buff so that we can send the net buff to the client with updated message Now connects to the address and port of the client which we stored earlier then send the buffer to the respective connection finally we will clear everything if there was any error during the binding, we will delete the connection if you remember from the UDP server raw project, the steps we performed were pretty much the same, creating a new UDP connection binding to the port and then receiving the data.

And once the data is received, we modify the message allocate the memory for the P buff, copy the message into the P buff connect to the destination address and port and send the buffer that's enough explaining now we will write the code and include the UDP server header file in the default task after initializing the L w i p we will initialize the UDP server this is it let's build the code and debug it I am going to use the Hercules as the UDP client run the code now enter the server address and port local port is the port of the client. Let's send hello world there is a response from the server this is exactly what we programmed in the UDP server you can see the server is responding well to every message sent by the client. Things are working well. And you saw the UDP server responding. This is it for the UDP server using the L WAP and Netcom. We saw how to configure the RMI connection type and also no memory configuration was required for the Ethernet. The next project will be about UDP client and I am going to use the H 745 MCU which have the Mi connection type and also need the Ethernet memory configuration.

EXAMPLE DUMMY CODE

To implement a NETCONN UDP server using FreeRTOS and lwIP on an STM32 microcontroller, you need to have FreeRTOS and the lwIP stack set up and running correctly on your STM32. Additionally, you should have the lwIP NETCONN API enabled in your project.

Below is an example code for a NETCONN UDP server using FreeRTOS and lwIP on an STM32 microcontroller. This code listens for incoming UDP packets on port 8888 and responds with a message when a packet is received.

```
#include "main.h"
#include "lwip.h"
#include "api.h"

#define UDP_SERVER_PORT 8888

// Task handle for the UDP server task
```

```c
TaskHandle_t udp_server_task_handle;

// UDP server task function
void udp_server_task(void *pvParameters) {
  struct netconn *conn, *newconn;
  err_t err;
  struct netbuf *buf;
  void *data;
  u16_t len;

  // Create a new UDP netconn
  conn = netconn_new(NETCONN_UDP);
  if (conn == NULL) {
   vTaskDelete(NULL);
  }

  // Bind the UDP netconn to the specified port
  netconn_bind(conn, NULL, UDP_SERVER_PORT);

  while (1) {
   // Wait for an incoming UDP packet
   err = netconn_recv(conn, &buf);
   if (err == ERR_OK) {
    // Get the data and length of the received
packet
    netbuf_data(buf, &data, &len);

    // Print the received data (assuming it is a
```

```c
null-terminated string)
    char received_data[len + 1];
    memcpy(received_data, data, len);
    received_data[len] = '\0';
    printf("Received: %s\n", received_data);

    // Free the received buffer
    netbuf_delete(buf);

    // Send a response back to the client
    const char *response_msg = "UDP Server
Response";
    buf = netbuf_new();
    netbuf_alloc(buf, strlen(response_msg));
    netbuf_copy(buf, response_msg,
strlen(response_msg));
    netconn_send(conn, buf);
    netbuf_delete(buf);
    }
  }
}

int main(void) {
  // Initialize the HAL, peripherals, and FreeRTOS
  HAL_Init();
  SystemClock_Config();
  MX_GPIO_Init();
  MX_LWIP_Init();
```

```c
    // Create the UDP server task
    xTaskCreate(udp_server_task, "UDP_Server",
configMINIMAL_STACK_SIZE, NULL,
tskIDLE_PRIORITY + 1,
&udp_server_task_handle);

    // Start the scheduler
    vTaskStartScheduler();

    // We should never reach here
    while (1) {
    }
}
```

In this example, we create a FreeRTOS task udp_server_task to handle the UDP server functionality. Inside this task, we create a new UDP netconn, bind it to port 8888, and then enter a loop to wait for incoming UDP packets. When a packet is received, we extract the data from the netbuf, print it to the console, and send a response back to the client.

Please note that this example assumes you have correctly configured lwIP and FreeRTOS in your STM32 project and that the network and hardware setup is correctly configured.

Additionally, you may need to adjust the task priorities, stack sizes, and other parameters based on your specific application requirements.

Keep in mind that this is a basic example to demonstrate the concept of a NETCONN UDP server. Depending on your application's complexity and specific use cases, you might need to handle more advanced scenarios and implement error handling.

NETCONN UDP CLIENT FREERTOS LWIP - 1

today we will see how to use STM 32 as a UDP client using the net con API. Here we will periodically send the data from the STM 32, which is a UDP client to the computer where we will create a UDP server. Along with that, whenever the server will send some data to the client, the client will also response to the server by sending some reply related to the data. We have already covered the UDP server using Netcom in the previous project, and most of the configuration will be similar to that project. So let's start the cube ID and create a new project I am using the STM 32 F 750 Discovery Board give some name to the project and click Finish let me clear the pinouts first if you have watched the previous project, you can skip to 11th minute and we will start with the clock configuration.

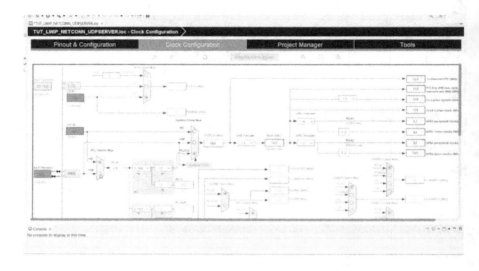

I have 25 megahertz crystal on board and I am running it as 200 megahertz clock All right now go to the Ethernet and enable the type of connection you have. As I mentioned earlier, this board have our Mi connection type. Let's start with the parameter configuration first, since we are using the onboard connector, the pH y address must be zero. Also change the RX mode to the interrupt mode. When you do this, you can see the Ethernet interrupt is enabled. Finally do check the pin outs and match it with the schematics of your board. Also make sure that the speed is set to maximum.

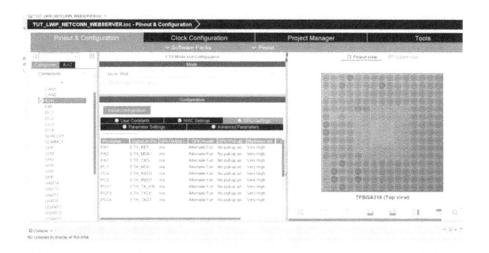

Next go to the free r t o s I am enabling the version two of the CM CIS no changes are needed to be made in the free RT O S Just leave everything to default. You can see there is a default task created and later the L wi P will use this task. So leave this to I am enabling the new library re entrant as it gives the error while generating the code. Now go to the L wi p here first of all we will disable the DHCP and manually enter the IP address subnet mask etc you can see here the RT o s usage is enabled by default as we have enabled it already. Anyway, leave everything else to default in the General Settings. In the key options, the only change we need to make is increase the heap memory size I am setting it to 10 kilobytes This is it for the L W IP configuration, leave everything else to default for now. Last but not least, since we are using the RTO s we have to use the time base as anything other than cystic I am using the timer six for this purpose All right, if you are not using Cortex M seven based MCU go ahead and generate the code. As I mentioned, I am using the F 750 Discovery Board and as st recommends we must enable the instruction and data cache for better processing. Also, this board has less flash memory and it won't be able to store all the variables in the flash. That is why I am going to use the external flash memory and for this purpose I must use the MPU set the MPU to background region privileged access only plus MPU will be disabled during hard fault. Now enable the MPU region. The base address will be the address of the external flash that is the QS p i which is at 9 million hexa. The size will be five 112 megabytes, and we will disable all the access in this region. As mentioned here in the memory description, the QS P eyes in the block four, which is 512 megabytes. This is why I blocked access to 512 megabytes of memory so as to prevent the speculative access to this region. If you don't understand this part, watch the MPU configuration series in the Cortex M seven playlist, the link is in the description the region to will start again the 9 million hexa and the size will be 16 megabytes. This is the actual size of the QS pi memory available on the board. Here we will permit the access and we will set the region to cacheable and buffer bubble. This was actually explained in my project about the memory configuration in Cortex M seven series MCU.

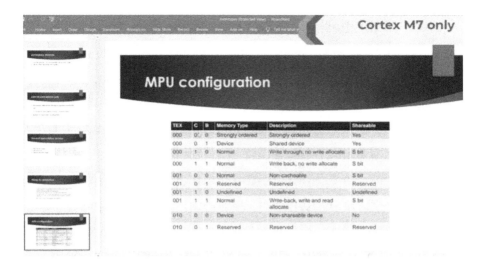

MPU configuration

TEX	C	B	Memory Type	Description	Shareable
000	0	0	Strongly ordered	Strongly ordered	Yes
000	0	1	Device	Shared device	Yes
000	1	0	Normal	Write through, no write allocate	S bit
000	1	1	Normal	Write back, no write allocate	S bit
001	0	0	Normal	Non-cacheable	S bit
001	0	1	Reserved	Reserved	Reserved
001	1	0	Undefined	Undefined	Undefined
001	1	1	Normal	Write-back, write and read allocate	S bit
010	0	0	Device	Non-shareable device	No
010	0	1	Reserved	Reserved	Reserved

We are trying to set this region as the normal memory region with the right back attribute. This is according to the STS recommendation for the Q SP I memory configuration, we will create one more memory region at 9 million hexa. But this time we will enable the instruction execution from this region this is it for the MPU configuration for the external flash. Click Save to generate the code you can see there is the default task getting created. And inside the default task, the L WAP gets initialized. Let's build the code wants to check for errors. All right, we have four errors. Let's solve them. The first one is about the multiple definitions of IRLO. It is defined in the middleware third party L W IP system OS sis arch file, let's open this file first. This must be where the redefinition is causing error. Let's comment out this line and rebuild the code. We still have some errors, but the error regarding redefinition is gone. Now the issue is related to the flash memory being overflowed. For this reason, we have already set up the MPU so that we can use the external flash memory to store the data. Let's go to the flash strip file to do the modification we have to change the origin of the flash to the Q SP II memory the address is 9 million hexa and the size is 16 megabytes. Save the file and generate the code again. And all the errors are gone. Now we have modified the flash script but this is not enough. We still need to make some changes in the system file go to System init function and we will add some code here. First we will reset the configuration register. And then we must relocate the vector table to the new flash base. This is all the setup needed for now. We will do the ping test first. And for that we don't need any functions. Let's build the code and debug it. Since I am using external flash, I need to use the external loader in the debugger. So here we will create a new debug configuration. Go to debugger tab, check external loader and click Scan. Now choose the MCU F 750 In my case, and click Apply to save the configuration.

Now click debug. Download verified successfully. Let's reset the controller and let's put a breakpoint in the error handler To make sure we don't hit it let's run the code let's ping to the board the ping test is successful. And before we go ahead I want to show you the configuration for the Ethernet. This time I have connected the controller directly with the computer without using any router. This is why I want to show the configuration for the Ethernet in the windows. Here I have changed the IP assignment to manual and you can see the rest of the configuration. I will upload these images along with the project so you can access them later also. Now as the ping is successful, let's include the UDP client library files. Let's see the UDP client source file we have the UDP client in IT function which creates two new threads. The UDP send thread will be used to periodically send the data to the server and the UDP in its thread will be used to initialize the UDP client. The stack size in both will be default one kilobytes and the priority is normal. Let's see UDP in its thread. Now. First of all, we will create a new Netcom connection. The net con UDP argument is used to initialize the UDP connection. If the connection is successful, we will bind the connection to the local IP address and the port seven the IP address will be the one we set up in the cube MX and the port will be the port of the client. Next we will convert the destination IP address to the integral format. This here is the IP address of the computer which you can find by typing IP config in the command window. Make sure you use the IP address of the Ethernet port. Next we will connect to the destination IP and port. This eight here is the port of the server. After the connection is successful, we will go into the while loop. Here we will wait for the server to send some data. The data sent by the server will be stored in the RX buff. RX buffer is actually a pointer to the net buffs structure that we have defined here. The net buffs structure contains the P buff, which contains the actual message, its length, etc. And other things like the address and port of the source. Here we get the message from the net buff, modify that message and store it in our AES message array. Then we call the UDP send function which will send this array to the server. Finally, we will delete the neck buff so that it can receive the new data. The next function is the UDP send function. It takes the argument as the pointer to the data that you want to send to the server. here first of all, we will allocate a new net buff, then the net buffer can be used to copy the data into the payload of the net buff structure. Once the data is copied, we will call the nephew Send to send the data to the server. Here the connection parameter contains the details like IP address and port of the server. And the buff parameter contains the data, its length and the IP and port of the client. After sending the data, we will deallocate the neck buff structure. So far, the client only sends the response to the server, but we want the client to send the data periodically. And this is why we need the UDP send thread. Here we will send the value of the index variable every 500 milliseconds. This way the client will always send the data to the server irrespective of whether the server responds or not. Let's write the main function now. Here include the UDP client header file.

Project Explorer ×
LWIP_UDPCLIENT_NETCONN_F7508
  Binaries
  Includes
  Core
    Inc
    Src
      freertos.c
      main.c
      stm32f7xx_hal_msp.c
      stm32f7xx_hal_timebase_tim.c
      stm32f7xx_it.c
      syscalls.c
      sysmem.c
      system_stm32f7xx.c
      udpclient.c
    Startup
  Drivers
  LWIP
  Middlewares
  Debug
  LWIP_UDPCLIENT_NETCONN_F7508.i
  LWIP_UDPCLIENT_NETCONN_F7508 C
  STM32F750N8HX_FLASH.ld
  STM32F750N8HX_RAM.ld

```
283     * @brief  Function implementing the defaultTask thread.
284     * @param  argument: Not used
285     * @retval None
286     */
287    /* USER CODE END Header_StartDefaultTask */
288    void StartDefaultTask(void *argument)
289    {
290      /* init code for LWIP */
291      MX_LWIP_Init();
292      /* USER CODE BEGIN 5 */          I
293      udpcl
294      /* Infinite loop */
295      for(;;)
296      {
297        osDelay(1);
298      }
299      /* USER CODE END 5 */
300    }
301
302    /* MPU Configuration */
303
304    void MPU_Config(void)
305    {
306      MPU_Region_InitTypeDef MPU_InitStruct = {0};
307
308      /* Disables the MPU */
309      HAL_MPU_Disable();
310
```

In the default task after the LW IP has initialized called the initialization of the UDP client. This will create the two new threads and everything will work from there. That's all the things we need to do in the main file. Let's build and debug the code I am going to use the Hercules as the UDP server. This is the address of the client. Seven is the port of the client and eight is the port of the server. The address of the server is same as the IP address of the computer. Let's run the code now. You can see the client is sending the value of the index variable. And when the server sends some data, the client modifies it and send it back. In the meantime, it continues sending the index value every 500 milliseconds.

TCP SERVER AND CLIENT NETCONN FREE RTOSLWIP

The STM 32 Ethernet series, and today we will see how to use the STM 32 as a TCP server and TCP client both using the L WAP and Netcom. Using free RT OS Of course, I have already covered the UDP server and client in my previous projects, and you can check them out in the Ethernet library. Before I start the project, there is important information I want to share with you guys. The controller's tech website now has the community feature where you can open a topic about the relevant issue. To do so, you have to go to the Community tab first. Here I have added a few microcontrollers so that you can create the topic in the relevant section, you have to first register on the forum. Once the registration is successful, you can go to the respective MCU and create a topic there. If you want more threads to be added, you can send me a mail about it. If the registration option doesn't show up in the menu, you can directly go to the register page and then register the work is still in progress, and sometimes it is misbehaving as of now. Anyway, let's continue with the project and we will create a new project in cube IDE I am using the STM 32 F 750 Discovery Board, give some name to the project and click Finish. The Cube MX configuration is similar to what we have seen in the previous two projects.

So, if you have already seen the previous two projects on the Ethernet, you can skip to the 11th Minute let me clear the pin outs first. We will start with the clock configuration. I have 25 megahertz crystal on board and I am running it as 200 megahertz clock All right now go to the Ethernet and enable the type of connection you have. As I mentioned earlier, this board have our Mi connection type. Let's start with the parameter configuration first, since we are using the onboard connector, the pH y address must be zero. Also change the RX mode to the interrupt mode. When you do this, you can see the Ethernet interrupt is enabled. Finally do check the pin outs and match it with the schematics of your board. Also make sure that the speed is set to maximum Next go to the free r t o s I am enabling the version two of the CM sis no changes are needed to be made in the free RT O S Just leave everything to default you can see there is a default task created and later the L wi P will use this task. So leave this to I am enabling the new library reentrant as it gives the error while generating the code. Now go to the L wi p here first of all we will disable the DHCP and manually enter the IP address subnet mask etc you can see here the r t o s usage is enabled by default as we have enabled it already. Anyway, leave everything else to default in the General Settings. In the key options, the only change we need to make is increase the heap memory size. I am setting it to 10 kilobytes This is it for the L W IP configuration. Leave everything else to default for now. Last but not least, since we are using the R TOS we have to use the time base as anything other than cystic I am using the timer six for this purpose. All right If you are not using Cortex M seven based MCU go ahead and generate the code. As I mentioned, I am using the F 750 discovery board. And as st recommends, we must enable the instruction and data cache for better processing. Also, this board has less flash memory and it won't be able to store all the variables in the flash. That is why I am going to use the external flash memory and for this purpose, I must use the MPU. Set the MPU to background region privileged access only plus MPU will be disabled during hard fault. Now enable the MPU region. The base address will be the address of the external flash that is the QS p i which is at 9 million hexa.

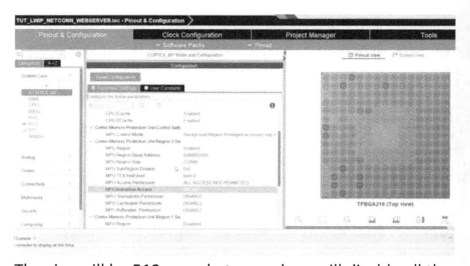

The size will be 512 megabytes, and we will disable all the access in this region. As mentioned here in the memory description, the QoS P eyes in the block four which is 512 megabytes. This is why I blocked access to 512 megabytes of memory so as to prevent the speculative access to this region. If you don't understand this part, watch the MPU configuration series in the Cortex M seven playlist. The link is in the description. The region two will start again the 9 million hexa and the size will be 16 megabytes. This is the actual size of the QS pi memory available on the board. Here we will permit the access and we will set the region to cashable and buffer bubble. This was actually explained in my project about the memory configuration in Cortex M seven series MCU we are trying to set this region as the normal memory region with the right back attribute. This is as according to the STS recommendation for the Q SP I memory configuration we will create one more memory region at 9 million hexa but this time we will enable the instruction execution from this region this is it for the MPU configuration for the external flash click Save to generate the code you can see there is the default task getting created. And inside the default task, the L WAP gets initialized let's build the code wants to check for errors All right, we have four errors. Let's solve them. The first one is about the multiple definitions of IRLO. It is defined in the middleware third party L w i P system OS sis arch file, let's open this file first. This must be where the redefinition is causing error. Let's comment out this line and rebuild the code. We still have some errors but the error regarding redefinition is gone. Now the issue is related to the flash memory being overflowed. For this reason, we have already set up the MPU so that we can use the external flash memory to store the data. Let's go to the flash strip file to do the modification we have to change the origin of the flash to the QS pi memory the address is 9 million hexa and the size is 16 megabytes save the file and generate the code again and all the errors are gone.

```
/* Highest address of the user mode stack */
_estack = ORIGIN(RAM) + LENGTH(RAM); /* end of "RAM" Ram type memory */

_Min_Heap_Size = 0x200 ; /* required amount of heap */
_Min_Stack_Size = 0x400 ; /* required amount of stack */

/* Memories definition */
MEMORY
{
  RAM    (xrw)  : ORIGIN = 0x20000000,  LENGTH = 320K
/* FLASH  (rx)   : ORIGIN = 0x08000000,  LENGTH = 64K */
  FLASH  (rx)   : ORIGIN = 0x90000000,  LENGTH = 16M
}

/* Sections */
SECTIONS
{
  /* The startup code into "FLASH" Rom type memory */
  .isr_vector :
  {
    . = ALIGN(4);
    KEEP(*(.isr_vector)) /* Startup code */
    . = ALIGN(4);
  } >FLASH

  /* The program code and other data into "FLASH" Rom type memory */
  .text :
  {
```

Now we have modified the flash script but this is not enough. We still need to make some changes in the system file go to System init function and we will add some code here. First we will reset the configuration register and then we must relocate the vector table to the new flashbay This is all the setup needed for now, we will do the ping test first. And for that we don't need any functions. Let's build the code and debug it. Since I am using external flash, I need to use the external loader in the debugger. So here we will create a new debug configuration. Go to debugger tab, check external loader and click Scan. Now choose the MCU F 750 In my case, and click Apply to save the configuration. Now click debug. Download verified successfully, let's reset the controller. Let's put a breakpoint in the error handler to make sure we don't hit it let's run the code let's ping to the board the ping test is successful. And before we go ahead, I want to show you the configuration for the Ethernet. This time I have connected the controller directly with the computer without using any router. This is why I want to show the configuration for the Ethernet in the windows. Here I have changed the IP assignment to manual and you can see the rest of the configuration. I will upload these images along with the project so you can access them later also. Alright, since the ping is successful, let's include the library files in our project. Here I have the files for TCP server and client and we are going to cover both of them in this project itself. Put the source files in the source directory and header files in the include directory.

Let's take a look at the TCP server first. Here I have defined two Netcom connections. One of them will be used as the identifier for the server and another one for the client which will connect with the server. The buffer is the pointer to the neck buff structure. And as we already know, the neck buff stores all the information about the data and also about the sender, like the address and port of the sender. I have also defined the variables to store the address and port in case you need the same for the client. And here we have the message arrays where we will store the message received and the message to be transmitted. The initialization of the server starts with the TCP server init function. Here we create a new thread whose name is TCP thread. The entry function is also the TCP thread, the argument passed to this thread is now the stack size is set to default, which is one kilobytes and the priority is set to normal. Let's see the TCP thread now. Here we will first create a new connection using the net con new function. The arguments net con TCP creates a TCP identifier then we will bind this connection to any available IP address it will automatically bind it to the IP that we set in the cube MX and this will be the IP address of the server and also the port for the server is set to seven. Now the server is ready and we will put it into the listen mode so that it can listen for the new client. If a client tries to connect to this server, we will accept the connection and the parameters of this connection will be saved into the new calm. The net can accept takes two arguments which net con is listening and where the connection will be stored. Once we have accepted the connection, this while loop will run forever. Here we will wait for the client to send some data net can receive takes two parameters again. The first is the connection from which the data is to be received, which in our case is the new con the client and the second is the pointer to the net buff structure which we have defined as the buff. If the data is received successfully, we will first extract the address and port of the client just in case if you need it. Then the string copy function is used to copy the payload from the network. off into our message array. You can use this data sent by the client in any way you want. But here I am just going to modify this data and send it back to the client as a response from the server. Net con right is used to send the data to the connection. The first parameter is the connection where you want to send the data to.

```
if (accept_err == ERR_OK)
{
    /* receive the data from the client */
    while (netconn_recv(newconn, &buf) == ERR_OK)
    {
        /* Extract the address and port in case they are required */
        addr = netbuf_fromaddr(buf);  // get the address of the client
        port = netbuf_fromport(buf);  // get the Port of the client

        /* If there is some data remaining to be sent, the following process will continue */
        do
        {
            strncpy (msg, buf->p->payload, buf->p->len);  // get the message from the client

            // Or modify the message received, so that we can send it back to the client
            int len = sprintf (smsg, "\"%s\" was sent by the Server\n", msg);

            netconn_write(newconn, smsg, len, NETCONN_COPY);  // send the message back to th
            memset (msg, '\0', 100);  // clear the buffer
        }
        while (netbuf_next(buf) >0);

        netbuf_delete(buf);
    }

    /* Close connection and discard connection identifier. */
    netconn_close(newconn);
    netconn_delete(newconn);
}
else
```

Then we have the data pointer itself, which in our case is the AES message array, then the length of the message. And at last, we have the API flag, which is Netcom copy. These flags are defined to handle the data we are sending. For example, when the Netcom copy flag is passed, the data is copied into internal buffers which are allocated for the data. This allows the data to be modified directly after the call. You can read more about these flags in the SDS documentation. But in these tutorials, we will stick with the Netcom copy. After sending the data, we will clear the array and then we will delete the buffer also, so that we can receive new data from the client, the server will again wait for the client to send some data and this loop will run forever. So the steps was simple. First, we create a new net con identifier, then bind the identifier to the local IP and port. Then we put the server in the listen mode. If some client tries to connect, the server will accept the new connection, then it will wait for the data to be sent by the client. And finally the server will send the response to that data. These are all the steps for the TCP server. Let's write the main file now. Include the TCP server header file. In the default task, we will just make a call to the TCP server init function which will eventually create the new thread and everything will begin let's build and debug the code so that we can see the working in real time I am using Hercules and since STM 32, is the server Herculis will act as the client here is the IP address and port of the server. Note that the IP address is the same as we configured in the cube MX. Let's connect to the server. Here is the message that the connection is successful. Now we will send some data to the server and you can see the server has sent the response. The pink color data is sent by the client and the black color is the response sent by the server. You can see the server is responding pretty well even for the larger data size. So our TCP server was working well. Now let's move to the TCP client. Here STM 32 will act as the TCP client which will send some periodic data to the server along with a response for any data sent by the server.

This is the TCP client source file just like the server here also we have appointed to the net cons structure and appointed to the net buffs structure there are variables for address and port also the message and less message array to store the data all right everything starts at the TCP client init function. Here first of all, we will create a new semaphore. The argument TCP Sam is defined in the beginning. The semaphore will be used to prevent the simultaneous access to this TCP send function which is used to actually send the data to the server and is being called by two different threads the TCP send thread and the TCP in it thread. We will use the semaphore to make sure that both threads don't call the function at the same time. The sis Sam knew takes two arguments. The first is the semaphore handler and the second is the initial count. I am setting the initial count to zero. So we must first release the semaphore before it can be acquired. And we will release it after the initialization of the client is complete. And then we will create two new threads one for initializing the TCP client, and another for periodically sending the data to the server. The stack size is default one kilobytes and priority is set to normal for both. Let's see the initialization thread first. Here we will first create a new connection identifier. The arguments net con TCP will create the TCP identifier. Once the identifier is created, we will bind it to the available IP address and the port seven, the IP address will be the same as the one we defined in the cube MX and this will be the address of the client. Now we will connect to the server. First we will convert the IP address of the server into the integral format. This address will be the same as the IP address of the computer, which you can find in Windows by using the command IP config. Make sure you use the address of the Ethernet and not the Wi Fi. The destination port is 10 and this is the port of the server. Now we will connect to the server using the Netcom connect function. Here the first argument is the connection identifier.

```
                                          38   {
Includes                                  39        /* Bind connection to the port number / (port of the client). */
Core                                      40        err = netconn_bind(conn, IP_ADDR_ANY, 7);
  Inc                                     41
 Src                                      42        if (err == ERR_OK)
  freertos.c                              43        {
  main.c                                  44            /* The destination IP adress of the computer */
  stm32f7xx_hal_msp.c                     45            IP_ADDR4(&dest_addr, 192, 168, 0, 2);
  stm32f7xx_hal_timebase_tim.c            46            dest_port = 10;   // server port
  stm32f7xx_it.c                          47
  syscalls.c                              48            /* Connect to the TCP Server */
  sysmem.c                                49            connect_error = netconn_connect(conn, &dest_addr, dest_port);
  system_stm32f7xx.c                      50
  tcpclient.c                             51            // If the connection to the server is established, the following will continue, else delete t
  tcpserver.c                             52            if (connect_error == ERR_OK)
 Startup                                  53            {
Drivers                                   54                // Release the semaphore once the connection is successful
LWIP                                      55                sys_sem_signal(&tcpsem);
Middlewares                               56                while (1)
Debug                                     57                {
LWIP_TCP_SERVER_CLIENT_NETCONN            58                    /* wait until the data is sent by the server */
LWIP_TCP_SERVER_CLIENT_NETCONN            59                    if (netconn_recv(conn, &buf) == ERR_OK)
STM32F750N8HX_FLASH.ld                    60                    {
STM32F750N8HX_RAM.ld                      61                        /* Extract the address and port in case they are required */
                                          62                        addr = netbuf_fromaddr(buf);  // get the address of the client
                                          63                        port = netbuf_fromport(buf);  // get the Port of the client
                                          64
                                          65                        /* if there is some data remaining to be sent, the following process will continu
                                          66                        do
```

Problems Tasks Console × Properties
<terminated> LWIP_TCP_SERVER_CLIENT_NETCONN Debug [STM32 Cortex-M C/C++ Application] ST-LINK (ST-LINK GDB server)   LWIP_TCP_SERVE
Download verified successfully   28-Apr-2022, 12

Then we have the pointer to the destination address and at last the destination port. If the connection is successful, we will release the semaphore so that the TCP send thread can send the data to the server. And here we will wait for the server to send some data to the client. Once the data is received, we will extract the address and port of the server just in case you need it. Now copy the data sent by the server into our message array. We will modify this message and send it back to the server. But before we can call the TCP send function, we would need to acquire the semaphore. This is to prevent the simultaneous access to the TCP send function by this thread and the TCP send thread. Let's see the TCP send thread now. Here we will convert the value of the index variable into the string format and then send this value to the server. But again before calling the TCP send, we must acquire the semaphore. This is a periodic task, and it will run every

500 milliseconds. In the TCP send function, we will first send the data to the server. Net con right takes four arguments. The first parameter is the connection identifier where you want to send the data to then we have the data pointer itself. Then the length of the message. And at last we have the API flag, which is Netcom copy. These flags are defined to handle the data we are sending. For example, when the Netcom copy flag is passed, the data is copied into internal buffers which are allocated for the data. This allows the data to be modified directly after the call. You can read more about these flags in the SDS documentation. But in these tutorials, we will stick with the Netcom copy. Once the data is sent, we will release the semaphore implying that it's safe to send the data now. So the task waiting for the semaphore can acquire it and call the TCP send function. This is it for the explanation part. Now let's write the main code. Here. Instead of TCP server, we will initialize the TCP client we also need to include the TCP client header file. Let's build and debug the code so that we can see the working of the client in real time. The STM 32 is acting as the TCP client so the Herculis will act as the TCP server this is the port of the server and it should be the same as whatever you set in the code. All right, let's run the code now. Put the server in the listen mode, the client is connected, and it is sending the index value every 500 milliseconds. You can see the confirmation in the status window. The value of the index variable started at six

because for the first five times, it was not able to acquire the semaphore.

As the server wasn't connected. You can see the client is also responding to the data sent by the server. The index value is updating every 500 milliseconds. So everything is working as expected. We saw how to intimate the STM 32 was the TCP server and TCP client and in both cases, our program worked as expected. The next few projects on Ethernet will cover the HTTP server where we will do one basic server and then implement some additional details for example.

EXAMPLE DUMMY CODE

Below is an example code for a TCP server and client using FreeRTOS and the lwIP NETCONN API on an STM32 microcontroller. This code demonstrates a basic TCP communication where the client sends a message to the server, and the server responds with an acknowledgment message.

TCP Server:

```
#include "main.h"
#include "lwip.h"
#include "api.h"

#define TCP_SERVER_PORT 5000

// Task handle for the TCP server task
TaskHandle_t tcp_server_task_handle;

// TCP server task function
void tcp_server_task(void *pvParameters) {
  struct netconn *conn, *newconn;
  err_t err;
  struct netbuf *buf;
  void *data;
  u16_t len;

  // Create a new TCP netconn
  conn = netconn_new(NETCONN_TCP);
  if (conn == NULL) {
```

```c
  vTaskDelete(NULL);
}

// Bind the TCP netconn to the specified port
netconn_bind(conn, NULL, TCP_SERVER_PORT);

// Listen for incoming connections
netconn_listen(conn);

while (1) {
  // Accept new client connections
  err = netconn_accept(conn, &newconn);
  if (err == ERR_OK) {
    while ((err = netconn_recv(newconn, &buf)) ==
ERR_OK) {
      // Get the data and length of the received
packet
      netbuf_data(buf, &data, &len);

      // Print the received data (assuming it is a
null-terminated string)
      char received_data[len + 1];
      memcpy(received_data, data, len);
      received_data[len] = '\0';
      printf("Received from client: %s\n",
received_data);

      // Send an acknowledgment back to the client
```

```c
        const char *ack_msg = "Message received";
        netconn_write(newconn, ack_msg,
strlen(ack_msg), NETCONN_COPY);
        netbuf_delete(buf);
      }

      // Close the connection with the client
      netconn_close(newconn);
      netconn_delete(newconn);
    }
  }
}

int main(void) {
  // Initialize the HAL, peripherals, and FreeRTOS
  HAL_Init();
  SystemClock_Config();
  MX_GPIO_Init();
  MX_LWIP_Init();

  // Create the TCP server task
  xTaskCreate(tcp_server_task, "TCP_Server",
configMINIMAL_STACK_SIZE, NULL,
tskIDLE_PRIORITY + 1, &tcp_server_task_handle);

  // Start the scheduler
  vTaskStartScheduler();
```

```c
  // We should never reach here
  while (1) {
  }
}
```

TCP Client:

```c
#include "main.h"
#include "lwip.h"
#include "api.h"

#define TCP_SERVER_IP "192.168.0.100" //
Replace with the IP address of your server
#define TCP_SERVER_PORT 5000

// Task handle for the TCP client task
TaskHandle_t tcp_client_task_handle;

// TCP client task function
void tcp_client_task(void *pvParameters) {
  struct netconn *conn;
  err_t err;

  // Create a new TCP netconn
  conn = netconn_new(NETCONN_TCP);
  if (conn == NULL) {
   vTaskDelete(NULL);
  }
```

```c
// Connect to the server
err = netconn_connect(conn, IP_ADDR_ANY,
TCP_SERVER_PORT);
if (err != ERR_OK) {
  vTaskDelete(NULL);
}

while (1) {
  // Send a message to the server
  const char *message = "Hello, TCP Server!";
  netconn_write(conn, message, strlen(message),
NETCONN_COPY);

  // Wait for the server's response
  struct netbuf *buf;
  void *data;
  u16_t len;
  err = netconn_recv(conn, &buf);
  if (err == ERR_OK) {
    // Get the data and length of the received
packet
    netbuf_data(buf, &data, &len);

    // Print the received data (assuming it is a null-
terminated string)
    char received_data[len + 1];
    memcpy(received_data, data, len);
```

```c
    received_data[len] = '\0';
    printf("Received from server: %s\n",
received_data);

    // Free the received buffer
    netbuf_delete(buf);
    }

    // Wait for a short period before sending the
next message
    vTaskDelay(pdMS_TO_TICKS(2000));
    }
}

int main(void) {
    // Initialize the HAL, peripherals, and FreeRTOS
    HAL_Init();
    SystemClock_Config();
    MX_GPIO_Init();
    MX_LWIP_Init();

    // Create the TCP client task
    xTaskCreate(tcp_client_task, "TCP_Client",
configMINIMAL_STACK_SIZE, NULL,
tskIDLE_PRIORITY + 1, &tcp_client_task_handle);

    // Start the scheduler
    vTaskStartScheduler();
```

```
    // We should never reach here
    while (1) {
    }
}
```

In this example, we have two tasks: tcp_server_task for the TCP server and tcp_client_task for the TCP client. The TCP server listens on port 5000 for incoming connections and responds to client messages. The TCP client connects to the server, sends a message, and waits for a response.

Please ensure that you have correctly set up the lwIP stack and FreeRTOS for your STM32 microcontroller, and that the network configuration is correct for both the client and server.

Keep in mind that this is a basic example to demonstrate TCP communication using FreeRTOS and lwIP on an STM32 microcontroller. Depending on your specific application requirements, you might need to handle more advanced scenarios and implement error handling.

BASIC HTTP SERVER NETCONN FREERTOS LWIP

Ethernet series and today we will see how to use the STM 32 as the HTTP server. In today's project, I will create a very simple web server which will use the get method for the request and then display the web pages accordingly. Later, we will cover a more detailed server using the Ajax but that will be in the upcoming projects. Let's start the Q ID and create a new project I am using the usual STM 32 F 750 Discovery Board give some name to the project and click Finish let me clear the pinouts All right, let's start with the clock setup. I am using the external high speed crystal for the clock.

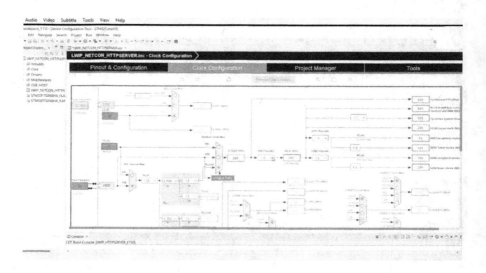

The board has 25 megahertz crystal and the system is running at 200 megahertz. All right now go to the Ethernet and enable the type of connection you have. As I mentioned earlier, this board have our Mi connection type. Let's start with the parameter configuration first, since we are using the onboard connector, the pH y address must be zero. Also change the RX mode to the interrupt mode. When you do this, you can see the Ethernet interrupt is enabled. Finally do check the pin outs and match it with the schematics of your board. Also make sure that the speed is set to maximum. Next go to the free AR t o s I am enabling the version two of the CM sis no changes are needed to be made in the free RT O S Just leave everything to default you can see there is a default task created and later the L wi P will use this task. So leave this to I am enabling the new library reentrant as it gives the error while generating the code. Now go to the L wi p here first of all we will disable the DHCP and manually enter the IP address subnet mask etc you can see here the RT o s usage is enabled by default as we have enabled it already. Anyway, leave everything else to default in the General Settings. In the key options, the only change we need to make is increase the heap memory size, I am setting it to 10 kilobytes. So far we did the usual setup whatever we did in the previous three four projects. For the HTTP server, we need to enable the L wi P httpd. If all these options don't show up, you need to check this box. Let's leave everything to default here for now. All right, if you are not using Cortex M seven based MCU go ahead and generate the code. As I mentioned, I am using the F 750 Discovery Board and as st recommends we must enable the instruction and data cache for better processing. Also, this port has less flash memory and it won't be able to store all the variables in the flash. That is why I am going to use the external flash memory and for this purpose I must use the MPU set the MPU to background region privileged access only plus MPU will be disabled during hard fault. Now enable the MPU region the base address will be the address of the external flash that is the QS p i which is at 9 million hexa.

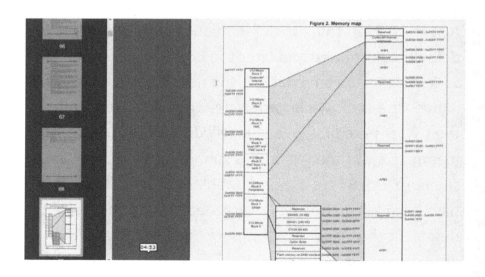

The size will be 512 megabytes and we will disable all the access in this region as mentioned here in the memory descript Can the Q S P eyes in the block for which is 512 megabytes. This is why I blocked access to 512 megabytes of memory so as to prevent the speculative access to this region. If you don't understand this part, watch the MPU configuration series in the Cortex M seven playlist. The link is in the description. The region two will start again the 9 million hexa and the size will be 16 megabytes. This is the actual size of the QS pi memory available on the board. Here we will permit the access and we will set the region to cashable and buffer bubble. This was actually explained in my project about the memory configuration in Cortex M seven series MCU. We are trying to set this region as the normal memory region with the right back attribute. This is as according to the STS recommendation for the Q SP I memory configuration, we will create one more memory region at 9 million hexa. But this time, we will enable the instruction execution from this region. This is it for the MPU configuration for the external flash. Click Save to generate the code. Before we go any forward, let's build the code once, we will see a lot of errors, and we will resolve them one by one. Here we have the error about the FS data custom dot c file, the file is not present in the directory, double click the error to see where it occurred. Here we will go to the definition of the customer s data and set it to zero. So now we are not using the FS data custom file. Apparently there is no way to disable it in the cube setting. So we have to manually do it here. Now we have another error about Fs data file and it is also not present in the directory. You can go to middleware third party I WAP source apps HTTP. Here you can see the FS data header file is present, but there is no source file. This file is actually generated based on your resources. And we need to use the make Fs data application to do that. Here we have the FS folder, which consists of all the resources we have for this project. By default, there are two HTML files index and 404. And I am leaving them as it is, this is how our index file will look like. And this is how the 404 file will look. You can create any HTML file and place it in this folder and then generate the FS data file. As I mentioned, I am keeping the files as it is and we will copy all these files into our HTTP directory. Now double click the FS data application and it will generate the FS data file for you. I will leave the link to this folder in the description below. And let's go back to our project and build it again we have seven errors now and most of them are about the multiple definitions. Now go to the FS data file we just created and excluded from the build let's build again all the errors regarding the multiple definitions are gone.

workspace_1.7.0 - LWIP_NETCON_HTTPSERVER/STM32F750N8HX_FLASH.id - STM32CubeIDE

le Edit Source Refactor Navigate Search Project Run Window Help

Project Explorer ×

LWIP_NETCON_HTTPSERVER

- Includes
- Core
- Drivers
- LWIP
- Middlewares
  - ST
  - Third_Party
- Debug
- LWIP_NETCON_HTTPSERVER.ioc
- STM32F750N8HX_FLASH.ld
- STM32F750N8HX_RAM.ld

LWIP_NETCON_HTTPSERVER.ioc   main.c   *STM32F750N8HX_FLASH.ld ×

```
4)
44 /* Memories definition */
45 MEMORY
46 {
47   RAM    (xrw)  : ORIGIN = 0x20000000,  LENGTH = 320K
48   FLASH  (rx)   : ORIGIN = 0x9b0000,    LENGTH = 64K
49 }
50
51 /* Sections */
52 SECTIONS
53 {
54   /* The startup code into "FLASH" Rom type memory */
55   .isr_vector :
56   {
57     . = ALIGN(4);
58     KEEP(*(.isr_vector)) /* Startup code */
59     . = ALIGN(4);
60   } >FLASH
61
62   /* The program code and other data into "FLASH" Rom type memory */
63   .text :
64   {
65     . = ALIGN(4);
66     *(.text)        /* .text sections (code) */
67     *(.text*)       /* .text* sections (code) */
68     *(.glue_7)      /* glue arm to thumb code */
69     *(.glue_7t)     /* glue thumb to arm code */
```

STM32F750N8HX_FLASH.ld

Problems ×   Tasks   Console   Properties

4 errors, 0 warnings, 0 others

Description   Resourc

∨ Errors (4 items)

Now. This Airavata flash overflow is specific to this board as I mentioned that the Flash has a low space and this is why I configured the MPU for the external flash. Now I will set the flash to the external location and this is done in the flash script file. If your board has enough flash memory, you don't need to do this. All right, there is one last error and it is about the multiple definition of Furneaux. Let's go to this location middleware third party L w i P system OS sis archtops. See here just comment out the definition of earn no All right, all the errors are gone now. Now since I have Using the external flash, I need to relocate the vector table. Again, this is specific to some boards. And if you did not set the external flash, you don't need to do this this is our main file. Here the default task is created. And once this task will run, it will initialize the L wi P. All right, everything is set now, and it's time to ping. Since I am using the external flash, I need to use the external loader in the debugger. Let's run it now. Now we will ping to our IP address. As you can see, the ping is successful, so everything seems okay so far, and we can proceed ahead with it. Let's include the library files now. Here I have the HTTP server source and header files. Put the source file in the source directory and header file in the include directory. The HTTP server header file only has one function HTTP server in it. Let's see its implementation in the source file. The HTTP server in it creates a new HTTP thread whose entry function is HTTP thread itself. The stack size is default one kilobyte and the priority is set to normal.

Inside the HTTP thread, we will create a new net comm connection. The argument is net con TCP and it will create a new TCP connection. If the connection is created successfully, we will bind it to the local IP address. This is the same as the one we set in the cube MX and this will be the address of the server the port of the server is set to 80. Once the binding is successful, we will put the server in the listen mode. Now the connection will listen for any client which is trying to connect to this server. Once the client connects to this server, we will accept the connection the net can accept takes two arguments. The first argument is the TCP connection, which is listening to the client. And the second argument is the pointer where the new connection is going to store. Our TCP listening connection is COMM And we will store the new connection in the new comm. Both of them are defined in the beginning of the function. Once the client connection is accepted by the server, we will call the HTTP server to handle the requests made by this client. In the HTTP server, we will receive the requests made by the client net con receive takes two arguments. The first is the connection. And the second is the net buffer structure where the request data is going to store. Next we will check what request was made by the client. And to do that, we will first get the data pointer and its length from the net buff structure. Net buffer data takes three arguments here. The first is the neck buff structure where we want to get the data from next is the pointer where you want to store the data pointer to and at last is the pointer where the length should be stored. So now the data pointer is stored in buff and the length is stored in buff Len. Now we will compare the data in the Data pointer to whatever requests you want to serve. For example, here I am checking if the client has requested the index dot HTML. If it did, then we will open the file index dot HTML. We will store the information about this file in the file structure. Now we will write this data to the connection. Net con right takes four arguments. The connection where the data is to be written the data pointer length of the data pointer. And the last one is the API flag. This API flag basically decides how the day Till will be written. For example, the net con copy will be used if you want to copy the data into the memory belonging to the stack. Here we are using no copy, and it means the data will be simply written without any conditions. After writing the data, we will close the file.

So we serve the requests made by the client to get the index dot HTML file. If you remember, I only have one file in the FS folder, and hence if any other request comes from the client, my server will show the 404 error page. You can see this in the else condition. Once the client request is served, we will close the connection and delete the neck buff. Finally, we will delete the connection itself so that a new clients can make another request. This while loop will keep running and the server will keep looking for the clients. All right, let's write the main code now. First of all, we will include the HTTP header file. Now in the default task, after the LW IP is initialized, we will initialize the HTTP server also. This will eventually create a new HTTP thread and everything will begin. Let's build and debug the code now.

lwIP - A Lightweight TCP/IP Stack

The web page you are watching was served by a simple web server running on top of the lightweight TCP/IP stack lwIP.

lwIP is an open source implementation of the TCP/IP protocol suite that was originally written by Adam Dunkels at the Swedish Institute of Computer Science but now is being actively developed by a team of developers distributed world-wide. Since it's release, lwIP has spurred a lot of interest and has been ported to several platforms and operating systems. lwIP can be used either with or without an underlying OS.

The focus of the lwIP TCP/IP implementation is to reduce the RAM usage while still having a full scale TCP. This makes lwIP suitable for use in embedded systems with tens of kilobytes of free RAM and room for around 40 kilobytes of code ROM.

More information about lwIP can be found at the lwIP homepage at http://savannah.nongnu.org/projects/lwip/ or at the lwIP wiki at http://lwip.wikia.com.

Let's open the index dot HTML page. You can see the page is being displayed. If we request the 404 page, the server displays it perfectly. As I mentioned, the server currently has two pages only. And if we request anything other than the index page, the server will show the 404 error. The HTTP Basic server is working all right.

EXAMPLE DUMMY CODE

Creating a complete and feature-rich HTTP server from scratch is quite involved and goes beyond the scope of a simple example. However, I can provide you with a basic outline and example code for a simple HTTP server using FreeRTOS and the lwIP NETCONN API on an STM32 microcontroller. This example serves a static HTML page when a client requests the root URL ("/") and returns a "Not Found" response for other URLs.

Please note that this example is minimal and lacks some critical features, such as handling various HTTP methods (e.g., GET, POST), serving other types of content (e.g., CSS, JavaScript, images), handling query parameters, and more. For more sophisticated HTTP server functionality, you might want to consider using existing HTTP server libraries built on top of lwIP or other dedicated libraries.

```c
#include "main.h"
#include "lwip.h"
#include "api.h"

#define HTTP_SERVER_PORT 80

// HTML content to be served
const char http_response[] =
  "HTTP/1.1 200 OK\r\n"
  "Content-Type: text/html\r\n\r\n"
  "<html><body><h1>Hello, STM32 HTTP Server!</h1></body></html>";

// Task handle for the HTTP server task
TaskHandle_t http_server_task_handle;
```

```c
// HTTP server task function
void http_server_task(void *pvParameters) {
  struct netconn *conn, *newconn;
  err_t err;
  struct netbuf *buf;
  void *data;
  u16_t len;

  // Create a new HTTP netconn
  conn = netconn_new(NETCONN_TCP);
  if (conn == NULL) {
   vTaskDelete(NULL);
  }

  // Bind the HTTP netconn to the specified port
  netconn_bind(conn, NULL, HTTP_SERVER_PORT);

  // Listen for incoming connections
  netconn_listen(conn);

  while (1) {
   // Accept new client connections
   err = netconn_accept(conn, &newconn);
   if (err == ERR_OK) {
     while ((err = netconn_recv(newconn, &buf)) ==
ERR_OK) {
       // Get the data and length of the received
```

```
packet
    netbuf_data(buf, &data, &len);

    // Parse the HTTP request (assuming it is a
GET request)
    if (len > 4 && memcmp(data, "GET ", 4) == 0) {
    // Check if the request is for the root URL
("/")
    if (memcmp(data + 4, "/", len - 4) == 0) {
    // Serve the HTML content
    netconn_write(newconn, http_response,
strlen(http_response), NETCONN_COPY);
    } else {
    // Return "Not Found" response for other
URLs
    const char *not_found_response =
"HTTP/1.1 404 Not Found\r\n\r\n";
    netconn_write(newconn,
not_found_response, strlen(not_found_response),
NETCONN_COPY);
    }
    }

    // Free the received buffer
    netbuf_delete(buf);
    }

    // Close the connection with the client
```

```c
      netconn_close(newconn);
      netconn_delete(newconn);
    }
  }
}

int main(void) {
  // Initialize the HAL, peripherals, and FreeRTOS
  HAL_Init();
  SystemClock_Config();
  MX_GPIO_Init();
  MX_LWIP_Init();

  // Create the HTTP server task
  xTaskCreate(http_server_task, "HTTP_Server",
configMINIMAL_STACK_SIZE, NULL,
tskIDLE_PRIORITY + 1, &http_server_task_handle);

  // Start the scheduler
  vTaskStartScheduler();

  // We should never reach here
  while (1) {
  }
}
```

In this example, we create a FreeRTOS task
http_server_task to handle the HTTP server

functionality. Inside this task, we create a new HTTP netconn, bind it to port 80 (standard HTTP port), and then enter a loop to wait for incoming HTTP requests. When a GET request is received, we parse the request and serve the HTML content for the root URL ("/"). For any other URL, we return a "Not Found" response.

Please ensure that you have correctly set up the lwIP stack and FreeRTOS for your STM32 microcontroller, and that the network configuration is correct.

Keep in mind that this is a basic example to demonstrate a simple HTTP server using FreeRTOS and lwIP on an STM32 microcontroller. For a more complete and robust HTTP server implementation, consider using existing libraries or more advanced solutions.

HTTP SERVER WITH AJAX - PART 1 NETCONN LWIP

Today we will see how to use the HTTP server with Ajax. The project was going to be very long and therefore we will cover it in two different parts. This part will only include the basic understanding of what exactly we are going to use. Also, we will try sending an empty request to the server, and the server should perform some operation on receiving the request. In the next project, we will update a specific part of the webpage by receiving the data from the server. And this whole operation will be done without loading the page. Again, as this is the continuation from the previous HTTP server project, I would advise that you watch that project first. In order to use Ajax, we use the XML HTTP request object. You can find more info about it in the Mozilla documentation, I will leave the link in the description.

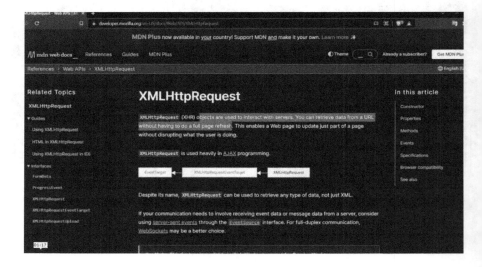

As mentioned here, the object is used to retrieve data from a URL without doing the full page refresh. I X stands for Asynchronous JavaScript and XML and it uses a number of technologies, especially the XML HTTP request.

We will see how to implement it as we proceed with the project. This is the project from my previous project about the HTTP server and I am going to continue with the same. Let's open the project in cube IDE. Here is the HTTP server file, which we will modify in a while. The most important part of this tutorial is the HTML files we use. To make it a bit more interesting. I have decided to use a larger webpage with images and more syntax. As I am too lazy to make it from scratch, I decided to use one from the STS examples. This is an example on the net con HTTP web server provided by the s t. Here we are only interested in this Fs folder. The home page looks like this. And this is good enough for the experiment. This is the 404 error page. We will modify the home page and add some buttons to it which will be used to send an empty request to the server. Let's create some buttons. First, I am going to use an online HTML editor to create the button. These look nice with the hover actions. Let me delete all this stuff from here.

First, we will create an onload event which will basically call the onload function once the entire page is loaded. Now we need to create this onload function and it must be defined under the script tag in the head. You can use JavaScript for larger code, but since I am using something very basic, I am writing the code here itself. First we will define a variable to store the XML HTTP request. Now we will define the onload function in which we will create a new XML HTTP request. The buttons we created, we must use the click functionality to them. So when the green button is clicked, we will call the function green which we will define in a while. Similarly, when the blue button is pressed, it will call the function blue. And we will define these functions inside our script tag again. So when the green button is pressed, we will initialize the ex HR request. The open method is used to initialize a new request or reinitialize an existing request. Here is the syntax for the same. The parameters are the request method, the URL, and the third one is optional. Here we will use the get method, the URL will be button color equals to G and just put true in the last parameter. After initializing the request, we will send it to the server with no parameters at all. This is not actually a request for data, but rather a test to see if the server is able to receive it. We will do the same for the blue button close the script tag after everything is finished, I am not good with HTML or JavaScript. So if I am missing some functions, or if you think using JavaScript is better here, you are free to do so please don't spam the comments section regarding this. We will test this with our server later. Now as I mentioned that I am going to use the files from the examples provided by S T. Let's copy them outside we will rename this to index dot HTML also let's rename this to the image folder it will be easier for us to deal with it now you can see the images are not loading as we need to update the path to these images in the code. Let's edit this index dot HTML file. This is the folder name where it is looking for the images we will change it to the IMG folder at all the locations in the code also we need to add the button code we just created let's copy the head section and replace the entire head from the index file we also need to add the onload event in the body of the file all right, the images are loading fine now.

STM32F7xx Webserver Demo
Based on the lwIP TCP/IP stack

Home page	List of tasks

STM32 F-7 Series

The STM32 F7 devices are the world's first ARM
Cortex M7 based 32-bit microcontrollers, setting
the benchmark in performance.

Taking advantage of ST's ART Accelerator as well
as an L1 cache, the STM32 F7 devices deliver the
maximum theoretical performance of the Cortex-
M7 no matter whether code is executed from
embedded Flash or external Memory: 1000
CoreMark/428 DMIPS at 200 MHz fCPU

The STM32F7xx home page

About this demonstration

This webserver is a part of a demonstration package developed on the top level of the lwIP TCP/IP
stack.   07:22

The package contains nine applications:

Now comes the button parts I want to add them somewhere in the middle of the page let's reload this page all right they are looking fine. You can see our script is also loading all right we need to change the folder name in the 404 file as well. Alright, right we will copy them in our project folder now. So go to middleware, third party I WAP source apps, HTTP Fs and paste them here now we need to generate the FS data file again. So double click this make Fs data application. Alright, let's build the code once. We have added a few images in the webpage, so we need to add the functions to serve those images. If you notice in the web server file, our code is only looking for the index dot HTML file. So we need to add the code for serving the image file also. If you check the HTML file again here you can see there will be a request for the IMG slash st dot GIF. So we will check if this request was made. And if it did, we will open the gift

from the image folder and send this data similarly, there
will be a request for the STM 32 dot jpg we will again
check this request and open the respective file and send it
in the 404 file, there will be another request for the logo
image all right other than the requests for these image
files, remember that we are also making a request when
clicking the buttons so we will check for the URL button
color equal to the next character will basically define
whether we clicked the green or the blue button.
Whatever it is, we will store it in the color variable, we
need to define this color variable and we will check its
value in the debugger. Let's build and debug the code
now.

Let's go to the server address which is the same as the
previous tutorial. All right, the web page is loaded
successfully with the images and the buttons. Keep an eye
on the debugger window as well where I have added the

color variable. When I click the green button, the color variable has the character G and on clicking the blue button, it changes to B. So the buttons are working fine. And the XML HTTP request is indeed made by the client. If we try to access any other page, it will show the 404 error page instead. Let's check the Wireshark. To understand the requests made by the client. We are analyzing the Ethernet requests. Also I am putting a filter for HTTP requests. Let me reload the page once. Here you can see the requests.

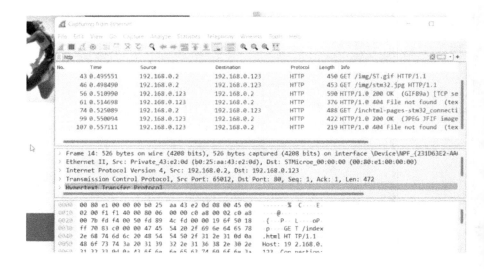

First one is the index dot HTML, which was successful. Then it requested the GIF and jpg file, which was successful as well. When I pressed the buttons, the button color requests were made by the client. The page did not reload while making these requests, which was exactly what we wanted it to do. When we open some other page, you can see the 404 page request followed by the logo file. So far things are working fine. You can play with these buttons, like using the buttons to control the LEDs. In the next tutorial, we will actually receive some data from the server and display it in some section on the webpage. And the objective is to achieve this without reloading the webpage again. Let me be clear again, I am not an expert in HTML, CSS or JavaScript. So if you notice any mistake in the webpage, please check out the comments before pointing them out.

HTTP SERVER WITH AJAX - PART 2 NETCONN LWIP

The STM 32 Ethernet series, and today we will be continuing the use of Ajax in the web server. we created XML HTTP request and our server, the SDM 32 was able to receive that request. Today, we will continue with it and we will receive some data from the server, then display the data on the web page without reloading the entire page. Before I continue with this tutorial, I want to share some important information. I was testing this with free RT o s cm since version two, and the code kept getting stuck at this particular location after some time, basically, the semaphore is getting corrupted for some reason. And this happens during the call to acquire the semaphore from the Ethernet input function. You can see on the right, the item size is supposed to be zero, but it's not. The value field on the webpage just gets empty at this stage as the server is not sending any data to the webpage. After I searched for the error, I found that this is a very common problem with the STM 32 Ethernet drivers. I will post the link to this thread in the description below. Here users have listed some solutions to overcome these issues. And using one of these solutions. I switched back to cm sis version one and the code worked perfectly. So I would advise you guys to use the CM sis version one of the free RT Rs in the Ethernet programming. Alright, since this is the continuation from the previous tutorial, let me rename the previous project to part two. Now let's load the project in the cube ID. In the meantime, let me show you the HTML file I have created for this project. I was testing it on the W three schools website.

So let me put it there itself. If I press the start button, the data gets loaded in the Value field. Notice that this data is refreshing every one second. By the way, this is fetching the data from the W three schools server, so it won't work anywhere else, we will modify it to work with our server. If you notice, under the script tag, we have the same code, we will create a variable to store the request, then the onload function will create a new XML HTTP request. This timer function is a new addition here, this function will be called periodically and inside it we will write another function which will be called whenever the status of the X HR changes. Here we will update the value of the text area which we have defined later in the body. The value will be updated based on what response is sent by the server when it receives the X HR request. Just like the previous tutorial, we have to initiate the X HR request by using the open method. As I mentioned before, this particular URL only works with this website, and you can just put it in the browser URL. So this is the data sent by the server when requested through this URL. We will change the URL later according to our server. Anyway, we use the open method to initialize the X HR request, then send the request to the server using the Send method. In the end, we will set the timeout for the function to be called periodically, I am setting the period to be one second. So the timer function will be cold every one second and only the Value field in the text area will be updated in each call. I have set this start button to call the timer function once and after that it will keep running every one second. If you don't want to set the start button and want to call the timer function automatically, you can call the timer function here just after the page gets loaded. And you can see this time it is displaying data without pressing the start button. But I will stick with the start button for now. All right now we will modify our previous index file and add this code to it. So open the project folder middleware third party TL WAP source apps HTTP and open the FS folder. Here is our index dot HTML file from the previous project. Let's open it in the editor. We already have a script tag from the previous project, we will just add the new function to it let's change the URL to get value. Later we will add this in the server file to look for this URL and send the value to the client. I am adding this timer function here just in case you guys want to display the values without the start button. Now we have to add these things in the body of our index file. Here are the green and blue buttons. Let's add the code after this let's see how it looks. This is fine. The button and text area positioning is perfect. All right, everything is fine so far. Now let's open the cube ID as I mentioned in the beginning, I am going to change to cm sis version one. Also I am disabling the new library reentrant save the project to generate the code we will have to deal with all the errors again. So let's start by generating the FS data dot c file first. Now build the code to see the errors.

All right, first, we have the error for Fs data custom file, go to its definition and set it to zero All right, the errors are gone. Now. We do have a few warnings, but I guess that's fine. We will see later if we have problems running the code. Let's continue with the HTTP server dot c file we will add one more condition to check for the get value URL. If the request is made using this URL, then first we will create a pointer to store the value we will be sending then allocates the memory for this variable. If you are using s printf then you must allocate using the PV port malloc otherwise the memory will get corrupted. I have explained it in one of the free RTLs projects, you can check on the top right corner, I am going to send the incremented value of this index variable then net con write will write the data similar to how we did in the previous tutorial. If you want to send any sensors value, like temperature, or pressure or any other ADC value, you have to first convert it to the string like I did, and then send it in the end, free the memory allocated for the buffer. Let's build and debug the code. And we will also check the requests on the Wireshark. Here I am going to filter the HTTP requests. All right, let's open the web page. You can see all the requests made on the Wireshark upon pressing the green button, the empty request is sent by the client, just like the previous tutorial.

And now let's press the start button. You can see the requests made by the client and how the Value field is updating every second. If we try to access any other page, it will show the 404 error the fact that only the value requests are visible on the Wireshark means the entire page is not reloading. Otherwise, you would see the requests for images as well. All right, let me show you one more thing where I will uncomment this timer function so that the function will be called after the page has been loaded. In this way, we don't need to press the stop button to start retrieving the values. We need to generate the FS data file again with this updated code. Let's build and run the code. All right, you can see the value started updating after the page loaded fully. So it depends on how you want this to work. We saw how the use of Ajax made it possible to only update a specific section of the webpage instead of reloading the entire page. I hope you understood the project. I know I didn't send any HTTP okay response. You can take care of that part if you are building an application for this.

EXAMPLE DUMMY CODE

Implementing a complete HTTP server with AJAX (Asynchronous JavaScript and XML) on an STM32 microcontroller is quite involved and goes beyond the scope of a simple example. AJAX allows web pages to request and exchange data with a server asynchronously, without requiring a full page reload.

To implement a functional HTTP server with AJAX, you'll need to use a web server library that supports AJAX, handle AJAX requests, and respond to them appropriately. AJAX typically involves handling HTTP requests and responses in the background and dynamically updating parts of a web page without reloading the entire page.

Below is a basic outline of the steps you would need to follow to create a simple HTTP server with AJAX:

Set up the web server: You need to use a web server library that supports AJAX, or you can write your own server using low-level socket or HTTP libraries. There are several lightweight web server libraries available for microcontrollers that can be used with lwIP or other networking stacks.

Handle AJAX requests: On the server-side, you need to handle AJAX requests coming from the client (web browser). The server should be able to distinguish AJAX requests from regular HTTP requests based on the request headers or other criteria.

Process AJAX data: After receiving the AJAX request, the server needs to process the data (if any) sent by the client and prepare the appropriate response.

Send AJAX response: The server should send the AJAX response back to the client. The response could be JSON data, XML data, or any other format that can be easily parsed by the client-side JavaScript.

Handle AJAX response on the client-side: On the client-side (web page), you need to write JavaScript code to make AJAX requests to the server and handle the server's responses. The JavaScript code will update the web page content dynamically based on the received data.

Creating a complete example of an HTTP server with AJAX would require a lot of code and would be quite extensive. Instead, I can provide a basic example of how to handle an AJAX request and respond with JSON data.

```c
// Server-side C code for handling AJAX request
and sending JSON response

#include "main.h"
#include "lwip.h"
#include "api.h"
#include <stdio.h>

#define HTTP_SERVER_PORT 80
```

```c
// Task handle for the HTTP server task
TaskHandle_t http_server_task_handle;

// AJAX response data
const char* ajax_response = "{\"message\":
\"Hello from server!\"}";

// HTTP server task function
void http_server_task(void *pvParameters) {
  struct netconn *conn, *newconn;
  err_t err;
  struct netbuf *buf;
  void *data;
  u16_t len;

  // Create a new HTTP netconn
  conn = netconn_new(NETCONN_TCP);
  if (conn == NULL) {
   vTaskDelete(NULL);
  }

  // Bind the HTTP netconn to the specified port
  netconn_bind(conn, NULL, HTTP_SERVER_PORT);

  // Listen for incoming connections
  netconn_listen(conn);
```

```c
while (1) {
  // Accept new client connections
  err = netconn_accept(conn, &newconn);
  if (err == ERR_OK) {
    while ((err = netconn_recv(newconn, &buf)) ==
ERR_OK) {
      // Get the data and length of the received
packet
      netbuf_data(buf, &data, &len);

      // Check if it is an AJAX request
      if (len >= 4 && memcmp(data, "POST", 4) ==
0) {
        // Prepare the response headers
        const char* headers = "HTTP/1.1 200
OK\r\nContent-Type: application/json\r\n\r\n";

        // Send the headers
        netconn_write(newconn, headers,
strlen(headers), NETCONN_COPY);

        // Send the AJAX response data
        netconn_write(newconn, ajax_response,
strlen(ajax_response), NETCONN_COPY);
      }

      // Free the received buffer
      netbuf_delete(buf);
```

```
    }

    // Close the connection with the client
    netconn_close(newconn);
    netconn_delete(newconn);
   }
 }
}


int main(void) {
 // Initialize the HAL, peripherals, and FreeRTOS
 HAL_Init();
 SystemClock_Config();
 MX_GPIO_Init();
 MX_LWIP_Init();

 // Create the HTTP server task
 xTaskCreate(http_server_task, "HTTP_Server",
configMINIMAL_STACK_SIZE, NULL,
tskIDLE_PRIORITY + 1, &http_server_task_handle);

 // Start the scheduler
 vTaskStartScheduler();

 // We should never reach here
 while (1) {
 }
}
```

In this example, we handle a POST request (you can customize the request method according to your needs) as an AJAX request and respond with JSON data. The JSON data is stored in the ajax_response variable.

Keep in mind that this is a very basic example and doesn't include all the complexities of a full-featured AJAX-enabled HTTP server. To build a more advanced and secure solution, you should consider using existing libraries or frameworks that support AJAX and provide more robust features for handling HTTP requests and AJAX responses.

STM32 ADC CONVERSION TIME FREQUENCY CALCULATION

I have already covered the ADC in STM 32. In my previous projects where we did single and multiple channels, there still are some doubts though. One of them is calculating the conversion frequency or conversion time. Today in this project we will talk about that also we will see how to use the internal temperature sensor which requires the particular conversion time in order to work. To show the differences in the ADC, I will be using two different microcontrollers in this project. The first half will cover the f1 03 Cortex M three controller and the second half will cover the F four series controllers other series would follow the same rules. Next, take a look at the reference manual of F 103. First it has 12 bit ADC which is fixed and we can't change the resolution now to calculate the conversion time, there are these formulas given in the manual.

Based on these I have written another formula to simplify this calculation basically conversion time is equal to the sampling time plus 12.5 cycles divided by the ADC clock. You will understand this as we progress further. Let's start by creating the project in cube Id give some name here and click finish first of all, I am enabling the external crystal for the clock.

$$T_{conv} = \frac{\text{Sampling time} + 12.5 \text{ cycles}}{\text{ADC CLOCK}}$$

$$T_{conv} = \frac{71.5 + 12.5}{5 \text{ MHz}} = 17 \text{ uS}$$

Also select serial wire here. Now in the ADC, select the internal temperature sensor. We will come back here let's first set the clock the ADC clock is 12 megahertz right now. Let's go back to ADC setup. We have no option to choose the resolution. As mentioned in the datasheet we can only use 12 bit resolution for ADC. Make sure you enable the continuous conversion. Here we have the sampling time. Now as according to the formula 12.5 cycles will continue. And if I select the sampling time of 71.5 cycles along with the ADC clock of five megahertz, I can get the conversion time of 17 microseconds. So why 17 microseconds. Let's see the temperature sensor details as the datasheet says we need the conversion time around 17.1 microseconds for the temperature sensor to work now we need to set these two values to their respective positions. Select 71.5 cycles and change the

ADC clock to five megahertz let's also include the DMA. Change it to Word and change the mode to circular. Now all set click Save to generate the project Let's create a variable to store the ADC value in the main function, start the ADC with DMA the parameters are ADC handler variable to store the data in and the number of channels we need to copy this conversion complete function in our main file when the ADC finishes the conversion we will convert the ADC value to the temperature the formula to do that is given in the respective reference manuals let's just copy this entire formula we need to replace these curly braces with the normal brackets now we need to define these values they can be found in the device datasheet.

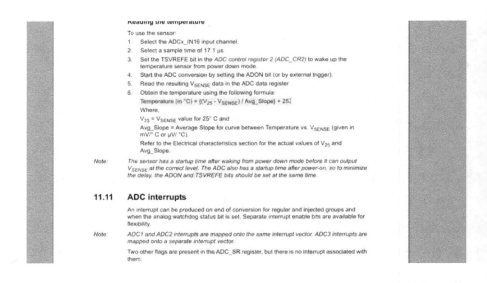

Just search for V sense and you can find all the values here we have average slope was 4.3 milli volts per Celsius let's define the average slope I am defining it in volts per Celsius V 25 value is 1.43 volts so we will use as it is now, V senses basically the voltage per ADC value 4096 is for 12 bit resolution as to power 12 is 4096 and based on the ADC value we will get the voltage here everything is set now, let's build and debug this code I have included both the variables in the live expression.

As you can see the temperature of the core is around 40 degrees Celsius. This is fine because the ambient temperature here is around 36 degrees. This temperature sensor could only work if the conversion time is selected properly. This is it for the F 103. Rest of the project will cover the F four series. If you want to know the difference, you should keep watching it this way you will better understand this entire process let's take a look at the reference manual of F 446 r e as you can see Now, we have options to select the different resolutions for the ADC. Let's scroll down here you can see the ADC clock is derived from the APB two clock and we have prescaler to further control this clock now here we have the formula to do the calculation for the conversion time. We will come back to this but first let's create a new project in cube ID. Like I said, I will be using a 446 R E, give some name to your project and click finish first of all, I will set up the clock I have eight megahertz external crystal.

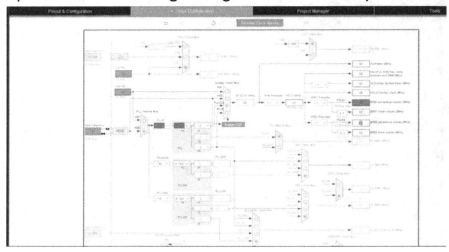

Now, if you remember, the ADC is connected to APB to clock, I will keep the APB two clock at 50 megahertz. The rest of the clocks will set up automatically. You will soon realize the reason behind keeping this at 50 megahertz. Let's go back to our setup and select the temperature sensor channel in ADC. We will deal with pre scalar in a while. These are the resolutions that we can select. Notice that there are different ADC clock cycles for these resolutions. Now this can be confusing, like what exactly these clock cycles are. To know this, let's go back to datasheet. By default, the formula here says 12 cycles. For 12 bit resolutions, the minimum conversion time can be calculated with three ADC cycles, and this totally gives up 15 ADC clock cycles. So this thing here you see is actually the minimum conversion time. Minimum conversion time for the 10 bit resolution can be 15 ADC clock cycles, and same for the rest of these resolutions. So our actual ADC cycles for the 12 bit resolution is 12 cycles, and for 10 bit it is 10 cycles. Now before going any further, let's take a look at the formula. This is the modified formula to do calculate the conversion time or frequency. Basically conversion time is equal to the sampling time plus the ADC cycles divided by the ADC clock ADC cycles will be 12 as I am using the 12 bit resolution. If you remember, I use the APB to clock as 50 megahertz and if we use the prescaler as four this will give us the ADC clock of 12.5 megahertz and now a sampling time of 112 cycles would give us the conversion time of 9.9 microseconds. Let's set the things in our setup now. So why do I need this 9.9 microseconds in the first place to know this go back to reference manual and see the temperature sensor section. Looks like we don't have all the details here. We need to open the datasheet for this controller search for V sense. We will directly come to the properties of temperature sensor as you can see here, the conversion time need to be around 10 microseconds for the temperature sensor to work and that That's why the 9.9 is the closest I got so everything is set up now just click Save to generate the project I forgot to add the DMA let's add it now select the circular mode and the data with FAS 32 bits in the Parameter Set Up enable the continuous conversion mode and the DMA continuous request create variables to store the ADC value and the temperature value next we need to write a conversion complete callback function.

$$T_{conv} = \frac{\text{Sampling time} + \text{Cycles}}{\text{ADC CLOCK}}$$

$$\text{ADC CLK} = \frac{\text{APB2 (50 MHz)}}{\text{PR (4)}} = 12.5 \text{ MHz}$$

$$T_{conv} = \frac{112 + 12}{12.5 \text{ MHz}} = 9.9 \text{ us}$$

Here we will convert the ADC value to the temperature using the formula provided in the manual all the constants used in the formula are defined in the datasheet so we will define them in our main file also. The value for average slope is given in milli volts per Celsius it's 2.5 milli volts per Celsius. I am writing this in volts per Celsius and that's why 0.00 to five V 25 is 0.76 volts and V cents depends on resolution this here will convert the ADC value to the respective voltage. Let's just quickly build this once so we don't have any errors till now. Now stopped the ADC with DMA in the main function. We only have one channel to convert, so one as the parameter here.

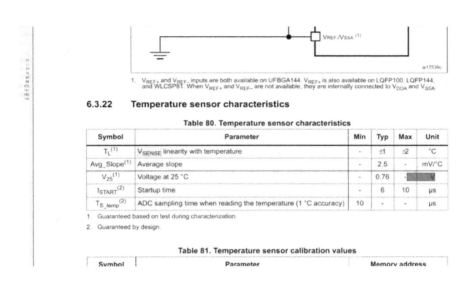

1. V_{REF+} and V_{REF-} inputs are both available on UFBGA144. V_{REF+} is also available on LQFP100, LQFP144, and WLCSP81. When V_{REF+} and V_{REF-} are not available, they are internally connected to V_{DDA} and V_{SSA}.

6.3.22   Temperature sensor characteristics

Table 80. Temperature sensor characteristics

Symbol	Parameter	Min	Typ	Max	Unit
T_L[1]	V_{SENSE} linearity with temperature	-	±1	±2	°C
Avg_Slope[1]	Average slope	-	2.5	-	mV/°C
V_{25}[1]	Voltage at 25 °C	-	0.76	-	V
t_{START}[2]	Startup time	-	6	10	µs
T_{S_temp}[2]	ADC sampling time when reading the temperature (1 °C accuracy)	10	-	-	µs

1. Guaranteed based on test during characterization.
2. Guaranteed by design.

Table 81. Temperature sensor calibration values

Symbol	Parameter	Memory address

Let's build and debug this now. As you can see the temperature is being displayed and it is very stable also, don't compare it with the temperature from the F 103. As I made these two pots of different times, the temperature here is accurate as the ambient temperature right now is around 27 degrees. This accuracy can only be achieved if you have the conversion time of 10 microseconds.

EXAMPLE DUMMY CODE

To calculate the ADC conversion time and frequency on an STM32 microcontroller, you need to know the ADC clock frequency, the number of ADC cycles required for the conversion, and the resolution of the ADC. The ADC conversion time is the time taken to complete one ADC conversion, and the ADC conversion frequency is the number of ADC conversions that can be performed in one second.

Below is an example code to calculate the ADC conversion time and frequency on an STM32 microcontroller using HAL (Hardware Abstraction Layer) libraries.

C

```c
#include "main.h"
#include "adc.h"

// Function to calculate ADC conversion time (in microseconds)
uint32_t
calculate_adc_conversion_time(ADC_HandleTypeDef *hadc) {
  uint32_t adc_clk_frequency =
```

```c
HAL_RCC_GetHCLKFreq(); // ADC clock frequency
in Hz
  uint32_t adc_resolution = hadc->Init.Resolution;
// ADC resolution (in bits)
  uint32_t adc_cycles = hadc-
>Init.NbrOfConversion;   // Number of ADC cycles

  // Calculate the conversion time (in
microseconds)
  // Note: The formula below assumes ADC is
operating in single conversion mode
  uint32_t conversion_time_us = (adc_cycles *
(1000000U)) / (adc_clk_frequency /
adc_resolution);

  return conversion_time_us;
}

// Function to calculate ADC conversion frequency
(in Hz)
uint32_t
calculate_adc_conversion_frequency(ADC_Handle
TypeDef *hadc) {
  uint32_t adc_clk_frequency =
HAL_RCC_GetHCLKFreq(); // ADC clock frequency
in Hz
  uint32_t adc_resolution = hadc->Init.Resolution;
// ADC resolution (in bits)
```

```c
  uint32_t adc_cycles = hadc-
>Init.NbrOfConversion;   // Number of ADC cycles

  // Calculate the conversion frequency (in Hz)
  // Note: The formula below assumes ADC is
operating in single conversion mode
  uint32_t conversion_frequency_hz =
adc_clk_frequency / (adc_resolution * adc_cycles);

  return conversion_frequency_hz;
}

int main(void) {
  // Initialize the HAL, ADC, and other peripherals

  // Start ADC conversion

  ADC_HandleTypeDef hadc;
  // Initialize ADC and its settings (resolution,
conversion cycles, etc.)

  // Perform ADC conversion
  HAL_ADC_Start(&hadc);
  HAL_ADC_PollForConversion(&hadc,
HAL_MAX_DELAY);

  // Get the ADC conversion time and frequency
  uint32_t conversion_time_us =
```

```
calculate_adc_conversion_time(&hadc);
  uint32_t conversion_frequency_hz =
calculate_adc_conversion_frequency(&hadc);

  // Do something with the calculated values (e.g.,
send them over UART, display on LCD, etc.)

  while (1) {
    // Your application code here
  }
}
```

In this example, we assume you have already
configured the ADC peripheral using the HAL
library. The calculate_adc_conversion_time
function calculates the ADC conversion time in
microseconds, and the
calculate_adc_conversion_frequency function
calculates the ADC conversion frequency in Hz.

Keep in mind that ADC conversion time and
frequency may vary based on the ADC resolution,
sampling time, and the number of channels being
converted. Additionally, the formula used in this
example assumes that the ADC is operating in
single conversion mode, and the ADC clock
frequency is derived from the HCLK (CPU clock)
frequency. If the ADC is running in continuous

conversion mode or other configurations, you may need to adjust the formulas accordingly.

Ensure that you set the ADC clock frequency and resolution correctly in your HAL initialization code, and take care of any other necessary configurations based on your specific STM32 microcontroller model and application requirements.

STM32 ADC MULTI CHANNEL WITHOUT DMA

Let's get into the project now. Well, this is yet another project on ADC AMS. Today I will again cover the multi channels part. I have already covered the multi-channel using DMA. But there was a problem with the while loop that it never gets executed.

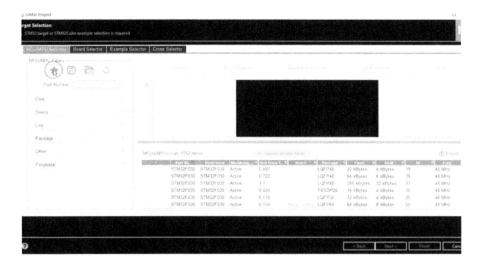

This happens because DMA interrupts triggers very frequently. And that's why the program never enters the while loop. Many users requested a way to use multiple channels without DMA and that's what we are going to cover today. So let's start by creating the project in cube Id first, I am using STM 32 F 446 r e controller give some name to the project and click Finish. Here is our cube MX I am selecting the external crystal for the clock. Let's accept the clock first. I have eight megahertz Crystal and I want the system to run at maximum clock I am going to select three channels of ADC one, Channel Zero channel one and the temperature sensor.

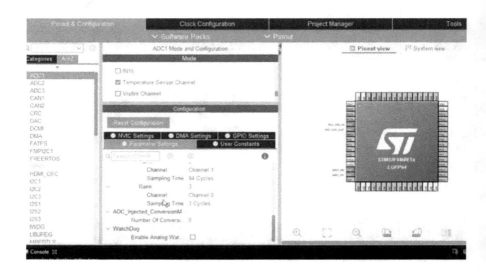

Select the scan mode. Since we are using multiple channels also select the continuous conversion mode I am not going to use any DMA I am using three channels so select three. Now set the ranks and sampling time according to your requirement that's all for the ADC setup. You can see that the two pins got selected for the respective channels I am also going to use D AC and then feed the output from pin PA four to the ADC Channel Zero select software trigger so it only triggers when we want that's all for the cube MX click Save to generate the project here is our main file. Let's go to the ADC init function first I am going to copy the configuration for these three channels and comment them out here so that they can't be configured in the beginning of the program also changed the number of conversions to one now let's write the function to select ADC channels zero. Here I am going to paste only the Channel Zero part you can see the

ADC channels zero and the sampling time. Now we will write another function for selecting channel one. And here we will only write the channel one related part also make sure that rank is set to one and now finally the temperature sensor channel and paste the related code here.

```
56  /* USER CODE BEGIN PFP */
57
58  /* USER CODE END PFP */
59
600 /* Private user code --------------------------------------------
61  /* USER CODE BEGIN 0 */
62
630 void ADC_Select_CH0 (void)
64  {
650         /** Configure for the selected ADC regular channel its co
66         */
67         sConfig.Channel = ADC_CHANNEL_0;
68         sConfig.Rank = 1;
69         sConfig.SamplingTime = ADC_SAMPLETIME_28CYCLES;
70         if (HAL_ADC_ConfigChannel(&hadc1, &sConfig) != HAL_OK)
71         {
72             Error_Handler();
73         }
74  }
75
76  void ADC_Select_CH1 (void)
77  {
78         |
79  }
80
81  /* USER CODE END 0 */
82
830 /**
84    * @brief  The application entry point.
85    * @retval int
86    */
```

Also change the rank to one next, I am going to define an array to store the ADC values these two variables will be used in da C and these are for the temperature sensor in the while loop, first of all I am going to assign a value to

241

the variable so that we can feed it to the VA see now increments the value if value is greater than 3.3 the reset it to zero we will use set value to set the value to the DA see I am using channel one and data alignment is to the right now stock the DA C now, for the ADC, first of all I am going to select Channels zero start the ADC poll for the conversion to finish get the ADC value and finally stop the ADC I am going to repeat the same steps in other channels also.

```
136     /* USER CODE BEGIN SysInit */
137
138     /* USER CODE END SysInit */
139
140     /* Initialize all configured peripherals */
141     MX_GPIO_Init();
142     MX_ADC1_Init();
143     MX_DAC_Init();
144     /* USER CODE BEGIN 2 */
145
146     /* USER CODE END 2 */
147
148     /* Infinite loop */
149     /* USER CODE BEGIN WHILE */
150     while (1)
151     {
152         /* USER CODE END WHILE */
153
154         /* USER CODE BEGIN 3 */
155         var = val*4096/3.3;
156         val+=0.1;
157         if (val>=3.3) val=0;
158         HAL_StatusTypeDef HAL_DAC_SetValue(DAC_HandleTypeDef *hdac, uint32_t Channel, uint32_t Alignment, uint32_t Da
159         HAL_DAC_SetValue(&hdac, DAC_CHANNEL, Alignment, Data);
160     }
161     /* USER CODE END 3 */
162 }
163
164 /**
165   * @brief System Clock Configuration
166   * @retval None
```

This is the statements to get the temperature and let's add one second delay here. Let's build it seems like we have some errors. I forgot to declare the ADC config type def just copied in all the ADC select functions so we don't have any errors now let's debug this I want to show you the connection before starting the debugger. So here the orange wire is connected between the output from the AC to the ADC Channel Zero and the ADC channel one is connected to the ground I have added the variables in the live expression you can see here var represents the DHCP value which is incrementing every second and ADC Channel Zero is also similar to this value. Channels zero is grounded and that's why the value is almost zero.

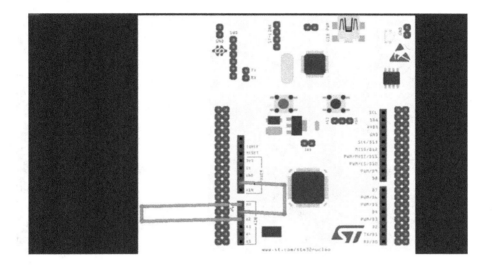

Now I am connecting the channel one to 3.3 volts and you can see the ADC is now reading the maximum value also the temperature is constant and the other ADC values are not affecting it the multiple channel works pretty good without the d m or to the advantage of this method is you can read the channels at any point in the code.

EXAMPLE DUMMY CODE

```c
#include "main.h"
#include "adc.h"

#define ADC_CHANNEL_COUNT 3

ADC_HandleTypeDef hadc;

// Array to store ADC conversion values
uint32_t adc_values[ADC_CHANNEL_COUNT];

// Function to perform multi-channel ADC conversion
void perform_adc_conversion(void) {
  for (uint8_t channel = 0; channel <
ADC_CHANNEL_COUNT; ++channel) {
    // Configure the ADC to use the desired channel
    hadc.Instance->CHSELR = (1 << channel);

    // Start the ADC conversion for the selected channel
    HAL_ADC_Start(&hadc);

    // Wait for the ADC conversion to complete
    HAL_ADC_PollForConversion(&hadc,
HAL_MAX_DELAY);

    // Read the ADC value and store it in the array
    adc_values[channel] = HAL_ADC_GetValue(&hadc);
  }
}
```

```
int main(void) {
  // Initialize the HAL and ADC

  // Configure ADC settings (resolution, sampling time,
etc.)

  while (1) {
    // Perform multi-channel ADC conversion
    perform_adc_conversion();

    // Process the ADC values as needed (e.g., send them
over UART, display on LCD, etc.)
  }
}
```

In this example, we assume that you have already
initialized the HAL and ADC settings in the main function.
The perform_adc_conversion function performs ADC
conversion on multiple channels sequentially using
polling mode.

Make sure to configure the ADC settings properly based
on your STM32 microcontroller model, such as setting
the resolution, sampling time, and any other necessary
configurations.

Please note that this example uses polling mode for ADC
conversion, which means the program will wait for each
ADC conversion to complete before moving on to the
next channel. In scenarios where you require higher
performance or non-blocking behavior, you may

consider using DMA for ADC conversion, which allows the ADC to transfer data directly to memory without CPU intervention.

STM32 DUAL CORE _1. GETTING STARTED WITH STM32 DUAL CORE CPUS STM32H745

the start of a new series, which will focus on the dual core processes by S T. We will cover a lot of things here, some of which are unique to these microcontrollers, like inter CPU communication, or hardware semaphores, et cetera. So let's start with the first step. And that is getting started with STM 32 dual core processes. This project will cover the basic things like how to create project how to debug both the cores simultaneously and how to turn off second core. Here I am using STM 32 H 745 discovery board it have a Cortex M seven MCU and a Cortex M four MCU. You can see it have a LCD attached to it. So a tutorial on L T DC will be coming soon. Let's start by creating a project in cube ID select the micro controller give some name to this project and click finish here you can see two different projects got created for M seven core and M four core.

Here is our cube MX there are a lot of pins here and they are initialized in their default states.

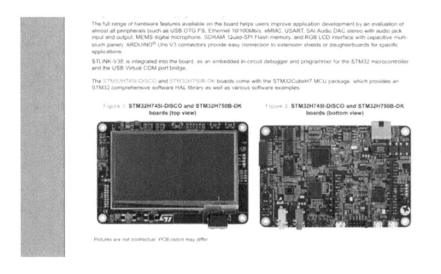

The full range of hardware features available on the board helps users improve application development by an evaluation of almost all peripherals (such as USB OTG FS, Ethernet 10/100Mb/s, eMMC, USART, SAI Audio DAC stereo with audio jack input and output, MEMS digital microphone, SDRAM, Quad-SPI Flash memory, and RGB LCD interface with capacitive multi-touch panel). ARDUINO® Uno V3 connectors provide easy connection to extension shields or daughterboards for specific applications.

STLINK-V3E is integrated into the board, as an embedded in-circuit debugger and programmer for the STM32 microcontroller and the USB Virtual COM port bridge.

The STM32H745I-DISCO and STM32H750B-DK boards come with the STM32CubeH7 MCU package, which provides an STM32 comprehensive software HAL library as well as various software examples.

Figure 1. **STM32H745I-DISCO and STM32H750B-DK boards (top view)**   Figure 2. **STM32H745I-DISCO and STM32H750B-DK boards (bottom view)**

Pictures are not contractual. PCB colors may differ

Let's clear this pin out first first of all I am selecting the external crystal for the clock. This is valid for both M seven core and the M four core let's go to the clock setup. Now this looks huge let's select PCL K and try setting up the clock at 400 megahertz it's showing the error no problem we will do the manual setup let's divided by five and then multiply by 160 and we got the 400 megahertz clock and four core can run at maximum 240 megahertz. So we will divide here by two also use the pre scalars have to hear everything looks good. Now. In case you want to run it at maximum 480 megahertz all you need to do is change the multiplier here to 192 and now the clock is at 480 megahertz in case you keep getting error make sure this voltage scale is selected least here in my case it is set to scale one also supply source should be direct SMP s supply let's enable the cash while the Cortex M seven. We will not be using MPU anytime soon. I am going to blink the onboard LEDs today. So let's take a look at the schematics to find out where they are connected to. You can see we have two LEDs here led one is green and led two is red. led one is connected to pin PJ two and led two is connected to pin pi 13. So let's search for these pins and select them as output Let's see the GP i o setup.

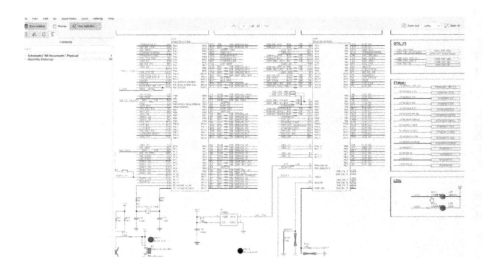

Now, here you see the pin context assignment is free by default, this means that the pin is not assigned to either of these cores and we can manually add them later, but we will not do that and we are going to assign each pin to the individual core I am assigning pi 30 into the Cortex M seven and P j two to the Cortex M four basically, that's how every peripheral is you can assign each peripheral to the individual core you have to turn the peripheral on for the respective core and then set it up we will cover those things some other time that's all for the setup click Save to generate the project this main file is for the M seven core and this one is for the M four core. Note here that the system clock is configured in the M seven core and not in the M four core. So, it is necessary that the M seven core runs first configures the system clock and all other necessary configurations and then the M four core can run to make this possible these steps are pre generated in the code. Here the CPU one waits for the CPU to to go into the STOP mode. If you look at the CPU two as soon as it boots it enters the STOP mode. After that, CPU one initializes the system clock and other necessary things and finally it releases the hardware semaphore. CPU to on the other hand before going into STOP mode activates the notification for the semaphore. When it receives the notification, it wakes up from the STOP mode and the rest of the code starts working as usual.

```
/*HW semaphore Clock enable*/
__HAL_RCC_HSEM_CLK_ENABLE();
/*Take HSEM */
HAL_HSEM_FastTake(HSEM_ID_0);
/*Release HSEM in order to notify the CPU2(CM4)*/
HAL_HSEM_Release(HSEM_ID_0,0);
/* wait until CPU2 wakes up from stop mode */
timeout = 0xFFFF;
while((__HAL_RCC_GET_FLAG(RCC_FLAG_D2CKRDY) != RESET) && (timeout-- > 0));
if ( timeout < 0 )

Error_Handler();

/* USER CODE END Boot_Mode_Sequence_2 */

/* USER CODE BEGIN SysInit */

/* USER CODE END SysInit */

/* Initialize all configured peripherals */
MX_GPIO_Init();
/* USER CODE BEGIN 2 */

/* USER CODE END 2 */

/* Infinite loop */
/* USER CODE BEGIN WHILE */
while (1)
{
    /* USER CODE END WHILE */

    /* USER CODE BEGIN 3 */
}
/* USER CODE END 3 */
}
```

CPU one also waits for the CPU to to wake up. This is how
both the cores initializes notes that the pin pi 13 is
initialized in the M seven core just like we set up in the
cube MX in the while loop we will toggle this pin every
500 milliseconds. Similarly, in the M four core, we will
toggle the pin p j two so that's it. Let's build it now. We
have to separately build both the projects let's debug
them now. This part is very crucial. So pay attention here.
Right now I have selected the M seven cause main file. Go
to debug configuration and double click here. It will
generate a debug configuration. Note here that this is for

the CM seven. Go to the debugger tab. Keep in mind what is this port number for the GDB here we have Cortex M seven. Check this whole tool cause this will basically hold both the cores and that way CPU two can't run on its own in the beginning. Shared st link must be checked. Now go to startup tab. Here we have the configuration for the CM seven. Click Add select C M for select debug and click OK. We are doing this because we want the Cortex M seven configuration to build and load the code for M four also. So that we don't have to load the code separately using the M for now click apply and and click Close. Now we will create the configuration for the Cortex M four. So go to the main file of Cortex M four and click debug configuration. Again, double click here, and it will generate the configuration for the M four core.

Go to debugger tab. This is the same port number as for the M seven, so we will increase it by at least three. Under the reset behavior, select none as we are already halting both the cores using M seven, go to startup tab. We are already downloading the code using the M seven so we don't need to do it here. Select Edit and uncheck the download option. Click Apply to save this. Now we will first launch the debugger using the M seven configuration. Once we are in the debugger, again launch the M for configuration so here we are, both the configurations are loaded successfully. Here you can see both the main files and we can switch between them depending on where we want to be. Let's set a breakpoint here. Before initializing the pin. I am setting it at the same statement in the M seven also. Now select both these with Ctrl button and click Run we need to run them together or else it will stuck it hit the breakpoint in the M four core. If we go to the M seven configuration, you can see this is also waiting if breakpoint. Keep checking the LEDs on the board, I will go to M seven file and step over these statements. Notice that the only the red LED is blinking as I am going through the statements. This means that the M four core is still waiting at that breakpoint. We will keep this red LED on and go to the second core. And as I step over these statements, only the green LED is blinking. So here we are able to debug the cause separately. Let's run this code now. Since I am running the M four code, the green LED is blinking while the red one is still on. Let's stop this one and run the M seven core and now only the red LEDs blinking. If you want to run both of them, you have to again select using the ctrl button and then hit Run.

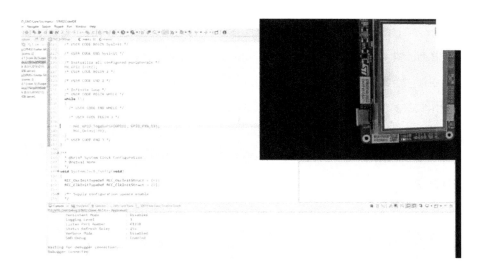

Everything is okay here but the problem is that you can't reset a single call whenever you want to reset you have to do for both cores and even after that, if we run it just like we run initially, this time the core two will not stop at the breakpoint. You can see that the core one has stopped at the breakpoint. But this is not the case with the core two and it is still running. As you can see the LED is keep blinking. I don't know why this happens. And if anyone have better idea, please comment below. Anyway, we can stop the core to manually This is it for the debugging part. Now let's say we want to run only one core and don't want the second core to consume power unnecessarily. In that case, we must stop the second core from booting. This can be done by modifying the option bytes. And to do this we will use the STM 32 Q A programmer, connect the device here and click option bytes. Here in the User Configuration, you can see the bits PCM four and BCM seven these bits controls which CPU will boot and which won't. If I uncheck this, that means the M four core will not boot click Apply to save this, it will take some time maybe around 30 seconds so we don't need this code anymore, since the second CPU is not booting, so it will definitely not go into the STOP mode.

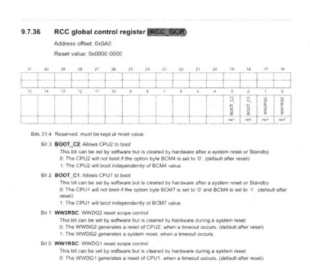

9.7.36   RCC global control register (RCC_GCR)

Address offset: 0x0A0

Reset value: 0x0000 0000

Bits 31:4 Reserved, must be kept at reset value.

Bit 3 **BOOT_C2**: Allows CPU2 to boot
This bit can be set by software but is cleared by hardware after a system reset or Standby
0: The CPU2 will not boot if the option byte BCM4 is set to '0'. (default after reset)
1: The CPU2 will boot independently of BCM4 value.

Bit 2 **BOOT_C1**: Allows CPU1 to boot
This bit can be set by software but is cleared by hardware after a system reset or Standby
0: The CPU1 will not boot if the option byte BCM7 is set to '0' and BCM4 is set to '1'. (default after reset)
1: The CPU1 will boot independently of BCM7 value.

Bit 1 **WW2RSC**: WWDG2 reset scope control
This bit can be set by software but is cleared by hardware during a system reset
0: The WWDG2 generates a reset of CPU2, when a timeout occurs. (default after reset)
1: The WWDG2 generates a system reset, when a timeout occurs.

Bit 0 **WW1RSC**: WWDG1 reset scope control
This bit can be set by software but is cleared by hardware during a system reset
0: The WWDG1 generates a reset of CPU1, when a timeout occurs. (default after reset)

Same thing here also, we can't wait for the second core to come out of STOP mode since it's not booting at all let's debug the M seven core if I run this you can see only the red LED is blinking and that means only the first core is running if we tried to debug the second core it won't work so how do we run the second call now we have to check the reference manual for that search for BCM four here you can see some details are given like which core will boot anyway let's search for Bootsy to. Here is an interesting thing in the RCCG CR register the third bit controls the CPU to Andy if we set it to one CPU two will boot the respective of the BCM for value now we will go back to the CPU one main file and after everything has been initialized we will set the Vic three of our CCG car let's build it all so go to the second coup main file and comment out all these lines we don't want the CPU to to go into STOP mode now I will debug with M seven core I am in the debugger. Now, if I tried to debug the M four I will get the error this is because the core is still not running. So what I will do is I will let this line execute and set the breakpoint here run it now it hit the breakpoint.

So second core must be running now. If we debug the second core, this time it will connect so this way we can control the boot for the second core. I will leave the BCM for on Let me quickly erase the flash once. Before we sum up this project, I want to show one last thing. If the LCD is on and you don't want to use it, you can turn off the backlight. Here you can see the LCD backlight is connected to pin p k zero so I will set the p k zero to output associated with either of those cores and set the output to low let's enable the functions that we disabled also enable the ones for the M four if we want to run the code, we can simply run for the M seven.

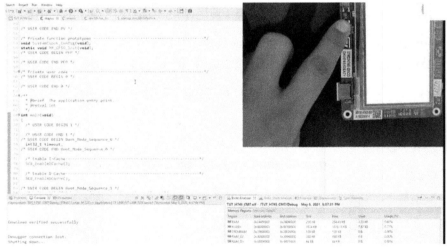

As we have configured that the M seven configuration will also load the program fine for we don't need to separately do the run for M four. As you can see both the LEDs are blinking together. So we can directly load the program using the configuration for M seven only. If you are directly running the program, you don't need to create a separate configuration for M four.

EXAMPLE DUMMY CODE

The STM32H7 series microcontrollers, such as STM32H745, come with dual-core CPUs - a Cortex-M7 core and a Cortex-M4 core. These cores can work independently and can be used for various tasks. Below is a basic example code to get started with STM32H745's dual-core CPUs using the HAL (Hardware Abstraction Layer) libraries.

In this example, we will blink an LED using both cores, where the M7 core handles LED blinking using a delay loop, and the M4 core handles LED blinking using FreeRTOS with a different blinking pattern.

Please note that to run FreeRTOS on the M4 core, you need to make additional configurations and setups. Here, we will assume FreeRTOS is set up correctly on the M4 core.

M7 Core (using delay loop for LED blinking):

```c
#include "main.h"
#include "gpio.h"

void M7_core_LED_blink(void) {
  while (1) {
    // Toggle the M7 core LED

HAL_GPIO_TogglePin(M7_CORE_LED_GPIO_Port,
M7_CORE_LED_Pin);
    HAL_Delay(500); // Delay for 500 milliseconds
  }
}

int main(void) {
  // Initialize the HAL and other peripherals
(including LED GPIOs)

  // Start the M7 core LED blinking task
  M7_core_LED_blink();

  while (1) {
    // M7 core main loop
  }
}
```

M4 Core (using FreeRTOS for LED blinking):

```c
#include "FreeRTOS.h"
```

```c
#include "task.h"

void M4_core_LED_blink(void *pvParameters) {
  while (1) {
    // Toggle the M4 core LED

HAL_GPIO_TogglePin(M4_CORE_LED_GPIO_Port,
M4_CORE_LED_Pin);
    vTaskDelay(pdMS_TO_TICKS(200)); // Delay for
200 milliseconds
  }
}

int main(void) {
  // Initialize the HAL and other peripherals
(including LED GPIOs)

  // Create the FreeRTOS task for M4 core LED
blinking
  xTaskCreate(M4_core_LED_blink,
"M4_LED_Blink", configMINIMAL_STACK_SIZE,
NULL, tskIDLE_PRIORITY + 1, NULL);

  // Start the FreeRTOS scheduler
  vTaskStartScheduler();

  // We should never reach here
  while (1) {
```

```
    }
}
```

In this example, we assume that the LED GPIOs (M7_CORE_LED_GPIO_Port, M7_CORE_LED_Pin, M4_CORE_LED_GPIO_Port, M4_CORE_LED_Pin) are initialized in the HAL initialization code.

Make sure you have correctly set up the dual-core environment in your STM32 project, including the linker scripts, system files, and memory configurations for both cores. Additionally, ensure that you have properly configured FreeRTOS on the M4 core, including setting up the tick timer, heap memory, and other necessary configurations.

This example demonstrates how you can utilize the dual-core architecture of STM32H745 to handle different tasks independently on each core. Depending on your specific application requirements, you can assign different tasks to each core to optimize performance and system utilization.

STM32 DUAL CORE _2. INTER CORE COMM USING HSEM NOTIFICATION SYNCHRONIZATION

I have decided to continue the projects on STM 32 Dual Core MC use, and for another couple of weeks, I will release projects on inter core communication using different means available. I have already made a project on how to get started with the dual core MCU where I covered how to program the MCU and how to debug it. Today we will start with the hardware semaphores also known as h Sam. As their name suggests, H Sam is just like the binary semaphore as we covered in the RT OS, but these are built on the hardware level. They are not used for the data transfer, but rather used for notification synchronization and for the shared resources. Today we will see how to use the hardware semaphore for the interCall notification for the core synchronization and how to use it to block the shared resource. Let's take a look at the reference manual of STM 32 h seven. Here we have the topic hardware semaphore.

11   Hardware semaphore (HSEM)

11.1   Hardware semaphore introduction

The hardware semaphore block provides 32 (32-bit) register based semaphores.

The semaphores can be used to ensure synchronization between different processes running between different cores. The HSEM provides a non blocking mechanism to lock semaphores in an atomic way. The following functions are provided:

- Locking a semaphore can be done in two ways:
  - 2-step lock: by writing COREID and PROCID to the semaphore, followed by a read check
  - 1-step lock: by reading the COREID from the semaphore
- Interrupt generation when a semaphore is freed
  - Each semaphore may generate an interrupt on one of the interrupt lines
- Semaphore clear protection
  - A semaphore is only cleared when COREID and PROCID match
- Global semaphore clear per COREID

11.2   Hardware semaphore main features

This block provides 32 Register based semaphores along with a non blocking mechanism to lock to semaphores. There are two ways to lock a semaphore. In a two step lock, we need to write the core ID and the process ID followed by a read check. And in a one step lock, we read the core ID from the semaphore we will be using the whole functions to lock and release the semaphores. So it will be a bit easier for us. Each semaphore can generate an interrupt and semaphores are released only when core ID and process ID matches with which it was locked. So there are 32 semaphores in total. The process ID can be eight bit in size, and the core ID can be for bid. You can read more about the semaphores. But we don't need too much info for today's tutorial. So I will skip this. Let's start the Q ID and create a new project I am using the STM 32 H 745 Discovery Board give some name to the project and click Finish. Let me clear the pin outs first I have already

262

covered the clock set up in the Getting Started project and I am following the same here the system is clocked by the external 25 megahertz crystal and is running at 400 megahertz for the M seven core and 200 megahertz for the M four core. There are two LEDs on board and I will use them to demonstrate the inter core communication LEDs are connected to the pins Py 13 and P j two. So I am setting them as output. Now we need to assign these pins to individual cores. I am assigning I 13 to the M seven core and j two to the M four core. These pins are inverted so we will pull them high initially so that the LEDs will be off by default.

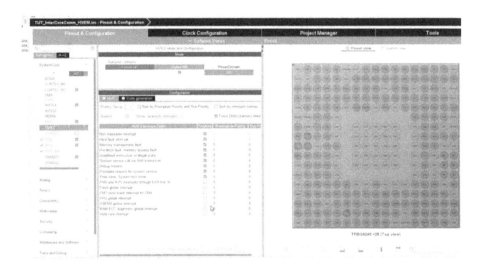

We also need to enable the interrupt for the semaphore the n vi c one is for the M seven core and two for the M four core. I am enabling the interrupt for the HSM to in the M four core. That's it for the cube MX click Save to generate the code. Here we have the two main files for the CM seven and cm four. Let's build them both before proceeding further. We will start with the core notification first. Here the M seven core will send notification to the M four core. The M seven will first take the semaphore with the ID zero. This is already defined by default, as the pre generated code also uses this semaphore number zero. After acquiring the semaphore we will toggle the LED 10 times with a delay of 250 milliseconds then the semaphore will be released. The fast tag function is used to take the semaphore without mentioning the process ID. When we use this function, the process ID is automatically assumed to be zero. When using the release function, the process ID must be mentioned and that's why it is set to zero. Now in the M four core, we will use the notification sent by the M seven In core, let's create a variable and assign it the value zero. If the note is received as one means the notification has been received, we will simply toggle the LED here, we need to activate the HSM notification in the main function we have activated the notification for the h seven zero. So when the M seven call will release the semaphore and interrupt will trigger and the H send free callback will be called. Inside the callback, we will set the variable note if received to one and activate the notification again. Let's understand it one more time. The note if received, it's set to zero so the code can't run in the beginning. The M seven core will toggle the LED 10 times and then release the semaphore this will trigger the interrupt in the end for core, the notice received variable will be set to one and the second LED will toggle Once this process will keep running forever. Let's build both the files. Now we will create the debug configuration so make sure you are in the M seven main file. Now click on the run configuration and double click here. The configuration should be generated for the M seven core. Go to the debug tab and check halt all cores. Now go to the startup tab and click the Add button. From the drop down menu. Select the CM four option. Make sure everything is checked here. Then click OK. Now we need to move the CM seven configuration to the top here. Everything is done, click Apply and run the configuration. This will load the code to both the cores but we need to manually reset the board after the loading has been finished. Here the red LED is controlled by the M seven core and the green is controlled by the M four core. The red LED is blinking five times and then the green LED toggles once basically the M seven core is toggling the red LED 10 times then it is sending the notification to the M four core.

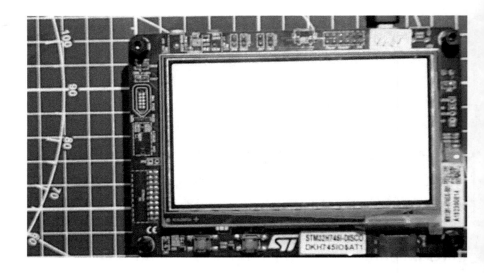

And finally the M four core toggles the green LED once so we were able to make one core send the notification to the second core using the hardware semaphores. Next, we will see how to synchronize both the cores. In this case the M seven core will first run and finish its job then the M four core will start doing its job. In this way the cores will be synchronized where the M four core can not run until the M seven has finished working. Here we will first write the code for the M seven. Let me toggle this part. And before uploading the final code, I will comment on it properly the M seven will toggle the LED 10 times then it will take the semaphore and release it now let's go to the M four main file here we will wait for the semaphore to be taken this function will return one once the semaphore is taken. The control will wait at this line until it happens and once it does return one we will turn the LED on for two seconds and then turn it off. Let's do the same thing for the M seven core also it will turn the LED on for two seconds and then turn it off then it will take the semaphore and this function will return one let's build and flash the code to the board here you can see the red LED is on for two seconds and then the green LED is on for another two seconds. Basically the M seven core is turning the LED on in the meantime the M four is waiting for the semaphore to be taken. When the red LED turns off, the M seven core acquires the semaphore the M four core can now proceed with turning the green LED on. So the M four core starts its job only after the M seven core has As finished, it's we were able to synchronize the cores to do their jobs sequentially. Now, we will see how to block the shared resource using the hardware semaphore, we have covered something similar as the binary semaphore in the RT O 's tutorial, where the semaphore must be taken before using the resource. And this is exactly what we will do here also, this time I am using the function h Sam take and it takes two parameters, the semaphore ID is still the same, and I am using the process ID 12. This is just a random process ID I have used. This statement will wait until the semaphore is acquired. And once it does, we will toggle the LED 20 times with a delay of 100 milliseconds. Now, the semaphore will be released, but make sure you use the same ID that you have used while locking the semaphore. We will use the same code in the M four core but with a small difference of blinking time just to differentiate between which core is blinking the LED. The shared resource in this case is going to be the LED connected to the pin Py 13, which is currently defined in the M seven file. We will define it in the M four file also.

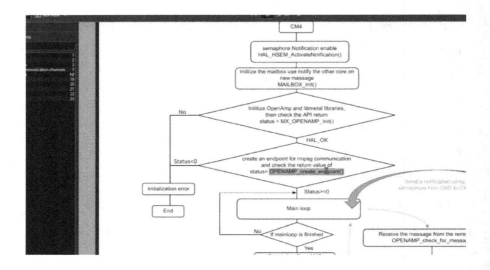

Let's build and flush this code to our board. Here you can see the LEDs blinking fast 10 times and then it's blinking slowly. Basically when the M seven core acquires the semaphore, it blinks the LED at a faster rate. And when the M four core acquires it, it blinks the LED at a slower rate. So the shared resource that is the LED is accessible by both the cause and they need to acquire the semaphore before accessing it. So we saw how we can use the hardware semaphore to send the notification between the cause how to synchronize the cores and how to use the shared resource between the cores.

EXAMPLE DUMMY CODE

The STM32H7 series microcontrollers provide an Hardware Semaphore (HSEM) mechanism to achieve inter-core communication and synchronization between the Cortex-M7 (M7 core) and Cortex-M4 (M4 core) processors. Below is an example code that demonstrates how to use the HSEM for notification-based synchronization between the two cores.

In this example, the M7 core will send a notification to the M4 core. The M4 core will be waiting for the notification, and upon receiving it, it will toggle an LED.

M7 Core Code:
```
#include "main.h"
#include "hsem.h"

int main(void) {
  // Initialize the HAL and other peripherals

  while (1) {
    // Perform M7 core tasks

    // Send notification to M4 core
    HAL_HSEM_FastTake(HSEM_ID_0); // Request
```

control of HSEM
```
    HAL_HSEM_Release(HSEM_ID_0, 0); // Release
HSEM and notify M4 core
    HAL_Delay(1000); // Wait for 1 second before
sending the next notification
  }
}
```

M4 Core Code:

```
#include "main.h"
#include "hsem.h"
#include "gpio.h"

void M4_core_LED_toggle(void) {
  while (1) {
    // Wait for the notification from M7 core
    HAL_HSEM_Take(HSEM_ID_0, 0); // Request
control of HSEM and wait for notification

    // Toggle the M4 core LED

HAL_GPIO_TogglePin(M4_CORE_LED_GPIO_Port,
M4_CORE_LED_Pin);
    HAL_Delay(500); // Delay for 500 milliseconds

    HAL_HSEM_Release(HSEM_ID_0, 0); // Release
HSEM after processing notification
```

```c
    }
}

int main(void) {
  // Initialize the HAL, peripherals (including LED
GPIO)

  // Create the FreeRTOS task for M4 core LED
toggle
  xTaskCreate(M4_core_LED_toggle,
"M4_LED_Toggle", configMINIMAL_STACK_SIZE,
NULL, tskIDLE_PRIORITY + 1, NULL);

  // Start the FreeRTOS scheduler
  vTaskStartScheduler();

  // We should never reach here
  while (1) {
  }
}
```
In this example, we assume that the LED GPIO
(M4_CORE_LED_GPIO_Port, M4_CORE_LED_Pin)
is initialized in the HAL initialization code.
Additionally, we assume that the HSEM interrupt
is properly configured and managed in the
system.

When the M7 core wants to notify the M4 core, it

takes control of the HSEM (HAL_HSEM_FastTake) and then releases it (HAL_HSEM_Release) with the specified semaphore ID (HSEM_ID_0). The M4 core is waiting for the HSEM with the same semaphore ID (HAL_HSEM_Take), and upon receiving the notification, it toggles the LED and releases the HSEM for further notifications.

Please note that this example assumes that you have properly configured and initialized the dual-core environment, including the HSEM, in your STM32 project.

This example demonstrates a simple inter-core communication mechanism using the HSEM for notification-based synchronization. For more complex synchronization scenarios, you might need to consider using additional mechanisms like mutexes, semaphores, or other communication methods, depending on your application requirements.

STM32 DUAL CORE _3. INTER CORE COMM USING OPENAMP AND RPMSG

I covered how to use the hardware semaphore for core notification and synchronization. Today we will see how to use the shared memory to transfer the data between the cores. To do so, we will use the open amp framework along with the remote processor messaging. You can find more info in the document number A n 5617. This documents specifically covers the inter process communication. That's why we need inter process communication in the first place. We can use it for Event Notification where one call can be used to monitor the event, and it can send the notification to the second core to wake up and process the event. We can use it to ask for the remote service where the cores will have to make the request via the IPC channel.

The figure below presents a conventional topology for a shared I/O resource manager (running on CPU2) and access abstraction using communication channels. The application task (CPU Task1) on CPU1 can request CPU2 services and do not have to run a second instance of I/O manager. This implementation reduces the resources allocated to CPU1 and the I/O manager task looks like it is running on the same CPU.

Figure 2 **Remote service request diagram**

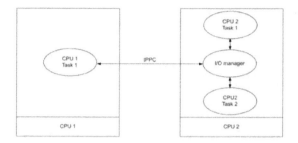

If it wants to use a certain resource, we can also use it for the payload processing where one core can be used to collect the data from the sensor and another core can process the data. Shared memory is one way to transfer the data easily between the cores. Here you can see in the h seven series MC use pretty much all the memories are accessible by both the cores using one way or another. So in a way, we can use any memory region as the shared memory for both the cores. But to keep things simple, I will go with the SRAM four region, which is available in the d3 domain. The main reason is that since the memory is in the d3 domain, it will remain accessible to both the cores even if the D one and D two domains are in the low power mode. The SRAM four region is widely used as the shared memory for the message exchange, so we will use the same there are different ways to notify the cause. They include the hardware semaphores, the external interrupts and the send event instruction, we will again use the hardware semaphore in this project. For the communication channel, we have the open amp, which stands for Open asymmetric multiprocessing along with the remote processor messaging our P message. Open amp is a framework that provides the software components for the development of the applications for the asymmetric multi processing system.

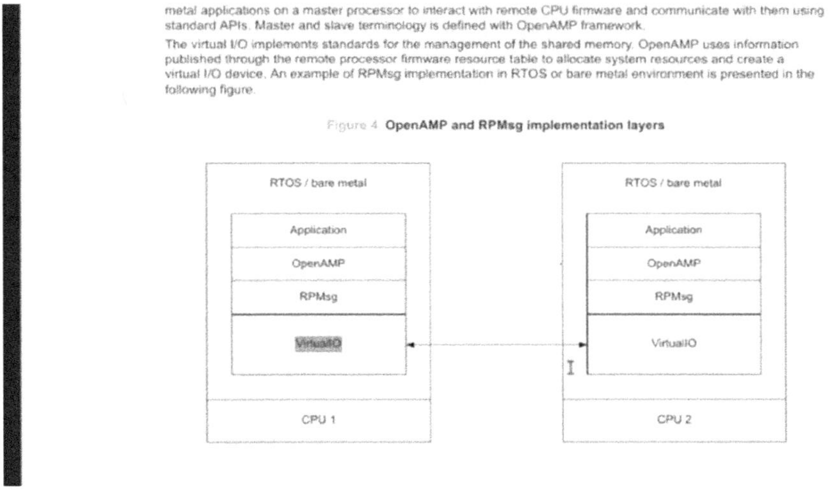

metal applications on a master processor to interact with remote CPU firmware and communicate with them using standard APIs. Master and slave terminology is defined with OpenAMP framework.

The virtual I/O implements standards for the management of the shared memory. OpenAMP uses information published through the remote processor firmware resource table to allocate system resources and create a virtual I/O device. An example of RPMsg implementation in RTOS or bare metal environment is presented in the following figure.

Figure 4 OpenAMP and RPMsg implementation layers

On the other hand, our P message is a component of the open amp framework, which allows the communication between applications running on different cores. The RP message library is based on virtual I O which actually does the communication. So this is our last layer of communication. On top of it we have the RP message and then the topmost layer is open amp for which we will actually write the code just like open amp and RP message we can also use the free RT OS along with the Stream Buffer for the inter process communication. We are not going to cover this for now. Then there are some hardware resources also like hardware semaphores XTi, controller and send event instruction and the dma's. I have covered the hardware semaphores in the previous project, and the rest of these channels will be covered in the upcoming projects to today we will focus on the open amp. In the open amp framework. One core acts as the master whereas another core acts as the slave master and slave both initialize the open amp individually, then the master creates a new service and an endpoint whereas the slave only creates the endpoint. The master sends the data, the slave receives the notification and the callback is called. The slave can then process data or it can send something back to the master. detailed instruction is given here on the very next page, but we will follow it while writing the code. We also need to modify the linker file in our project for this to work. So let's start and create a new project in cube ID. I am using the STM 32 H 745 discovery board. Give some name to the project and click Finish. Let me clear the pinouts First, we will start with the clock setup. And it will be the same as what we did in the previous projects. Now the first thing we need to do is enable the hardware semaphore interrupts for both the cause now go to middleware open and for the M four core and enable it, I am making the M four as the slave, the rest of the configuration is kept as default, the M seven core has automatically become the Master, the Master will send the data to the slave and then the slave will send it to the UART. The board has the virtual comport connected to the pins P V 10 and PB 11. These are the TX and RX pins of the UART three so, I am enabling the UART three for the slave core that is Cortex M for now, let's configure the MPU. We will start with enabling the cache for the Cortex M seven. Let's also enable the MPU. Let's see the memory configuration first. Here I have the reference manual of the STM 32 H 745. Here in the d3 domain, we have the SRAM for this is connected to the B DMA is also connected to the D two domain via the HB bus. And also to the D one domain via another a H V bus.

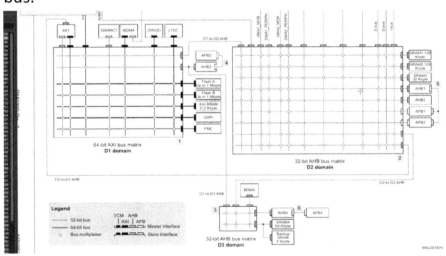

So all the domains can access the SRAM for and since it is in a separate domain, it can still work even if the other domains are in low power mode. Let's check the memory

277

organization. Here you can see the start address of the SRAM for is at 38 million hex. In the MPU configuration, we will set this region as non cashable. So to avoid data coherency. The RAM size is 64 kilobytes. If you don't understand this, check out the MPU configuration projects in the M seven playlist. That's all the setup we need. Click Save to generate the project. Let's build the main files once before we go ahead. Here you can see a separate folder for open amp has been created under both the cause. I am going to start with the M four core that is the slave. Here I have defined the RP message service name. The variable message receive will be used to indicate if the message has been received. received data will contain the actual data received. The RP endpoint is the RP message endpoint structure. Next we have the RP message received callback, which will be cold when a new message arrives. Then we have the receive message function which we will write to receive the data, we will write the callback and the receive message function later. Now inside the main function, after all the initialization has been done, we will write the code for the open amp. Let's understand this as per the instructions given in the document. Right now I am writing for the slave that is the M four core, we need to first initialize the mailbox which is done here. Then initialize the open amp and check for the status. If the status is not okay, the error function will be called.

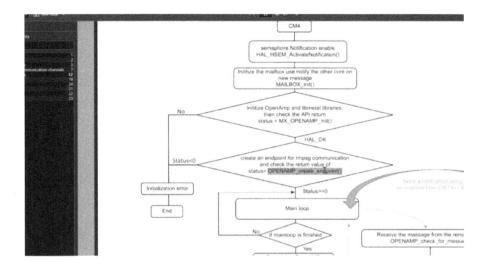

Here we are doing the same. The function takes the RP message role as the parameter which in this case is our p message remote the slave. The second parameter is to bind the new service but since the service is created by the master here, we will just pass the null. The next step is to create the endpoint. Here we will pass the address of the ERP message endpoint structure that we defined in the beginning. The next is the name we which is also defined, then the destination, which is set to any available address, then the callback, which we defined earlier. And finally the unbind callback, which will be null since the service has not been created by the slave. Now after creating the endpoint, the main loop begins where we receive the data from the master. Once the mail loop is done, we can D initialize the open amp. Here for the main loop, we will receive the data, then convert it to the string format, and then send it to the UART. Let's define this data array to store the data in the character format. Finally, we will D initialize the open app, we still need to write the callback function and the receive message function. In the callback function, we will first typecast the data to the unsigned int, since this is the format of our variable. After the data has been stored in the variable set the message received variable to one indicating that the data has been received. This received data variable contains the actual data, and we are converting the data stored in it to the character format. Since the data type is unsigned int we need to use the appropriate format specifier.

All right, now the function to receive the message while the message received variable is zero, we will keep checking for the data open and check for messages used to poll for the incoming message. Once the data is received, the message received callback will be called the variable will be set to one and it will break out of this loop. Here the code is written to receive the data only once and after receiving the open amp will be d initialized. Later in the project we will set it to receive infinitely in a while loop. I haven't defined the status variable. Let's define it here. All right, we have some errors, but they are related to the linker file. So we will fix them in the end. Let's write the code for the M seven core that is the master and here we have the similar defines that we used in the M four core. This time I have defined the RP message channel name and it is the same open amp test. The message variable is the actual message that we will send via the open amp. This is an integer value and after receiving it, the M four call will convert it to the character format before sending it to the UART we have the similar variables here the message received is used to indicate if the message has been received. Similarly, the service created will be set to one once the service has been created by the master received data variable will contain the actual data received by the master. And the RP endpoint is the endpoint structure. We have similar functions for the message received callback and for receiving the message. Other than them. We also have the callback functions for the service created in service destroyed. These callbacks will be called when a new service is created or destroyed. We will write these functions in a while let's write the main code. First. Let's take a look at the document again and understand this code. Here we are not using the RT O S, so this part is irrelevant. After initializing the mailbox, we need to also initialize the RP message endpoint. Note that we are only initializing the endpoint it will be created later. Next, initialize the open arm. The role is the master and this time we need to bind the new service callback here. This is because the service is created by the master and once the service is successfully created, the respective callback will be called inside the callback we will create the endpoint so here we will wait for the endpoints to become ready. Now once the endpoint is ready, send the message using open amp send function. Now wait for the service to be destroyed and then D initialize the open amp next right the function we defined earlier. Here is the message received callback. And this is similar to what we did for the slave. Although the master is not going to receive any data in today's project, we will use this function in the next one. When the remote endpoint is destroyed, the service destroyed callback will be called. And here we will simply set the variable to zero. Similarly, when the service created callback is called, we will create the endpoint. Here the name and destination is fetched from the new service callback, we have to pass the message received callback and the service unbind callback. Basically, once the open amp is initialized, the new service callback will be called then the end point will be created. Finally, we can send the message to the slave

All right, let's edit the linker file. Now. We will start with the M seven file first. Copy this part from the document and paste it in the linker file. We still need to add one more line for the resource table. Now scroll down and at the section path below the user heap stack we need to do the same for the Cortex M for Linka file also. That's it let's build the code for both the cores. The M seven core will send the integer message the M four will receive the message converted to the character format and then send it to the UART. Let's flash the code to the board. I am fast forwarding this part. As this is already covered in previous projects. I am using the Herculis for the serial monitor. Here you can see the number 1234 has been printed on the monitor. This value was sent by the M seven core to the M four core, which then converted it to the character format and sent to the UART. Let's reset the board the value has been printed again. Whenever I reset the board the value prints once. So we can say the open amp is working well with the shared memory. Now let's assume the master wants to continuously send the message to the slave. Here I am incrementing the value and let's set the start value at one here I am putting a while loop which will run until the message value reaches 15. Let's add a 500 millisecond delay between two consecutive cents. We also need to modify the M for code so that it can receive the message continuously.

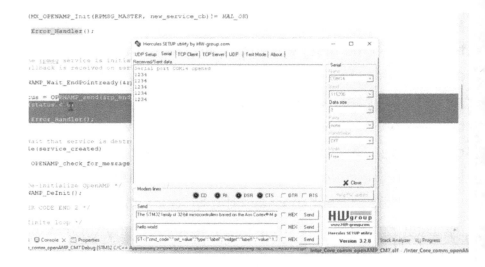

So we will put this much part in the while loop and comment out the D initialization for now. Let's build and flash the code into the board. Let me reset the board. So you can see the message values are being printed every 500 milliseconds and they only print up to 14. So we saw how to send some integral value between the cores. In the next project we will use free RT o s with open amp and we will transfer a string rather than just some value.

EXAMPLE DUMMY CODE

Inter-core communication using OpenAMP and RPMsg is a powerful mechanism for communication and synchronization between the Cortex-M7 (M7 core) and Cortex-M4 (M4 core) processors in STM32H7 series microcontrollers. OpenAMP provides a framework for remote

processor management, and RPMsg facilitates messaging between the cores.

Below is an example code that demonstrates how to use OpenAMP and RPMsg for inter-core communication on the STM32H7 microcontroller.

M7 Core Code:

```
#include "main.h"
#include "openamp.h"
#include "rsc_table.h"

// RPMsg endpoint handle
struct rpmsg_endpoint my_ept;

// Function to handle RPMsg received data
void rpmsg_receive_callback(struct
rpmsg_endpoint *ept, void *data, size_t len,
uint32_t src, void *priv) {
  // Process the received data here
  // For example, you can toggle an LED based on
the received message

HAL_GPIO_TogglePin(M7_CORE_LED_GPIO_Port,
M7_CORE_LED_Pin);
}
```

```c
int main(void) {
  // Initialize the HAL and other peripherals
  // Initialize OpenAMP
  MX_OPENAMP_Init(RPMSG_REMOTE, (void
*)&app_rsc_table, rpmsg_receive_callback,
NULL);

  // Wait for the remote processor to be ready
  while (!rpmsg_is_link_up(&my_ept)) {
    // Handle any background OpenAMP
processing
    MX_OPENAMP_Process();
  }

  while (1) {
    // Perform M7 core tasks
    // Send a message to M4 core
    rpmsg_send(&my_ept, "Hello from M7 core!",
strlen("Hello from M7 core!"));
    HAL_Delay(1000); // Wait for 1 second before
sending the next message

    // Handle any background OpenAMP
processing
    MX_OPENAMP_Process();
  }
}
```

M4 Core Code:

```c
#include "main.h"
#include "openamp.h"
#include "rsc_table.h"

// RPMsg endpoint handle
struct rpmsg_endpoint my_ept;

// Function to handle RPMsg received data
void rpmsg_receive_callback(struct
rpmsg_endpoint *ept, void *data, size_t len,
uint32_t src, void *priv) {
  // Process the received data here
  // For example, you can toggle an LED based on
the received message

HAL_GPIO_TogglePin(M4_CORE_LED_GPIO_Port,
M4_CORE_LED_Pin);
}

int main(void) {
  // Initialize the HAL and other peripherals
  // Initialize OpenAMP
  MX_OPENAMP_Init(RPMSG_MASTER, (void
*)&app_rsc_table, rpmsg_receive_callback,
NULL);
```

```
  // Wait for the remote processor to be ready
  while (!rpmsg_is_link_up(&my_ept)) {
    // Handle any background OpenAMP
processing
    MX_OPENAMP_Process();
  }

  while (1) {
    // Perform M4 core tasks
    // Handle any background OpenAMP
processing
    MX_OPENAMP_Process();
  }
}
```

In this example, we assume that the LED GPIOs
(M7_CORE_LED_GPIO_Port, M7_CORE_LED_Pin,
M4_CORE_LED_GPIO_Port, M4_CORE_LED_Pin)
are initialized in the HAL initialization code. The
rpmsg_receive_callback function is a callback that
will be called when the M7 core receives data
from the M4 core.

The M7 core sends a message to the M4 core
every second, and the M4 core responds by
toggling an LED upon receiving the message.

The MX_OPENAMP_Init function initializes

OpenAMP with RPMsg as the communication channel, and MX_OPENAMP_Process is called in a loop to handle any background OpenAMP processing.

Please note that this example assumes that you have properly configured and initialized the dual-core environment and OpenAMP library in your STM32 project. You also need to define the resource table (app_rsc_table) that describes the resources available for communication.

Inter-core communication using OpenAMP and RPMsg offers more flexibility and advanced features compared to the simple Hardware Semaphore (HSEM) mechanism. It allows you to exchange complex data structures, share resources, and implement sophisticated inter-core communication protocols. OpenAMP and RPMsg are particularly beneficial for complex multi-core applications where seamless communication between cores is required.

STM32 DUAL CORE _4. INTER CORE COMM FREERTOS OPENAMP IPC SHARED MEMORY

And today we will see how to use the free RT OS with the open amp. This is the continuation from the previous project, so if you haven't watched it, please watch the previous project first, I will continue from where I left off in that project, we will basically do the same with the M seven core which is the master will send the data to the M four core the slave the data will be then sent to the UART by the M four core. The explanation has been covered in the previous project. So I will just focus on the RT o s part. This is the previous project we covered, we need to enable the RT O S.

So let's go to the cube MX enable the free RT O S for Cortex M four, go to the tasks and queues tab. Here the default task is already created. So we will just change its name to the RX task, the RX task will be used to receive the data from the master. Note that its priority is set to normal. Let's create one more task the TX task it will be used to send the data to the UART we will keep its priority lower than the RX task. So I am setting it to below normal. Now I have one binary semaphore so that we can restrict TX task from sending data continuously. That's it for the Cortex M four enable the RT OS for the Cortex M seven, we will again create two tasks here, one for sending the data to the slave and another one for receiving the data from the slave. Though we are not going to receive any data from the slave, we still need to check for the message to know if the service has been destroyed by the slave. We don't need any semaphore here as we will send the data periodically. Since we are using our t o s, we need to use a time base other than the cystic so I am enabling the timer six for the Cortex M seven and timer seven for the Cortex M for now select the appropriate time base source. That's it for the configuration. Click Save to generate the project. There is a warning about the new library reentrant but that's all right, go ahead and generate the code.

Let's build both the files once. I will start with the Cortex M for first this part is used to initialize the open amp and creates the endpoint we will put it inside the RX task and it will only run once in the beginning. Since the RX task has higher priority, it will run first and initialize the open amp. After the initialization is over, it will acquire the semaphore. So, the TX task does not run the TX task is responsible for sending the data to the UART So, this part goes there we will shield this with the semaphore. So, to send the data first it has to acquire the semaphore. Since we are using our t o s, we will use the malloc and free functions to create an array of characters. So, the TX task needs to acquire the semaphore before sending the data, but the semaphore is already acquired by the RX task. Therefore, once the message is received, we will free the semaphore so that the TX task can acquire it and send the data now inside the RX task, we will continuously check for the data sent by the master Finally, the RX task is as follows. Once the control enters it, the open amp will be initialized, then the endpoint is created and it will acquire the semaphore. And then it will continuously check for the data sent by the master every 10 milliseconds. Once the data that has received the data will save in the variable and the semaphore will be released. After that the TX task will send the data to the UART and again try to acquire the semaphore let's delete this also the data is defined in the TX task itself. That's all for the slave. Now we will write the code for the master. Here I am leaving the message as one we will again copy the initialization inside the RX task after the initialization is over the RX task will check for the message from the slave. And now the transmission of data will take place in the TX task it will run every second. As I mentioned, the slave is not sending any data. So the check for message is only used to check if the service is destroyed by the slave. The master should only check for message if the service is created.

And if it is destroyed, the open amp will D initialize. All right let's build and flashed the code I am using the same debug configuration from the previous project let's reset the board here you can see the message is being printed on the console every one second.

```
88  #define RPMSG_SERVICE_NAME                "openamp_test"
89
90  static volatile int message_received;
91  volatile unsigned int received_data;
92  static struct rpmsg_endpoint rp_endpoint;
93  char data[100];
94
95  static int rpmsg_recv_callback(struct rpmsg_endpoint *ept, void *data, size_t len, uint32_t src, void *priv)
96  {
97      received_data = *((unsigned int *) data);
98      if (osSemaphoreRelease(txSemHandle) != osOK)
99  
100     return 0;
101  }
102
103  unsigned int receive_message(void)
104  {
105      while (message_received == 0)
106      {
107          OPENAMP_check_for_message();
108      }
109      message_received = 0;
110
111      return 0;
112  }
113
114
115
116  /* USER CODE END 0 */
117
118  /**
119   * @brief The application entry point.
120   * @retval int
121   */
122  int main(void)
```

So our project is working fine so far. Now let's say I want to D initialize the open amp after some time. If the message value is equal to 15, the slave will D initialize the open amp and also terminate the TX and RX tasks. This will destroy the service and the master should also do the same. When the tasks are terminated, an ideal task should run in both the cause and we will see this while debugging the project terminating tasks is not the ideal solution. Rather, you can just suspend them and write a separate task for initializing the open amp again and then resume the tasks to do their job. I am just terminating them so that the TX task does not try to send data while the open amp is D initialized. for debugging. We use the same configuration for M seven core but make sure the M four file here is on the top. Then go to the Cortex M four main file and create a new debug configuration select non under the reset behavior. Make sure the port number is at least four higher than the M seven. Go to the startup tab, double click on the configuration and uncheck the download option. Now debug using the M seven configuration. When fully loaded, again, load the M four configuration. file right now select both the main files using the control button and click Run. The message is being printed and it stopped at 14 Because as soon as it reached 15 The open app was D initialized and the tasks were terminated. Hey In statistics tasks could not send the message to the console. If you pause the debugger, now you can see the ideal tasks are running in both the cause. So we saw how to D initialize the open amp after a certain condition was met. Now let's quickly see how to transfer a string or some character data. Here I am creating another variable in the M for call. This is a character pointer.

```
314    /* USER CODE END 5 */
315  }
316
317  /* USER CODE BEGIN Header_StarttxTask */
318  /**
319  * @brief Function implementing the txTask thread.
320  * @param argument: Not used
321  * @retval None
322  */
323  /* USER CODE END Header_StarttxTask */
324  void StarttxTask(void *argument)
325  {
326      /* USER CODE BEGIN StarttxTask */
327      /* Infinite loop */
328      for(;;)
329      {
330          if (osSemaphoreAcquire(txSemHandle, osWaitForever) != osOK) Error_Handler();
331          char *data = pvPortMalloc(100);
332          sprintf(data, "%u\n\r", received_data);
333          HAL_UART_Transmit(&huart3, (uint8_t *)data, strlen(data), 100);
334          vPortFree(data);
335          osDelay(1);
336      }
337      /* USER CODE END StarttxTask */
338  }
339
340  /**
341  * @brief  Period elapsed callback in non blocking mode
342  * @note   This function is called  when TIM7 interrupt took place, inside
343  * HAL_TIM_IRQHandler(). It makes a direct call to HAL_IncTick() to increment
344  * a global variable "uwTick" used as application time base.
345  * @param  htim : TIM handle
```

Inside the receive callback function, we will simply typecast the data into the character pointer. Since we are receiving the data in the character form, we will use the S format rather than you know, the rest of the code remains unchanged. For the Master, I am first defining the string I am going to send and while sending the data I am using the string length function to calculate the length here make sure to add one to the length it should be an array All right, let's run the code again. You can see the string is being displayed on the console. So I hope you understood how to use the open amp with free RT O 's and how to send the string or characters between the cores.

EXAMPLE DUMMY CODE

Inter-core communication using FreeRTOS, OpenAMP, and IPC (Inter-Processor Communication) with shared memory is a powerful approach for communication and synchronization between the Cortex-M7 (M7 core) and Cortex-M4 (M4 core) processors on STM32H7 series microcontrollers. It enables efficient data exchange between the cores through a shared memory region.

Below is an example code that demonstrates how to use FreeRTOS, OpenAMP, and IPC shared memory for inter-core communication on the STM32H7 microcontroller.

M7 Core Code:

```
#include "main.h"
#include "openamp.h"
#include "rsc_table.h"

// RPMsg endpoint handle
struct rpmsg_endpoint my_ept;

// Shared memory buffer for communication with
M4 core
```

```c
#define SHARED_MEM_SIZE 64
uint8_t
shared_memory_buffer[SHARED_MEM_SIZE];

// Function to handle RPMsg received data
void rpmsg_receive_callback(struct
rpmsg_endpoint *ept, void *data, size_t len,
uint32_t src, void *priv) {
  // Process the received data here
  // For example, you can toggle an LED based on
the received message

HAL_GPIO_TogglePin(M7_CORE_LED_GPIO_Port,
M7_CORE_LED_Pin);
}

int main(void) {
  // Initialize the HAL and other peripherals
  // Initialize OpenAMP
  MX_OPENAMP_Init(RPMSG_REMOTE, (void
*)&app_rsc_table, rpmsg_receive_callback,
NULL);

  // Wait for the remote processor to be ready
  while (!rpmsg_is_link_up(&my_ept)) {
    // Handle any background OpenAMP
processing
    MX_OPENAMP_Process();
```

```c
}

    // Create a FreeRTOS task to handle
communication with M4 core
    xTaskCreate(M7_core_IPC_task, "M7_IPC_Task",
configMINIMAL_STACK_SIZE, NULL,
tskIDLE_PRIORITY + 1, NULL);

    // Start the FreeRTOS scheduler
    vTaskStartScheduler();

    // We should never reach here
    while (1) {
    }
}

// FreeRTOS task for M7 core IPC
void M7_core_IPC_task(void *pvParameters) {
    while (1) {
    // Perform M7 core tasks

    // Write data to the shared memory buffer for
M4 core
    // For example, you can send a message or data
structure to M4 core
    // In this example, we write a simple message
"Hello from M7 core!"
    snprintf((char *)shared_memory_buffer,
```

```c
SHARED_MEM_SIZE, "Hello from M7 core!");

    // Notify M4 core that data is ready in the
shared memory buffer
    MX_OPENAMP_Notify();

    HAL_Delay(1000); // Wait for 1 second before
sending the next message
    }
}
```

M4 Core Code:

```c
#include "main.h"
#include "openamp.h"
#include "rsc_table.h"

// RPMsg endpoint handle
struct rpmsg_endpoint my_ept;

// Shared memory buffer for communication with
M7 core
#define SHARED_MEM_SIZE 64
uint8_t
shared_memory_buffer[SHARED_MEM_SIZE];

// Function to handle RPMsg received data
void rpmsg_receive_callback(struct
```

```c
rpmsg_endpoint *ept, void *data, size_t len,
uint32_t src, void *priv) {
  // Process the received data here
  // For example, you can toggle an LED based on
the received message

HAL_GPIO_TogglePin(M4_CORE_LED_GPIO_Port,
M4_CORE_LED_Pin);
}

int main(void) {
  // Initialize the HAL and other peripherals
  // Initialize OpenAMP
  MX_OPENAMP_Init(RPMSG_MASTER, (void
*)&app_rsc_table, rpmsg_receive_callback,
NULL);

  // Wait for the remote processor to be ready
  while (!rpmsg_is_link_up(&my_ept)) {
    // Handle any background OpenAMP
processing
    MX_OPENAMP_Process();
  }

  // Create a FreeRTOS task to handle
communication with M7 core
  xTaskCreate(M4_core_IPC_task, "M4_IPC_Task",
configMINIMAL_STACK_SIZE, NULL,
```

```
    tskIDLE_PRIORITY + 1, NULL);

    // Start the FreeRTOS scheduler
    vTaskStartScheduler();

    // We should never reach here
    while (1) {
    }
}

// FreeRTOS task for M4 core IPC
void M4_core_IPC_task(void *pvParameters) {
    while (1) {
        // Wait for notification from M7 core
        MX_OPENAMP_Wait();

        // Read data from the shared memory buffer
sent by M7 core
        // For example, you can process the message or
data structure received from M7 core
        // In this example, we simply print the received
message
        printf("Received message from M7 core: %s\n",
shared_memory_buffer);
    }
}
```

In this example, we assume that the LED GPIOs

STM32 MPU CONFIGURATION NEED FOR THE MEMORY PROTECTION UNIT

There will be few more projects on this topic, and they all will be mostly the theory based as due to the lack of proper resources. I have put together a few conclusions from different documents, and I will share them with you. If something you think is lacking. Let me know in the comments. I will put them all together and release another project. So let's start with the first one today. And here we will see what is MPU. And why do we need it. Memory Protection Unit is a piece of hardware which is attached to the MCU itself. The main purpose of MPU is to prevent any process from accessing the memory location that hasn't been assigned to it. It does that by allowing the privileged access for the process in the allocated location. Privileged Access means that the process can use all the instructions and have access to all the resources. The Memory Protection Unit monitors all the transactions including the instruction fetching, and any violation of the access by the process will trigger fault exception. This could result in unpredictable behavior, and sometimes hard fall to we can control the MPU. With the attributes provided in the Cortex M seven, such as shareability, cache ability, et cetera, we will cover them in upcoming projects. There are three main reasons that I can think of to use the MPU. The first one is to prevent speculative access to the some memory locations, then we have DMA limitations obviously, and the third is not a reason. But we can manage our T OS tasks in much better ways. Let's start with speculative access. Speculative access is when CPU access some memory locations in advance and fetches the instructions or data from them, so that the wait cycles can be reduced. This accessing is done by the CPU on its own without any provided instruction, and it helps improve the performance. But the problem arises when CPU accesses memory locations that are not available, like external memories. This could sometimes result in hardware fault, and we need to prevent this speculative access to such locations. There are three types of speculative access in Cortex M seven speculative read speculative instruction fetch and speculative cache line fills. Speculative read is when the CPU tries to read the data in advance from the normal memory regions. I said normal memory region, and this is a type of memory regions available in Cortex M seven, we will cover it in the next project. Anyway, CPU tries to read data from this location, even if the data might not be needed. It does that so to reduce the wait cycles and improve the performance, but if the memory location is unavailable, it can cause faults in the system. There you could see errors like this, the CPU is trying to access a location which isn't available, we can use MPU to block the access to such memory locations. Here is the memory map of Cortex M seven, and you can see the addresses from 6 million to a million belongs to the external memories.

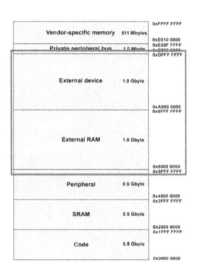

These addresses are already available in the core irrespective of whether the memory is available or not. So in case we are not using any external memory, we must block the access to these locations to prevent speculation reads to external memories. Next is the speculative instruction fetch. Here the CPU fetches the instructions in advance, so to increase the performance, but sometimes the instruction is not needed. Or sometimes it fetches the instructions that aren't even valid. We could use MPU to block the instruction access to any location, and this would prevent CPU to fetch instruction from that memory location. cache line fill means when the processor recognizes that an information being read from memory is cashable, the processor reads an entire cache line into the appropriate cache slot. We can make the region not cashable to prevent speculative cache line fill. That's all about the speculative access. Now let's talk about the second major issue and that is de ma. The DMA can't work in the cashable regions because it needs data coherency. As of now, the hardware support for data synchronization is not available in STM 32 F seven, and h seven series MC us, we can achieve the coherency using the software also typically by cleaning the cache and invalidating it, but an easier way is to use MPU to set the region as non cashable so that the DMA can synchronize with CPU or another DMA. We will see more about data coherency in the upcoming projects. Another thing we can do using MPU is the task management. We can restrict any task within certain region to prevent its access to other resources. This is a good example to understand it. You can read more about it on the source website. Basically, here the task A has been restricted to the green memory zone. While the task Lee is allowed to access the entire memory region.

STM32 MPU CONFIGURATION CACHE POLICIES

Let's start with the cache itself. Cache is a technique of storing a copy of data into a very fast memory. Very fast means where the read and write can take place at very high speed. Cortex M seven processes uses the level one cache to increase the performance. There are two types of cache used in STM 32. And they are instruction cache and data cache. Let's see some of the terms that we are going to use in this project. First one is cache hit and cache miss. If we are performing the right operation, the cache hit occurs if the address to be written is found in the cache memory. And if the address is not present in the cache, it's termed as cache miss. In case of the read operation, the cache hit occurs if the requested data is found in the cache. And if the data is not present in the cache, it's called cache miss. Another term that we are going to use is dirty bit. dirty bit indicates whether the cache has been modified or not modified. Every cache block contains one dirty bit. Generally, whenever the master writes the data into the cache, it sets the dirty bit to indicate the modification. The data right from cache to memory is only done if the dirty bit is set. This way the rights to the memory are reduced. Now let's talk about the cache policies in Cortex M seven processes. Here we have four cash policies right through Right back, right allocate and read allocate. Let's start with right through as it is the simplest one. In the write through policy, the data is simultaneously updated in the cache and to the memory. Take a look at the flow diagram, we will keep the focus on the writing part. If there is cache hit, the data will be written to the cache and then to the memory. And if there is cache miss, then the data is directly written to the memory. Basically, no matter what the data is written to the memory in a single instruction, this method is useful to handle the data coherency. But here we are performing more writes to the memory. And that defies the entire purpose of using cache. Next is the write back policy. Here, if there is cache hit, the master will write the data to the cache and set the dirty bit, the data can be updated later in the memory. To be precise, the data will be written to the memory only when the new data is about to be written in the cache. But if there is cache miss, that means if the address to be written is not present in the cache, then it completely depends on the right allocate.

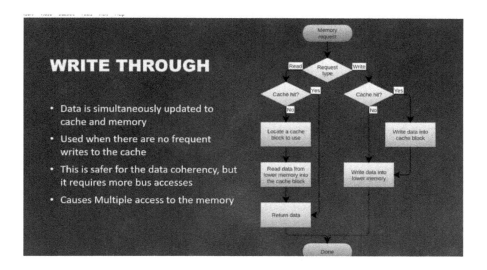

WRITE THROUGH

- Data is simultaneously updated to cache and memory
- Used when there are no frequent writes to the cache
- This is safer for the data coherency, but it requires more bus accesses
- Causes Multiple access to the memory

In right allocate, the data is loaded from memory into cache, and then it's updated in the cache. And the dirty bit is set so that the next cycle can get a cache hit, and the memory can be updated with new data. This is exactly how it's described in the diagram on the right. In case of the cache hit, the data is written to the cache and the dirty bit is updated. In case of the Miss, it will first locate some cache block which can be used for this purpose. If the block is already dirty, the previous data will be written to its respective memory. And then it proceeds further with copying data from memory to this cache. But if the block is not dirty, it will copy the data from the memory to this cache, then the data is updated in the cache and the dirty bit is set so that the next cycle we'll update the data to the memory in STM 32. The write back policy is mostly used with write allocate. Next is the read allocate every cashable location in Cortex M seven is read allocate, in case of the cache miss the cache lines are allocated for that particular data. So the next access to cash will be a hit. Here is the picture from SDS document about the policies used in STM 32 Cortex M seven, we have right through with no write allocate. In case of the hit, the data will be updated in the cache and the memory. But in case of miss the data will be updated in the memory and that memory block will not copied into the cache. Since this is no write allocate, then there is right back with no write allocate. In case of the hit the cache will be written and the dirty bit will be set, the main memory is not updated instantly, that's how the right back works. In case of Miss, the data will be updated in the memory and that memory block will not be copied into the cache. Since this is no write allocate. The last one is right back with write and read allocate. In case of the hit, the cache will be written and the dirty bit will be set. The main memory can update later. That's how the write back works. In case of the Miss, the memory block is updated, and the block is copied into the cache. This is because now we have both read and write allocate. Here is the cache policies for the memory locations. Remember that every cashable region is read allocate by default. Out of these locations, we are most interested in the SRAM region. If you remember the data coherency. We talked about where the CPU and DMA are not coherent in the cashable region. This kind of issues takes place in the write back policy regions, and that is the SRAM, we will see some cases of data coherency issues now, and also how to solve these issues. I made this PDF by collecting some important things from one of the microchips document, the link to the original document is at the bottom of this PDF. Let's start with the first issue when the DMA writes the data into the SRAM. Here DMA is copying data from the peripheral into the ES RAM and CPU is trying to copy this data from SRAM to some other location.

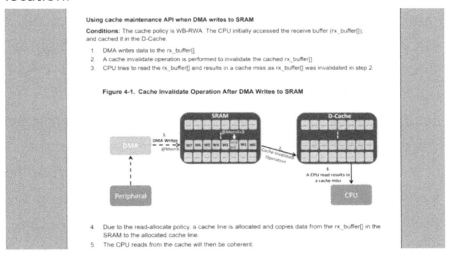

Using cache maintenance API when DMA writes to SRAM

Conditions: The cache policy is WB-RWA. The CPU initially accessed the receive buffer (rx_buffer[]), and cached it in the D-Cache.

1. DMA writes data to the rx_buffer[]
2. A cache invalidate operation is performed to invalidate the cached rx_buffer[]
3. CPU tries to read the rx_buffer[] and results in a cache miss as rx_buffer[] was invalidated in step 2.

Figure 4-1. Cache Invalidate Operation After DMA Writes to SRAM

4. Due to the read-allocate policy, a cache line is allocated and copies data from the rx_buffer[] in the SRAM to the allocated cache line.
5. The CPU reads from the cache will then be coherent.

Also, note that the cache policy of SRAM is right back with read and write allocate DMA reads data from peripheral and updates the data into the receive buffer in SRAM, but since we are using data cache, CPU will read the data from the cache, which hasn't been updated. So we have the data coherency issue here. To solve this, we can invalidate the cache. Let's see how, again, DMA will read the data from the peripheral and writes it in the receive buffer. As soon as DMA is finished, we will invalidate the cache or the receive buffer region. Now when CPU tries to access the cache, it's not available, so there will be a cache miss. Since the SRAM have read allocate policy, in case of the cache miss, a cache line will be allocated in the cache memory and the receive buffer will be copied there. Now when the CPU tries to access this cache, it will have the same data as the receive buffer. This is how the coherency issue can be solved using the cache invalidate. Here is the sample code. But this is as per the microchips protocol. But we will just focus on what's happening instead of the functions they are using. This handler is called when the D ma finished the transfer, we have transfer complete callback for that. Inside the handler, we have to invalidate the cache by address. The address is the address of the receive buffer and the size is the transfer size or the buffer size. This function is exactly the same across all Cortex M seven devices. In the main function, we can wait for the transfer to finish and then copy the data using the CPU. The next issue is when DMA reads the data from the SRAM. Here the CPU updates the data in the transmit buffer, but due to write back policy, the memory is not updated until the next right now in DMA read the cache, it will always read the old data and not the latest one. I hope you remember when I mentioned this, that the data to the memory is written when the new data is about to be written in the cache. Due to this there is always coherency issue between the CPU right and DMA read. We can solve this by cleaning the cache, CPU writes the data into the cache. Cache clean operation is performed to flush the cache into the SRAM. Now DMA read the data which will be coherent with the CPU right? This is the sample program First Data is being copied into the transmit buffer. Then we will perform clean cache by address and finally enable the DMA transfer. This way the DMA can read the latest data from the transmit buffer and the coherency issue can be solved. So we saw we can use cache invalidate and cache clean to solve the data coherency issues. We can also just make the region non cacheable through the MPU configuration and it will work just fine.

STM32 MPU CONFIGURATION CUBEMX SETUP

We saw the data coherency ESU, and how to resolve it. This project will show an actual working example of what we saw in the previous project. Also, we will see how to configure the MPU in the cube MX let me show you the configuration first. Here I have enabled the instruction cache and the data cache. Other than that everything is set to default setup. Here I have created two buffers receive and transmit and both of them have been assigned a particular location in the memory.

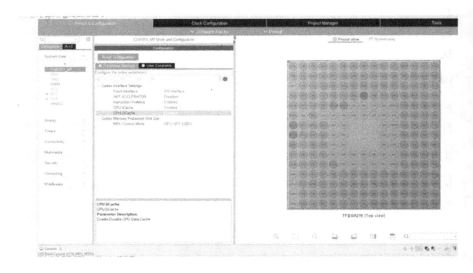

Here is the assignment. They are both placed in the SRAM one. I am doing this because the RAM in my case starts from dtcm region and it's not cacheable therefore the demonstration will not be valid in this region. You can watch the memory management project to understand this. Check it in the Cortex M seven playlist. Let's see example from the previous project we talked about two different coherency a sews first when DMA writes to SRAM and second when DMA reads from es RAM. I am using a memory to memory transfer for the DMA. So first we will write some data to the TX buffer and then we will use the CPU to copy the data from the TX buffer to the RX buffer. I am using the CPU transfer first. Let's test this part to see if the transfer works in the cashable region. Here you can see the location of the TX buffer and the RX buffer they are just where we have allocated them to be. Here I have put both the buffers in the live expression so the transfer is working all right, the CPU can copy data around without any issue. That's why the cases are very specific to DMA. Now instead of mem copy, let's try to use the DMA to transfer this data. Here the source address is the TX buffer and destination addresses RX buffer 100 milliseconds will be enough to do the transfer for both the DMA so that we can start it again All right, let's run it you can see the TX buffer is updating but the RX buffer is not changing.

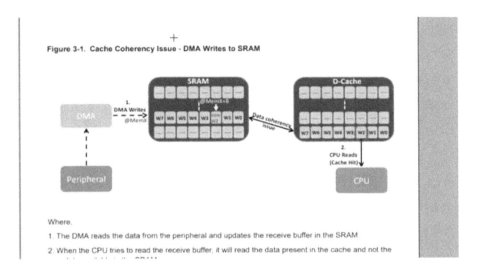

Figure 3-1. Cache Coherency Issue - DMA Writes to SRAM

Where,

1. The DMA reads the data from the peripheral and updates the receive buffer in the SRAM

2. When the CPU tries to read the receive buffer, it will read the data present in the cache and not the

This brings us to the issue we discussed in the previous project. Here both these issues are taking place at the same time because the DMA is reading from the s ram that is Tx buffer and D Ma is writing to s ram that his RX buffer. Let's start from the solution for the DMA reading from s ram. Here after the CPU writes the data to the s RAM, we must perform a cache clean operation which will

315

flush the cached TX buffer into the SRAM. So after copying the data into the TX buffer, we must clean cache by using clean D cache by address let's call the function here the address will be the address of the TX buffer and the size will be the size of the TX buffer. Now let's see for the DMA writing to the SRAM. After the DMA is finished writing, we must invalidate the cache we can do it in the transfer complete callback I will just do it here for now, invalidate the cache by address the addresses the address of the RX buffer and the size is the size of the RX buffer nets tested. All right, the first set of data is copied. The second set got copied to its working all right now. So whenever we are using multiple masters, we must perform these steps. Before the DMA reads the data we must perform cache clean and the invalidate cache must follow. After the DMA writes the data in is the SRAM, this was the software solution to maintain coherency. If this seems too much for you, there is another way around it. And I personally prefer using the MPU to solve the coherency issue. So let's see the MPU configuration first of all, here we will select the third option MPU region privileged access only and MPU disabled during hard fault. Now here we have a bunch of settings for different regions. There are 16 regions for me, but this might be different for you. We will start with the region zero. Let's enable it.

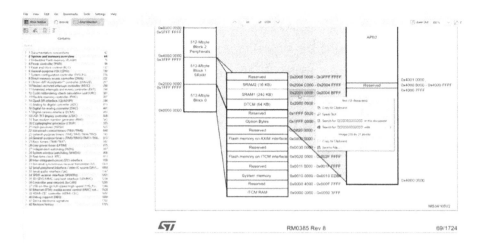

The first parameter is the base address. Here we will put the address of our buffers the buffers are starting from this particular address next is the region size. I have placed the buffers at different locations in the memory and together they take around 63 bytes of space from the beginning. Note that the buffer size are 10 bytes each. So they take 20 bytes. But since I have kept them at different locations, the region between them is also covered in this 63 bytes. So we will choose the next possible size and that is 64 bytes. This is the image I showed you in the previous project, and this have the configuration settings for different regions. Here we can choose the region type that suits best. For example, we can make the memory as the shared device where we can make it shareable and buffer oval or we can keep it as normal, but as a non cacheable memory. I will go with the shareable device type just to demonstrate that the normal memory can also be made to behave as a device type. So the text field will be zero. instruction should be disable, as there are no instructions available here and make it shareable non cacheable and buffer VUL this is as per the requirement mentioned here similarly, if you want to set another memory region you can choose here and configure it as per the requirement now since we have configured the MPU we don't need this software solutions.

Let's just disable them and see if the DMA can handle the transfer. You can see the RX buffer is updating just fine. So the DMA is able to read and write to SRAM without any issue. I have shown you two different methods to handle the data coherency issues and you can choose according to your convenience, just to show you that it is working because of the MPU configuration. Let's disable the MPU config and see what happens. Now the data is not updating in the RX buffer. So configuring the region as a shared device made the DMA transfer possible. This is it for this project. I hope you understood the MPU configuration data coherency Su and how to solve it. This is the end for the MPU configuration series. There is one more topic remaining, which is about the sub regions in the MPU but we will skip it for now. It's not important unless you are writing a very complicated program if required, I will cover it in the future.

STM32 MPU CONFIGURATION MPU SUB-REGION SETTING

This is the picture from one of the SDS Project and it shows how the region is divided a region can be divided to eight sub regions only if the region size is greater than 256 bytes.

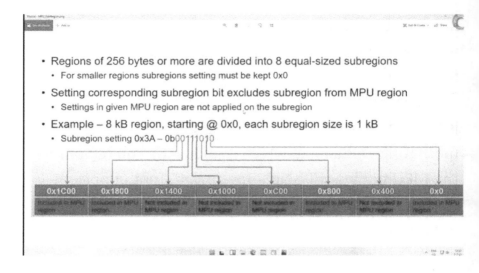

- Regions of 256 bytes or more are divided into 8 equal-sized subregions
  - For smaller regions subregions setting must be kept 0x0
- Setting corresponding subregion bit excludes subregion from MPU region
  - Settings in given MPU region are not applied on the subregion
- Example – 8 kB region, starting @ 0x0, each subregion size is 1 kB
  - Subregion setting 0x3A – 0b00111010

0x1C00	0x1800	0x1400	0x1000	0xC00	0x800	0x400	0x0
Included in MPU region	Included in MPU region	Not included in MPU region	Not included in MPU region	Not included in MPU region	Included in MPU region	Not included in MPU region	Included in MPU region

Another important point is that the setting a corresponding sub region bid will exclude the sub region from the MPU region. For example, if we have this eight kilobytes region in the MPU if we are using sub region, then this eight kilobytes region will be divided into eight sub parts. This means each sub part will be one kilobyte in size. Now, if the sub region setting is zero cross three A then all the positions that are set to one will not be a part of the MPU configuration, this region will exhibit the default memory behavior and all the positions that are set to zero will be a part of MPU configuration, we will see the working of this here I have already created a project. So I will directly take you to the cube MX configuration here The clock is set as usual. In the MPU configuration, I have selected the background region privileged access, the base address is set to 3 million. This is actually the address of one of the s rams. I am also using the eight kilobytes size. Let's disable the sub regions at first. So it will be easier to compare when we enable it or access are permitted and the region is set as shareable and non cashable. I am also using a DMA just like the previous project. Here we have two buffers each 10 bytes in size and they are defined at some particular locations in the memory. Here, the copy buffer is located at the start of the SRAM and the paste buffer is located at an offset of one kilobyte from the start of the SRAM. Let's build it once.

You can also see the buffers in the memory details. Here is the C data at the start of the s ram and the P data is at

400 offset. I have created a callback for the DMA and this flag will be set when the data transfer is finished. And here I am registering the callback for the DMA memory to memory transfer DMA don't have the callbacks, so we need to register manually. This parameter here defines when the callback will be called. This you can find in the DMA dot h file, and this is the ID for the full transfer. And at last, we have the callback itself now in the while loop, we will first set the data in the C data buffer and then start the DMA to transfer this data. Here C data is the source and P data is the destination then we will wait for the transfer complete flag to set in the callback and we will repeat the process again. As for now we have made this region non cacheable. So this transfer should work the Before we run this, let me show you how the region is set right now. Here is the setting for the region. Even if we consider that the region is divided into eight sub parts, here, all the sub parts are set to zero, and everything will be included in the MPU region. Let's see the working now. Here are both the buffers in the live expression. Let's run it. So everything seems to be working all right. Both the data buffers have the same data, so no coherent CSU.

0	0	0	0	0	0	0	0
1C00 – 1FFF	1800 – 1BFF	1400 – 17FF	1000-13FF	C00 – FFF	800 – BFF	400 – 7FF	0 – 3FF
						Pdata	Cdata

This is working because we set the eight kilobytes of non cashable region in the MPU and both the buffers are placed in that region. Now, let's go back to the Kulin Max and configure the sub regions. Right now, every region is included in the MPU. And we will exclude the PII data from it. To do that, we need to set a one in the second position. And that means we need to write zero cross zero to in the MPU sub region settings. Everything else will remain unchanged, and we will just exclude the P data region from the MPU configuration. This means the P data region will exhibit the default memory behavior where it is a cashable region. Let's see what happens with this configuration. We will keep our program same as before and run it. So everything is working fine here. Also, let's understand what's going on. Remember that we have only excluded the P data region, but the C data region is still non cashable. So the CPU writes the data to this region.

And since the region is non cacheable, the DMA is able to copy the latest data from it. That's why we see the same data in the P data buffer also. But if we make the C data region cacheable, the coherence CSU should start. To do that, we will set the region setting to zero cross 01. This will exclude the C data region from the MPU and this region will say to the default behavior, which will make it cashable. Let's test it now the P data region is not updating. This is because the C data region is cacheable. And the DMA is keep fetching the cached data, which was the initial data in the buffer. This was explained in the previous project, and is also known as data coherency. As you saw, we saw even the region was set to non cacheable. But with the sub region configuration, the C data becomes cacheable. And we have to face the coherency ESU. Now let's see what happens if we change the location of the C data buffer.

0	0	0	0	0	0	0	1
1C00 – 1FFF	1800 – 1BFF	1400 – 17FF	1000-13FF	C00 – FFF	800 – BFF	400 – 7FF	0 – 3FF
				Cdata		Pdata	

Here I am going to put the C data in some other location which is set to zero in the sub region settings. C 100 would be fine. So if we put the C data buffer at this new location, it should follow the MPU configuration and the buffer should be non cashable. Let's make the changes in the location of the C data buffer. Here I am updating the location in the flash script. So we have some error. Here it's mentioned that the memory counter cannot go backwards. Well this is happening because we have defined the higher location before the lower one We need to define the locations in their increasing order now it builds up successfully. All right, let's see the working now as expected, now the DMA works perfectly. It's able to copy the newest data from the C data buffer, because the C data buffer is in the non cashable region. Now, remember that only the first sub region was excluded from the MPU. So if the C data is placed in that region, it will follow the default properties of that memory region. But now we have changed the location of C data buffer.

EXAMPLE DUMMY CODE

To configure the MPU (Memory Protection Unit) and set up MPU sub-regions on STM32 microcontrollers, you can use the HAL (Hardware Abstraction Layer) functions provided by

STMicroelectronics. The MPU is used to define memory access permissions and regions to protect specific memory areas from unauthorized access.

Below is an example code that demonstrates how to configure the MPU and set up MPU sub-regions on an STM32 microcontroller using the HAL libraries.

```
#include "main.h"
#include "mpu.h"

// Memory region to be protected
#define PROTECTED_MEMORY_BASE_ADDRESS
0x20010000
#define PROTECTED_MEMORY_SIZE 0x1000

void configure_mpu(void) {
  MPU_Region_InitTypeDef mpu_init;

  // Disable MPU
  HAL_MPU_Disable();

  // Configure region 0 as a normal memory
region with full access permissions
  mpu_init.Enable = MPU_REGION_ENABLE;
  mpu_init.BaseAddress = 0x00000000;
```

```c
  mpu_init.Size = MPU_REGION_SIZE_4KB;
  mpu_init.AccessPermission =
MPU_REGION_FULL_ACCESS;
  mpu_init.IsBufferable =
MPU_ACCESS_NOT_BUFFERABLE;
  mpu_init.IsCacheable =
MPU_ACCESS_NOT_CACHEABLE;
  mpu_init.IsShareable =
MPU_ACCESS_NOT_SHAREABLE;
  mpu_init.Number = MPU_REGION_NUMBER0;
  mpu_init.TypeExtField = MPU_TEX_LEVEL0;
  mpu_init.SubRegionDisable = 0x00;
  HAL_MPU_ConfigRegion(&mpu_init);

  // Configure region 1 as a sub-region of region 0
with restricted access permissions
  mpu_init.Enable = MPU_REGION_ENABLE;
  mpu_init.BaseAddress =
PROTECTED_MEMORY_BASE_ADDRESS;
  mpu_init.Size = MPU_REGION_SIZE_1KB; // Sub-
region size (1KB in this example)
  mpu_init.AccessPermission =
MPU_REGION_PRIV_RO;
  mpu_init.IsBufferable =
MPU_ACCESS_BUFFERABLE;
  mpu_init.IsCacheable =
MPU_ACCESS_CACHEABLE;
  mpu_init.IsShareable =
```

```c
MPU_ACCESS_NOT_SHAREABLE;
  mpu_init.Number = MPU_REGION_NUMBER1;
  mpu_init.TypeExtField = MPU_TEX_LEVEL0;
  mpu_init.SubRegionDisable = 0x0F; // Enable all
sub-regions (4 sub-regions in 1KB)
  HAL_MPU_ConfigRegion(&mpu_init);

  // Enable MPU
  HAL_MPU_Enable(MPU_PRIVILEGED_DEFAULT);
}

int main(void) {
  // Initialize the HAL and other peripherals

  // Configure the MPU
  configure_mpu();

  while (1) {
    // Your application code here
  }
}
```

In this example, we first disable the MPU, configure Region 0 as a normal memory region with full access permissions, and then configure Region 1 as a sub-region of Region 0 with restricted access permissions.

The MPU sub-regions allow you to define smaller portions within a larger memory region and apply different access permissions to those sub-regions. In this example, we set up Region 1 as a 1KB sub-region of Region 0 (4 sub-regions with 256 bytes each), and we restrict access permissions to read-only (privileged access only) with bufferable and cacheable attributes enabled.

Please note that the exact configuration will depend on your specific application requirements and memory layout. Ensure that you properly configure the MPU according to the memory protection needs of your system.

Before using the MPU, you need to enable it in the system (usually in the startup code) and set up appropriate MPU regions and sub-regions based on your application's memory requirements. Also, note that enabling the MPU may require proper handling of memory attributes, access permissions, and alignment to avoid unexpected behavior or hard faults.

STM32 CAN MULTIPLE DEVICES

This is yet another project in the console series and today we will see how to use multiple devices in can. I thought I have explained the filter configuration properly. But apparently some of you still have problems with multiple IDs. So in this project, I will try to clarify that issue using the three different can modules. I am not going to explain everything here. And for that you must watch the previous projects about Ken this one will typically focus on using multiple IDs. And that's it. So before we jump into the code, let me show you what I am trying to achieve. Here is the picture of the connection. You can see there are three modules and they are connected to three microcontrollers.

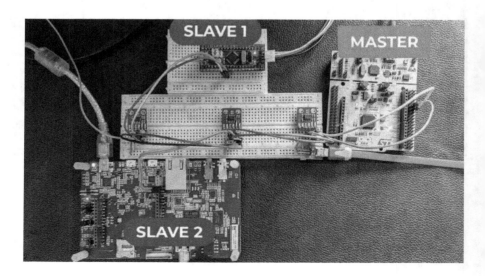

Also note that there are 120 ohms resistors connected at each node just like it was in the previous project. Let's assume that the nucleo is master and the other two are slaves. The can protocol don't have master and slave Slyke i to see but for now we can treat the nucleo as master as it is going to request the data from the other two. The nucleo will request the data from the two slaves and after receiving the data, it will send it to the UART so it will be easier for us to see which slave is sending the data. Let's see the code now. This is the main file for NUCLIO our master here the initial defines are same as the last project I have added these variables to check which slave has sent the data. Now in the pending callback, first we will receive the message from the FIFO then we will further check the ID of the slave these IDs are allocated to the other slave devices and you will see them in their main files. Based on which slave sent the data we will set the respective flag. So this whole process is like an additional filter on top of the hardware filters we already got. I will explain this failsafe in a while and then we do our usual process we start the can and configure the TX header. Note here that DLC is for as I am going to send four data bytes to the slaves and this is the ID assigned to the nucleo then we will load this particular string in the TX data and send the message now if you remember, we set some flags in the interrupt callback. Basically, if the data is received from the F 103 Then this flag will set and if the data is received from F 750 then this one will set in the while loop we will check if the either of these flags are set. If they are that means some data has been received and we will send the data to the UART.

And if the data was received from F 103 Then we will request the next data from F 750 and vice versa. This way the communication will be continuous and we don't need to intervene now let's see the failsafe. I have defined a value for failsafe here and in the interrupt file it keeps on decreasing every one millisecond. If this value goes less than zero, we will transmit the data again. This is kind of precaution in case of communication failure Also we need to keep updating this value so that it doesn't reach zero. And we do that whenever we receive data from the slave This is it for the master. Now let's see the code for the F 103. The first slave device here are also the things are same in the beginning, in the callback function, we will receive the data from the FIFO as you know, there are multiple devices connected to the same CAN bus. So, we want this slave to respond only when the master requests the data from it. To do that, we need one additional filter and here it is, we will check the received data from the master if the data is F 103, we will set this flag this will serve as a confirmation that the data is requested from F 103. Now if the flag is set, we will turn on the LED then send this data to the master now remember one thing that all the transactions are taking place on the same CAN bus. So which data will be received by which device this will be decided by the filter configuration. Here the filter is configured to pass through the data from the F 446 that is from the master only. So when the second slave send the data over the CAN bus, our first slave which is F 103 will not let the data in Alright, right now we have reached the second slave. Everything is same here, except that the check will be performed for the F 750. By the way, this is the ID for the second slave, I forgot to show it for the blue pill. Here it is 211 I have chosen these IDs for some particular reason. And you will see that in a while. And similar to the first slave, if the data is requested from this one, we will send some data to the master note here the filter is also configured to pass the message from the master only. Okay, so we saw the filter configurations for the slaves. And now we will see for the Master The Master is supposed to receive data from the two different slaves. So let's see how the filter is configured for the same. As you already know, we have two important registers, Id register and mask register. Those are the IDs of the F 750 and F 103. And we want the message from both of them to pass through. To do so we can just check for the common bits in both the IDS like both the IDs of one of these positions, let's fill the zeros in the rest this makes up 201. Now my mask register will be something like this.

If you remember from the first tutorial, I have explained this when the bit of the mask register is set to one the ID register will be compared with incoming ID. The mask register is one here. So this bit of the ID register will be compared with the bits of the incoming IDs. Again it is one here and that means this bit will be compared with The incoming IDs, it is zero here. So this bit will not be compared. So wherever the mask register is set to one, only those bits of the ID register are compared. And if all the comparing bits match with the ID register, the message will pass through, we can make it easier for this particular case and only compare these particular bits so, now only this bit and this bit and this will be compared because the mask register is only set at these positions so, basically, these other bits of the ID registers are don't care bits now, they match or don't match, it doesn't matter any more, since the mask bits are zero there, so they are not compared anyway. So, I will set to 01 for the ID and the mask register now, everything has been explained. So let's see the working here is the logic analyzer and this is connected to one of the the receive line I am also opening a serial port to see the data sent by Master let's start we are receiving some data. Here you can see the transactions taking place on the RX line. And you can also see the data from both the slaves. Let's see what's happening on the RX line. Here you can see the ID of the sender and this is the data from the second slave. If we check the next transaction here the data is sent by the master notice that the data here is f 103. So the master received the data from the second slave in the previous transaction and now it's requesting from first slave the gap here is around 2.5 seconds. This means that there was some transaction failure and here the master sends the same data again.

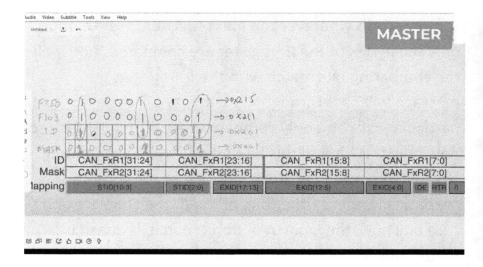

This happened because of the failsafe variable we used now the first slave sent the data after receiving the data from the first slave the master requests from the second slave and here is the data sent by the second slave. So this process will keep repeating forever you see the transactions taking place on the RX line. And when there is a big gap that means there was a failure and the master requests the data again here you can see the data is updating continuously. So this is it for this project. I hope you understood how to use multiple devices, specially the part where we configured the filters.

EXAMPLE DUMMY CODE

To demonstrate how to use the STM32 CAN peripheral to communicate with multiple devices, we will create a simple example where an STM32 microcontroller (CAN transmitter) sends messages to two other STM32 microcontrollers (CAN receivers). The receivers will process the incoming messages and perform specific actions based on the received data.

In this example, we assume that the CAN bus is properly set up with three STM32 devices connected to it. The first STM32 (transmitter) sends messages to the other two STM32s (receivers) through the CAN bus.

Transmitter Code (CAN Tx):

```
#include "main.h"
#include "can.h"

#define CAN_TX_ID_1 0x101   // Identifier for CAN message 1
#define CAN_TX_ID_2 0x102   // Identifier for CAN message 2

// Function to send CAN messages
```

```c
void send_can_message(uint32_t id, uint8_t*
data, uint8_t len) {
  CAN_TxHeaderTypeDef tx_header;
  uint32_t tx_mailbox;

  // Configure the CAN message
  tx_header.StdId = id;
  tx_header.ExtId = 0;
  tx_header.RTR = CAN_RTR_DATA;
  tx_header.IDE = CAN_ID_STD;
  tx_header.DLC = len;
  tx_header.TransmitGlobalTime = DISABLE;

  // Send the CAN message
  HAL_CAN_AddTxMessage(&hcan, &tx_header,
data, &tx_mailbox);
}

int main(void) {
  // Initialize the HAL and CAN peripheral

  uint8_t data1[8] = {1, 2, 3, 4, 5, 6, 7, 8}; // Data
for CAN message 1
  uint8_t data2[8] = {10, 20, 30, 40, 50, 60, 70, 80};
// Data for CAN message 2

  while (1) {
    // Send CAN message 1 to the first receiver
```

```c
  send_can_message(CAN_TX_ID_1, data1,
sizeof(data1));

  // Send CAN message 2 to the second receiver
  send_can_message(CAN_TX_ID_2, data2,
sizeof(data2));

  HAL_Delay(1000); // Send messages every 1
second
  }
}
```

Receiver Code (CAN Rx):

```c
#include "main.h"
#include "can.h"

#define CAN_RX_ID_1 0x101   // Identifier for CAN
message 1
#define CAN_RX_ID_2 0x102   // Identifier for CAN
message 2

// Function to process received CAN messages
void process_can_message(uint32_t id, uint8_t*
data, uint8_t len) {
  // Perform actions based on the received
message ID and data
  if (id == CAN_RX_ID_1) {
```

```
    // Process message 1 data
    // For example, toggle an LED or take any other
action based on the data
    // In this example, we toggle an LED when
receiving message 1
    HAL_GPIO_TogglePin(LED_GPIO_Port, LED_Pin);
  } else if (id == CAN_RX_ID_2) {
    // Process message 2 data
    // For example, perform another action based
on the data
    // In this example, we don't perform any action,
just receive the message
  }
}

int main(void) {
  // Initialize the HAL and CAN peripheral

  CAN_RxHeaderTypeDef rx_header;
  uint8_t rx_data[8];

  while (1) {
    // Check if a CAN message is received
    if (HAL_CAN_GetRxFifoFillLevel(&hcan,
CAN_RX_FIFO0) > 0) {
      // Receive the CAN message
      HAL_CAN_GetRxMessage(&hcan,
CAN_RX_FIFO0, &rx_header, rx_data);
```

```
    // Process the received CAN message
    process_can_message(rx_header.StdId,
rx_data, rx_header.DLC);
    }

    // Your application code here
  }
}
```

In this example, the transmitter STM32 sends two different CAN messages (message 1 and message 2) to the receivers. The receivers process the received messages in the process_can_message function and perform actions based on the message ID and data.

Make sure that the CAN bus is correctly configured with the appropriate bit rate and proper termination resistors. Also, ensure that each receiver knows the unique identifier (ID) for the messages it is expecting to receive from the transmitter.

Note: The actual hardware setup and CAN bus configuration will depend on the specific STM32 microcontroller and your application requirements. Additionally, you need to properly initialize the GPIO pins, enable the CAN peripheral, set up the bit rate, and handle any possible CAN bus errors or interrupts as needed.

STM32 CAN Communication NORMAL Mode

This is part two of the tutorial on can peripheral and today we will see how to communicate between two devices. I have already covered the basics of the can protocol and you must watch that project before this one. You can see the project on the top right. So let's start with this project. Now, I am using the blue pill and the f4 for six R E controllers and the connection is as shown here. The RX and the TX pins from the transceivers are connected to the respective microcontrollers. Then can high and can low are connected with each others. Note that there must be a 120 ohms resistance connected at each node just as it is shown in figure.

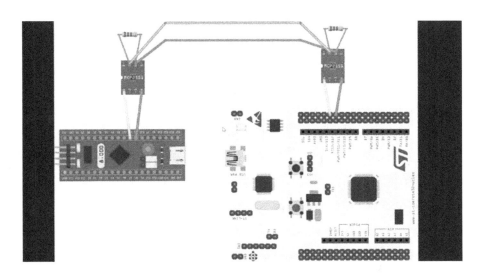

Some transceivers have this resistance on the breakout board itself and other don't. So make sure you check the resistance. Here is how the connection is I have twisted the wire pair connected between can high and can low. You could try with simple wires, but if doesn't work, try a twisted pair here is the 120 ohms resistance connected between the can high and low. I have it connected on the other node to p 11. And pa 12 from blue pill are connected to the first transceiver and the same pins from nucleo are connected to the second transceiver. The transceivers are powered with five volts from the microcontrollers. This is all about the connection. Now let's start the project for the nuclear first. So here we are in the cube MX first of all, I am selecting the external crystal for the clock I have eight megahertz Crystal and I want the system to run at maximum 180 megahertz. Notice here that the 446 have to can peripherals as mentioned in the reference manual, the can one is the master cam and the cam two is the slave can also they have 28 filter banks all together let's configure the cam one. Now here I am going to set the baud rate to 500,000 bits per second I am just modifying these parameters to get that here I got the baud rate. Now make sure that the operating mode is set to Normal and I am going to use FICO zero to store the incoming message.

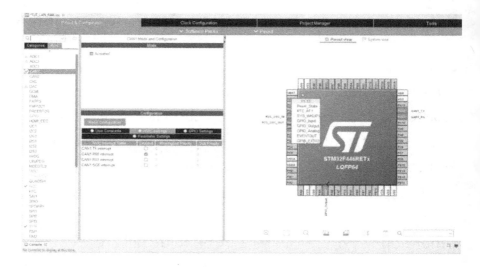

So in the ENV I see I am enabling the RX zero interrupt this is it for can set up. Now I am setting the P A five as output for the onboard LED. Also I am selecting the external interrupt for the user button which is connected to the PC 13 This is it now click Save to generate the project I hope you remember things from previous project because I am going to skip some explanation here. Let's write the program now. This is where the transmit header data will be stored. Our X header will store the header from the incoming message let's create the arrays to store the TX data and the RX data and at last the variable for the TX mailbox now in the main function stopped the can activate the notification for the data pending in the RX FIFO. Everything I am doing has already been covered in the previous project. Kindly watch it if you don't understand something here After activating the notification, we will load data in the TX header I am going to send two data bytes. So DLC is two we will be using standard ID and the ID will be zero cross 446. This is the ID of F 446 R E. Whenever this controller will send the message, this ID will act as the ID of the sender. Now before I send data, let me explain what I actually want to achieve here. This controller will send the two data bytes. The first data byte will act as delay for the LED on the second board. And the second data byte will act as the number of times that LED will blink when the second controller receives this message the LED on it will blink according to these instructions. I am not going to send the data here, but instead let's send it in the 60 callback function. When the user button is pressed, this function will be called and we will send the data here the delay will be 100 milliseconds and the loop will be repeated 10 times now we will send the data using Hall connect TX message here we have activated the notification for the receive when this controller will receive message from the blue pill, a message pending callback will be called. Inside this callback, we will receive the data from the FIFO zero the header will be stored in our x header and the data will be stored in the RX data let's create a flag we will just do one more check if the data length is two bytes then the flag will set if the flag is set we will blink the LED the number of times it will blink will be the second bite of the RX data and the time delay will be the first bite and finally reset the flag so that there is no false blink. Let's build it once I think I forgot to enable the interrupt for the XD line. Let's enable it. Next we have to configure the filters we will configure inside the can initialization function. Here is the filter configuration that I am using enable the can filter. I am assigning 20 filter banks to the can one out of these 20 I am using filter bank number 18. This is the ID that should pass through. This ID will be assigned to the blue pill later. And the same value in the mask ID register also, I am using FIFO zero to store the incoming message. This configuration is explained in the previous project. So make sure you watch it. Let's build it now. Now since I am going to connect both the control As the same computer I don't want the SD links to mix up. So I am going to assign the respective SD links to their controllers right now I have connected only the F 446 And if I scan the SD link here it will only show one so we will keep this st link assigned to this board that's all for this now let's create another project for blue pill I am doing the basic setup and running the system at maximum clock activates the can peripheral we have to select the same baud rate here that is 500,000 bits per second. Here I will use the FIFO one for receiving the message This is just to demonstrate PC 13 Is the LED on board so select it as output that's it click Save to generate the project I am going to use same code that I used in 446 so copy everything from here we are not using the external interrupts in blue pill let's copy this part now here we don't have can one or can too instead it's just can as I said I am using FIFO one here so replace all FIFO zero with FIFO one the transmitter ID for blue pill will be zero cross 103 Now let's copy the while loop here the LED is PC 13 Now since we are not using the external interrupt here we will send the data in this loop itself let's define the data that we will send and after the LED is finished blinking we will send the data using Paul F TX message now copy the filter configuration hear the start slave bank does not matter like I explained in the previous project and the filter bank should be between zero to 13 the ID that will be allowed to pass is zero cross 446 the ID of the f4 controller okay this should be can and we are using FIFO one all right, it's correct now, so I have removed the f4 st link and now only the blue pill is connected. If we scan the st link, only one shows up and we will assign it to the blue pill now the code has been loaded into both the microcontrollers. Let's see if it works as expected.

```
                                    58   /* USER CODE BEGIN 0 */
 ▾ ▣ TUT_CAN_F446                    59
   › 🗂 Includes                     60   CAN_TxHeaderTypeDef TxHeader;
   ▾ 🗂 Core                         61   CAN_RxHeaderTypeDef RxHeader;
     › 🗂 Inc                        62
   ▾ 🗂 Src                          63   uint8_t TxData[8];
     › C main.c                      64   uint8_t RxData[8];
     › C stm32f4xx_hal_msp.c         65
     › C stm32f4xx_it.c              66   uint32_t TxMailbox;
     › C syscalls.c                  67
     › C sysmem.c                    68
     › C system_stm32f4xx.c          69   void HAL_GPIO_EXTI_Callback(uint16_t GPIO_Pin)
     › 🗂 Startup                    70   {
   ▾ 🗂 Drivers                      71       if (GPIO_Pin == GPIO_PIN_13)
     › 🗂 CMSIS                      72       {
     ▾ 🗂 STM32F4xx_HAL_Driver       73           TxData[0] = 100;   // ms Delay
       ▾ 🗂 Inc                      74           TxData[1] = 10;    // loop rep
         › 🗂 Legacy                 75
         › C stm32f4xx_hal_can.h     76           HAL_CAN_AddTxMessage(&hcan1, &TxHeader, TxData, &TxMailbox);
         › C stm32f4xx_hal_cortex.h  77       }
         › C stm32f4xx_hal_def.h     78   }
         › C stm32f4xx_hal_dma_ex.h  79
         › C stm32f4xx_hal_dma.h     80   /* USER CODE END 0 */
         › C stm32f4xx_hal_exti.h    81
         › C stm32f4xx_hal_flash_ram 82   /**
         › C stm32f4xx_hal_flash.h   83    * @brief  The application entry point.
         › C stm32f4xx_hal_gpio_ex.h 84    * @retval int
         › C stm32f4xx_hal_gpio.h    85    */
         › C stm32f4xx_hal_pwr_ex.h  86   int main(void)
         › C stm32f4xx_hal_pwr.h     87   {
         › C stm32f4xx_hal_rcc_ex.h  88       /* USER CODE BEGIN 1 */
         › C stm32f4xx_hal_rcc.h     89
         › C stm32f4xx_hal_tim_ex.h
```

I have also connected The analyzer to see the data flow. Channel Zero is connected to the TX Of 446 and channel one is connected to the TX of blue pill. Pay attention to the LEDs on both the microcontrollers, the communication will start only when the button on the 446 is pressed. As you can see, when I press the button, the LED on blue pill blinks for some time, and then the LED on 446 starts blinking and then everything stops until the button is pressed again. This is exactly what we programmed it to do. Let's see the data.

This is the message sent by 446 You can see the ID the control field the two data bytes once this message is received by the blue pill, the LED will blink and once the LED finished blinking the blue pill will send the message and here you can see the message sent by blue pill you can see the same process will repeat every time we press the button let's try changing the data for both of them. You can see the LED is blinking somewhat longer now. Also observe the message on the analyzer. There is almost a delay of four seconds here we are sending the 100 milliseconds delay and 40 times blink to the blue pill and that's why this four seconds so this works pretty good now if you don't want to press the button every time you can just send this data after the blinking is finished just like we are doing in the blue pill.

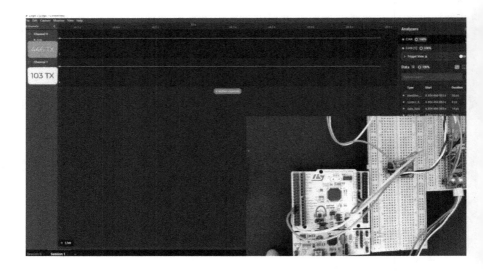

This way the process will keep going forever without any manual intervention let's run it now I will start the process by pressing the button once you can see the LED on blue pill is blinking and now the LED on the 446. And this process is keep repeating by itself. This is how we can use the can for the communication. We can send up to eight data bytes at a time. Filters allow the message filtering at the hardware level itself so the CPU don't have to do that work.

EXAMPLE DUMMY CODE

Below is an example code for STM32 CAN communication in NORMAL mode. In this example, we'll configure one STM32 microcontroller as the transmitter and another as the receiver. The transmitter will send a simple

message, and the receiver will receive the message and process it.

Transmitter Code (CAN Tx):

```c
#include "main.h"
#include "can.h"

// CAN message structure
CAN_TxHeaderTypeDef tx_header;
uint8_t tx_data[8] = {0x11, 0x22, 0x33, 0x44, 0x55, 0x66, 0x77, 0x88};
uint32_t tx_mailbox;

int main(void) {
  // Initialize the HAL and CAN peripheral

  // Configure the CAN message
  tx_header.StdId = 0x321; // Set the CAN ID for the message (11-bit standard ID)
  tx_header.ExtId = 0;   // Not used in this example (extended ID)
  tx_header.RTR = CAN_RTR_DATA; // Set the message type to data frame
  tx_header.IDE = CAN_ID_STD;   // Use standard ID (11 bits)
  tx_header.DLC = 8;     // Data length (bytes)
  tx_header.TransmitGlobalTime = DISABLE;
```

```c
  while (1) {
    // Transmit the CAN message
    HAL_CAN_AddTxMessage(&hcan, &tx_header,
tx_data, &tx_mailbox);
    HAL_Delay(1000); // Send message every 1
second
  }
}
```

Receiver Code (CAN Rx):

```c
#include "main.h"
#include "can.h"

// CAN message structure
CAN_RxHeaderTypeDef rx_header;
uint8_t rx_data[8];

int main(void) {
  // Initialize the HAL and CAN peripheral

  while (1) {
    // Check if a CAN message is received
    if (HAL_CAN_GetRxMessage(&hcan,
CAN_RX_FIFO0, &rx_header, rx_data) ==
HAL_OK) {
      // Process the received CAN message here
```

```
    // For example, you can toggle an LED or take
any other action based on the received data
    // In this example, we don't perform any
action, just receive the message
    }

    // Your application code here
    }
}
```

In this example, one STM32 microcontroller is set up as the CAN transmitter, and the other is set up as the CAN receiver. The transmitter periodically sends a CAN message with a specific CAN ID (0x321). The receiver continuously checks for incoming CAN messages in the receive FIFO and processes them when available.

Ensure that the CAN bus is properly configured with the appropriate bit rate, and both transmitter and receiver are configured with the same bit rate settings. Also, ensure that both transmitter and receiver have the same CAN IDs, so they can communicate with each other.

Note: The actual hardware setup and CAN bus configuration will depend on the specific STM32 microcontroller and your application

requirements. Additionally, you need to properly initialize the GPIO pins, enable the CAN peripheral, set up the bit rate, handle any possible CAN bus errors or interrupts, and perform other necessary configurations as needed.

STM32 CAN LOOPBACK MODE FILTER CONFIGURATION

There is a lot to cover in the cam peripheral, so I will do multiple parts for it. This project will cover the basic can protocol, how to use it in the loopback mode and also how to configure the filters. We will not use the extended version of this can in the beginning but focus on the basic cam. Let's start with the can protocol first. As you can see, the can data frame is quite big, but we will not discuss everything here we will only focus on the region I have highlighted with r1 other than this region, we will write the data obviously, but the rest is handled by the whole library region r1 contains the arbitration field and the control field.

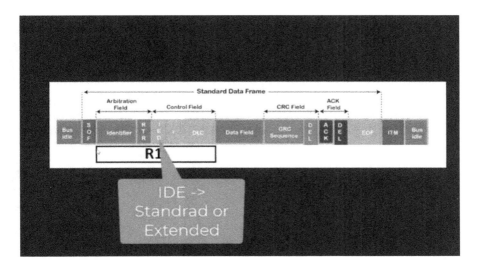

Here we have the 11 bit identifier which is more like the ID of the transmitting node, then we have our TR remote transmission request it defines either we are sending Remote Frame or data frame then we have ID which decides whether we are using standard ID or extended ID for the cam R is the reserved bit de l c is the data length in bytes. And finally we have the data field we will see them all today. Let's start by creating the project in cube ID I am using STM 32 F 103 ch controller give some name to the project and click Finish let's also take a look at the reference manual here is the cam peripheral blue pill can support basic and extended can protocols. The bit rate here can be up to one Mbps in the reception part it have to FIFO to receive the data for the devices with two can peripherals there are 28 filter banks and for the devices with one can peripheral there are only 14 filter banks. We will discuss filter banks later in this tutorial. blue pill only have one can peripheral so we only have 14 filter banks here here is how the can transceiver is connected it is connected to the CAN controller via the TX and the RX pins and the can high and can low from the transceiver are connected to the CAN bus. All other can transceivers are also connected to this bus and that's where the data transfer takes place.

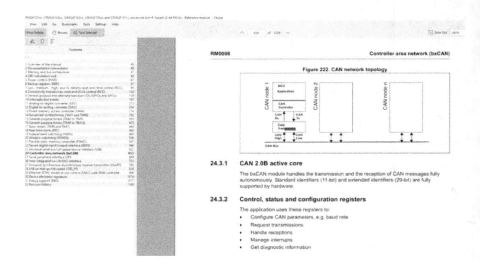

This is the can transceiver I have it is MCP 2551 Can transceiver and as you can see it have four data pins TX RX can high and can low for the transmit purpose it have three transmit mailbox and we can transmit data using these three mailbox we will check this in a while now comes the loopback mode. This is basically a test mode where we can test the transceiver whatever data we send, it should be able to loop back Okay, that's all for now let's set up the things in cube MX. I am enabling the external crystal for the clock I have eight megahertz Crystal and I want the system to run at 72 megahertz let's also enable the serial wire debug. Enable the can peripheral. You see here p 11. Is the can Rx pin and p 12. Is the can TX This is how the connection is p 11. is connected to RX p 12. To Tx and I have shorted the can high and can low since we are using loopback mode. There should be 120 ohms resistor here between these two let's set up the baud rate I am trying different setups to get the baud rate of 500,000 bits per second here I got it let's change the operating mode to loopback mode leave everything as default now go to the N V i c tab and select the FIFO interrupt you can use either of these FIFO but I will show the working for both so I am enabling both interrupts here is the Canon initialization function I will explain all these but let's quickly test the loopback mode first we need to configure the filters let's put it here after the initialization have a lot of elements in it for now I am going with this configuration but don't worry I will explain this in a while now we will call the filter configuration function we need to set the TX header before transmitting the data also we will check the RX header after the data has been received.

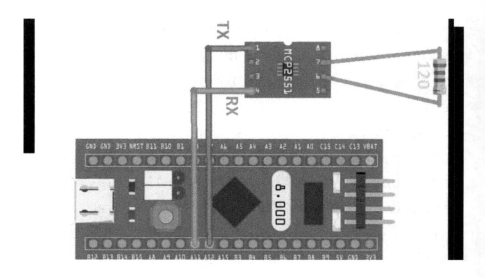

Let's create a mailbox to send the data also create buffer for transmit and receive now inside the main function stop the can let's activate the notification of receiving data. Here we need to write the interrupts type the type are defined in the can header file here we will look for the message pending in the FIFO zero now once this interrupt gets triggered, the interrupt callback function will be called. We will receive data in this message pending callback. But for now, let's just increment the count. Now before sending the data to the Can we have to modify the header basically set the arbitration and the control fields. We will do this in the TX header that we defined earlier. The first member is the DLC. This specifies the length of data that we are going to send I am planning on transferring only one byte of data. Next member is the extended ID. Since we are using basic can protocol today we will keep it zero.

Next is the IDE. This specifies the type of identifier Basically whether it's a standard identifier or extended ID we are using standard one today. So we will keep it standard ID. Next is the RT R. This specifies whether we are transferring data or Remote Frame. As we are sending data we will set it to data next is the standard identifier. Here we can give any identifier for this can peripheral. If there are other devices connected on the CAN bus, they all will receive this header and based on identifier we can filter the messages from a particular device. This identifier can be 11 bit wide and this serves as the ID for the can device. Next is the transmit global time. Let's not go into this and we will keep it disabled we will send this data to the cam to send the data use Hall cam AV TX message. Here we will send the TX header and data using this TX mailbox the data is received back in the RX FIFO zero and as we have activated the notification for the FIFO zero message pending interrupt the callback will be called let's test this much part first build and debug the code I am going to use the analyzer to visualize the data let's run the code now.

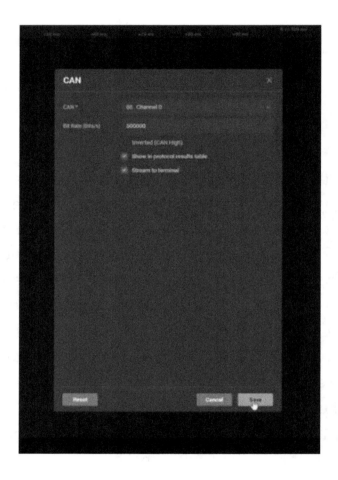

Here we got something on the transmit line. So we have the can identifier just like we have assigned the control field is zero cross 01. This include all those RTR D LC IDE bits and then we have the data field which contains the data for some reason the receiver is not able to receive I guess some issue with the wire. Anyway, let's not worry about that. We will check the received directly in our program itself. Inside the callback function, we will get the RX message the data will be received from FIFO zero the header will be stored in the RX header and the data will be saved in the RX data looks like some issue here the header is a pointer so let's give the address here. Let's run it now. We got the hit here. As you can see the RX header have the same parameters that we set in the TX header. The standard IDs zero cross 103 The DLC is one Also the RX data is same that we sent to the cam. So the things are working all right, the loopback mode works pretty well. Now let's take a look at the config filters. Here the first parameter is filter activation. This basically specifies whether you want to enable or disable the filters. We need it enabled since we are using the filters. Next parameter is the filter bank. This parameter specifies which filter bank you want to use. This parameter is associated with slave start filter bank. To understand this, let's take a look at the reference manual. As it's mentioned here, if there are two kin peripherals, there are 28 filter banks. Out of these two can peripherals one is termed as master and another is slave slave start filter bank is basically the filter bank after which the rest of the banks will be allocated to the slave can peripheral. For example, if I write 13 Here, the banks from 13 to 27 will be allocated for the can two or we can also say that banks from zero to 12 are assigned to the can one the master can. It's mentioned here that if there is only one can peripheral, then this parameter is useless. Now filter bank is the filter bank number that you want to use. For the controllers with single camera peripheral this can be between zero to 13. But for the controllers with two can peripherals you can use any filterbank that you have assigned for the respective Can I am using filterbank 10. And the comment here is for the devices with two can peripherals. Next we have filter FIFO assignment. This specifies which FIFO must be assigned to this particular filter, the incoming data will be saved to the FIFO that we assign here, we have two FIFO and I am using FIFO zero, we will cover this part but before that, let's check the filter mode.

Here we have to choose the type of filter that we are going to use. We have two types of filters, the ID mask mode and the idealist mode. In mask mode, the identifier registers and the mask registers can be used to look for the particular bits in the identifier. I will explain this part in detail. Also, we will be using 32 bit scale, which means the ID and the mask registers will be 32 bit wide. Now let's go back to the identifier and the mask registers. These registers are used to filter the incoming data. Basically, we can configure these registers to filter the data and let it pass through only when some particular conditions are met. These are 32 bit wide registers. The Read block is the highest 16 bits and the green block is the lower 16 bits. Since we are not using extended ID, we will keep our focus on the yellow color boxes. Now if you remember, the standard identifier that we used during the transmit was zero cross 103. As you can see here, the standard identifier is the part of the highest 16 bits of these registers. When some device send the data over the CAN bus. Every can device receives this ID. Let's say that this is the incoming ID. Also let's assume that we have same value set in the ID register and the mask register Now pay attention to what will happen here. Since these bits are set in the mask register, only these bits of the ID register will be compared with the incoming ID. And if the bits in the incoming ID matches to that of the ID register, the message will pass through. Let's see the application now. Remember that the ID of the transmitter was zero cross 103. So I am setting the same ID here in the ID high register. Also, I am using the same value in the mask high register. So why am I shifting it by five places? Well, that's because the extended ID is also the part of ID high register. And if you notice here, the extended if takes first five bits of this register, so the standard ID starts from the fifth position let's test this part first. I am adding a breakpoint here. And we hit the breakpoint. The ID is zero cross 103. So this was as expected. Now let's change this transmitter ID to zero cross 102 and see if it is passing through the filter. This time the filter didn't let it pass. This is because the incoming IDs 102 And the value in the ID register is 103. Also, since this mask bit is set to one, so these bits will be compared. If these bits are not same, the message will not pass. And that's what happened in this case. But what will happen if I don't write a one here in the mask Register Now these two bits will not be compared. And even if we have the ID 103 in the ID register the data should pass through. I am going to change the mask register value so that the fifth bit is zero Let's see the result now. As expected, the message got through the filter. Here the ID is 102 and it was passed through even if the ID Register was set to 103. So this entire process depends on the mask register, which decides which bits should be compared. Now let's say we want to pass multiple IDs. In that case, I have decided to only check this bit now only this 13th bit in the ID register will be compared to the incoming ID and if they are same, the message will pass through any other bits in the incoming ID don't matter anymore let's test this I am writing a one in the 13th position in the mask register.

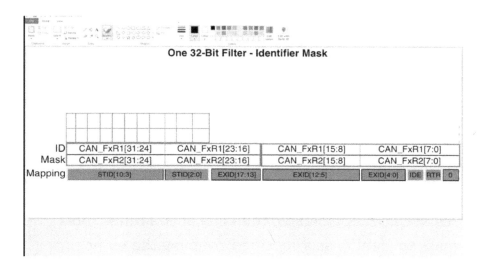

Let's change the ID to 123 so this is passed through because the 13th position in the incoming ID was one. Let's try with 523 This was also passed through the filter five to three will be like this and this have a one in the 13th position and since all that matter right now the message was passed through. Also if I write a one in this position in the mask register, then this particular bit will be compared in the ID register and the incoming ID. If these are same, the data will be okay. This is how the filter works. I hope you understood the logic here I am writing this so that it's easier to set the breakpoint the another filter type we have is the ID list filter.

dependent on the mode and the scale of each of the filter banks.

Concerning the filter configuration, refer to Figure 230.

Figure 230. Filter bank scale configuration - register organization

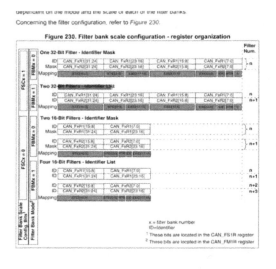

Here instead of having one mask register, we have two ID registers. Thus, instead of defining an identifier and a mask to identify as a specified doubling the number of single identifiers, all bits of the incoming identifier must match the bits specified in the filter registers. We will not be looking into this one today. Now the filters are done, let's take a look at the transmit mailbox. As mentioned here, it supports up to three transmit mailbox. The detailed description for this is given in the reference manual. Basically, the mailbox was empty at first, then we write some data into it. Once we do the transmit, it goes into the pending state. From there it gets sheduled and finally it transmits while the mailbox is in the pending state it can be aborted let's see how can we use these mailbox I am going to create an array of form mailbox and now I will send three mailbox one by one let's modify this so that we know if we have some error. I am going to send different data fields with each mail box let's run this now Okay, so everything was fine. And note here that we received the data from first mailbox again from the second mailbox and now from the third mailbox, things are going well till now. Now I will send the fourth mailbox and see what happens. You see we are not hitting the breakpoint anymore. And here we are in the error handler. So what happens is when it tried sending that fourth mailbox, it went into the error handler. This is because this can peripheral can support up to three mailbox and sending any more will result in failure. When all three mailbox were in pending states. You can change their priorities also. You Check this section of the datasheet as I am not going into the depth for now.

EXAMPLE DUMMY CODE

In STM32 CAN peripheral, the loopback mode allows the transmitter to directly connect to the receiver without involving the physical CAN bus. This is useful for testing and debugging the CAN communication without connecting to an external network. In this example, we will configure one STM32 microcontroller in loopback mode and send a message to itself.

Please note that this example assumes you have

already configured the CAN peripheral and initialized the HAL (Hardware Abstraction Layer) for STM32 microcontrollers.

```c
#include "main.h"
#include "can.h"

// CAN message structure
CAN_TxHeaderTypeDef tx_header;
CAN_RxHeaderTypeDef rx_header;
uint8_t tx_data[8] = {0x11, 0x22, 0x33, 0x44, 0x55, 0x66, 0x77, 0x88};
uint8_t rx_data[8];

int main(void) {
  // Initialize the HAL and CAN peripheral

  // Configure the CAN message for transmission
  tx_header.StdId = 0x321; // Set the CAN ID for the message (11-bit standard ID)
  tx_header.ExtId = 0;   // Not used in this example (extended ID)
  tx_header.RTR = CAN_RTR_DATA; // Set the message type to data frame
  tx_header.IDE = CAN_ID_STD;  // Use standard ID (11 bits)
  tx_header.DLC = 8;     // Data length (bytes)
  tx_header.TransmitGlobalTime = DISABLE;
```

```c
// Configure the CAN filter for loopback mode
CAN_FilterTypeDef can_filter;
can_filter.FilterBank = 0;          // Use filter
bank 0
can_filter.FilterMode =
CAN_FILTERMODE_IDMASK; // Set filter mode to
mask mode
can_filter.FilterScale = CAN_FILTERSCALE_32BIT;
// Set filter scale to 32-bit
can_filter.FilterIdHigh = 0x0000;      // Set filter
ID high value (not used in mask mode)
can_filter.FilterIdLow = 0x0000;       // Set filter
ID low value (not used in mask mode)
can_filter.FilterMaskIdHigh = 0x0000;   // Set
filter mask ID high value (not used in mask mode)
can_filter.FilterMaskIdLow = 0x0000;    // Set
filter mask ID low value (not used in mask mode)
can_filter.FilterFIFOAssignment =
CAN_RX_FIFO0; // Use RX FIFO 0 for the filter
can_filter.FilterActivation = ENABLE;   // Enable
the filter
HAL_CAN_ConfigFilter(&hcan, &can_filter);

while (1) {
  // Transmit the CAN message in loopback mode
  HAL_CAN_AddTxMessage(&hcan, &tx_header,
tx_data, NULL);
```

```
    // Wait for the message to be received (in
loopback mode, it should be instantaneous)
    HAL_CAN_GetRxMessage(&hcan,
CAN_RX_FIFO0, &rx_header, rx_data);

    // Process the received CAN message here
    // For example, you can toggle an LED or take
any other action based on the received data
    // In this example, we don't perform any
action, just loop back the message

    // Add a delay before sending the next
message
    HAL_Delay(1000);
  }
}
```

In this example, we use a mask filter (32-bit filter
with all bits set to 0) to accept all incoming
messages and put them into RX FIFO 0. The CAN
peripheral is configured to operate in loopback
mode, so the transmitted message is directly
looped back and received without going through
the physical CAN bus.

Please ensure that the CAN bit rate and other
CAN peripheral settings are configured

appropriately for your application. Also, take care of proper GPIO initialization, enabling the CAN peripheral, and handling any possible CAN bus errors or interrupts as needed.

STM32 FLASH PROGRAMMING SECTOR TYPE M4 M7

I covered how to store data in the flash memory of F 103 microcontroller, it have memory distributed in pages. Today in this project, we will see how to store data in the flash memory of those controller whose memory is distributed in sectors.

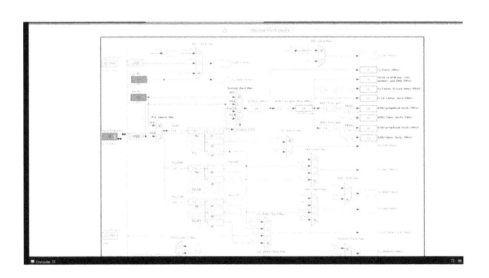

This would include Cortex M four and M seven series controllers. I am using STM 32 F 446 r e here is the cube MX I am selecting external crystal for the clock we don't need to do any setup in the clock setup, crystal is eight megahertz and I want the system to run at 180 megahertz click Save to generate the project first we will include the library in the project copy the header file into the include folder and C file into the source folder let's refresh the project and you can see the files here. Now include the flash sector dot h in the main file let's build it once to check for any errors. There are no errors. Let's take a look at the flash sector door see file get sector ID is used to get the sector number where the memory addresses located. This is the reference manual for a 446 R E. As you can see here we have seven sectors some of these are 16 kilobytes or 64 kilobyte and rest are 128 kilobytes This is the manual for a 407 microcontroller this one has 11 sectors, your controller may have 15 or 23 sectors also you have to comment after number of sectors you have mine have seven sectors. So I have commented the rest if you have 11 sectors include this portion also if you have 23 than include everything. Next flash write data will write the respective data to the flash memory. It takes the memory address as the parameter along with the address of 32 bit data variable that you want to write. It will first calculate the number of words based on the size of the data then it will get the start tech the number based on the length of data it will calculate the memory location of the end sector and then the end sector number and finally, the number of sectors needed to be written. It will then erase the required sectors and write the data into the NetID memory location. Flush reads data reads the data from the memory and save it in the entered variable. Convert to str converts the 32 bit data into the string Let's start now. I am creating a 32 bit variable to store the string. RX data will store the data that we will read from the memory string is to store the converted string In Flash write data will write the data to the given memory location, I will use this memory address pass the address to the data.

The OTP area contains 16 additional bytes used to lock the corresponding OTP data block.

 – Option bytes to configure read and write protection, BOR level, watchdog software/hardware and reset when the device is in Standby or Stop mode.
 • Low-power modes (for details refer to the Power control (PWR) section of the reference manual)

Table 4. Flash module organization

Block	Name	Block base addresses	Size
Main memory	Sector 0	0x0800 0000 - 0x0800 3FFF	16 Kbytes
	Sector 1	0x0800 4000 - 0x0800 7FFF	16 Kbytes
	Sector 2	0x0800 8000 - 0x0800 BFFF	16 Kbytes
	Sector 3	0x0800 C000 - 0x0800 FFFF	16 Kbytes
	Sector 4	0x0801 0000 - 0x0801 FFFF	64 Kbytes
	Sector 5	0x0802 0000 - 0x0803 FFFF	128 Kbytes
	Sector 6	0x0804 0000 - 0x0805 FFFF	128 Kbytes
	Sector 7	0x0806 0000 - 0x0807 FFFF	128 Kbytes
System memory		0x1FFF 0000 - 0x1FFF 77FF	30 Kbytes
OTP area		0x1FFF 7800 - 0x1FFF 7A0F	528 bytes
Option bytes		0x1FFF C000 - 0x1FFF C00F	16 bytes

Flash read data will read the data from the same location and store it in the RX data and finally convert the received data to the string let's build it I will connect my controller now hit the debug button now I will add the memory location to observe this is data from my previous extra minutes but we are writing in this location so that's where we need to focus I will add a breakpoint here. So we hit the breakpoint let's step in number of words are eight based on the address it have determined that the start sector is sector four which is exactly where we chose the address and sector address will be calculated based on the number of words and the end sector number is also the same as start sector. number of sectors needs to be deleted is one and now we will exit this function I will add RX data in the live expressions first. As you can see the data is written here. There were eight words so 832 bit memory locations are used. Let's read the data. Now. The data is stored in the RX data array. I have defined the array of six words, but I needed eight words. Anyway, let's finish this execution so the converted data is stored in the string. And of course, it's not the entire data because of the size of our x data. Let me quickly correct this I am increasing the size of the array and string also. let's debug now. Okay, you might also get this error if you try to debug again. Go to debug configuration debugger tab, reset behavior and choose None click apply and debug now. Data is already stored in the location. So you won't see any change here are x data now have all the data. And the string now shows the entire string. This was the result of programming flash memory from the start of the sector. Let's see can we get the same result if we programmed the front end of the sector. Now I will start writing from this address and eight words means it will come up to this address.

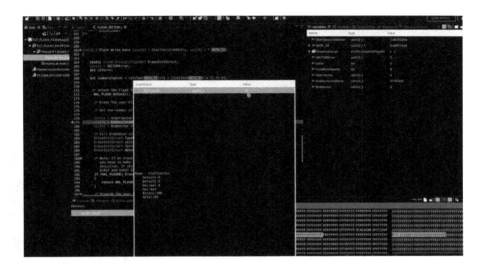

Here we are covering two sectors to write the data and that's exactly what we want to test. This is the memory location of sector three. And while writing data we will come to Sector four. Let's see the address of this location. The addresses zero cross 800 f f f four enter the memory location in the flash write data and in Flash read data also let's center in the flash write data the number of words are eight as the data is same start sector is sector three as that's where the address is located this is the address of the memory location where the data will be written up to this location is in Sector four the number of sectors needed to be raised are two now notes that this pre written data here will be raised when the sectors are erased. Now our data has been stored in the desired memory location which covers two different sectors the same data can be read and converted to string also. Keep one thing in mind that the entire sector will be erased before writing data.

EXAMPLE DUMMY CODE

In STM32 microcontrollers, the Flash memory is divided into sectors of varying sizes. Different STM32 devices have different sector layouts. The M4 and M7 cores share the same Flash memory, so the sector types are common for both cores. Below is an example code to demonstrate how to program the Flash memory in both M4 and M7 cores using the HAL (Hardware Abstraction Layer) libraries.

In this example, we'll use the STM32H7 series microcontroller, which has 128KB of Flash memory organized into eight 16KB sectors. We'll write a simple program to erase a Flash sector and then program it with new data.

C

```c
#include "main.h"
```

```c
#include "flash.h"

#define FLASH_START_ADDR   0x08000000   //
Start address of Flash memory
#define SECTOR_TO_ERASE   FLASH_SECTOR_2   //
Sector 2 (16KB) to erase
#define DATA_TO_PROGRAM   0x12345678   //
Data to program into the Flash

void erase_flash_sector(uint32_t sector) {
  FLASH_EraseInitTypeDef erase_init;
  uint32_t error;

  // Unlock the Flash memory
  HAL_FLASH_Unlock();

  // Erase the specified Flash sector
  erase_init.TypeErase =
FLASH_TYPEERASE_SECTORS;
  erase_init.Sector = sector;
  erase_init.NbSectors = 1;
  erase_init.VoltageRange =
FLASH_VOLTAGE_RANGE_3;
  HAL_FLASHEx_Erase(&erase_init, &error);

  // Lock the Flash memory
  HAL_FLASH_Lock();
}
```

```c
void program_flash_data(uint32_t address,
uint32_t data) {
  // Unlock the Flash memory
  HAL_FLASH_Unlock();

  // Program the data into the specified Flash
address

HAL_FLASH_Program(FLASH_TYPEPROGRAM_WO
RD, address, data);

  // Lock the Flash memory
  HAL_FLASH_Lock();
}

int main(void) {
  // Initialize the HAL and other peripherals

  // Erase the Flash sector
  erase_flash_sector(SECTOR_TO_ERASE);

  // Program data into the erased sector
  program_flash_data(FLASH_START_ADDR +
(SECTOR_TO_ERASE * FLASH_SECTOR_SIZE),
DATA_TO_PROGRAM);

  while (1) {
```

```
    // Your application code here
  }
}
```

In this example, we use the HAL_FLASH_Unlock
and HAL_FLASH_Lock functions to unlock and lock
the Flash memory for writing operations. The
HAL_FLASHEx_Erase function is used to erase the
specified sector, and the HAL_FLASH_Program
function is used to program the data into the Flash
memory.

Please note that Flash programming is a critical
operation, and you need to be careful while
writing to the Flash memory. It is essential to
follow the correct sequence and ensure proper
error handling.

The sector layout and sector numbers can vary
depending on the specific STM32 microcontroller
you are using. Refer to the STM32 reference
manual for your device to determine the correct
sector numbers and Flash memory layout.

Also, make sure to take proper precautions while
erasing and programming the Flash memory, as
incorrect usage can lead to the loss of your
program and data. Always test the Flash

STM32 FLASH PROGRAMMING WRITE AND READ PAGE MEMORY TYPE

Many of you guys requested this. So today we will see how to program the flash memory in STM 32. This project only cover those micro controllers whose memory is organized in pages for example, Cortex M three series or m zero series, I will make another video about the controllers whose memory is distributed in sectors like in Cortex M four or M seven devices.

	Reserved	0x4002 2018 - 0x4002 201B	4
	FLASH_OBR	0x4002 201C - 0x4002 201F	4
	FLASH_WRPR	0x4002 2020 - 0x4002 2023	4

Table 5. Flash module organization [medium-density devices]

Block	Name	Base addresses	Size (bytes)
Main memory	Page 0	0x0800 0000 - 0x0800 03FF	1 Kbyte
	Page 1	0x0800 0400 - 0x0800 07FF	1 Kbyte
	Page 2	0x0800 0800 - 0x0800 0BFF	1 Kbyte
	Page 3	0x0800 0C00 - 0x0800 0FFF	1 Kbyte
	Page 4	0x0800 1000 - 0x0800 13FF	1 Kbyte
	Page 127	0x0801 FC00 - 0x0801 FFFF	1 Kbyte
Information block	System memory	0x1FFF F000 - 0x1FFF F7FF	2 Kbytes
	Option Bytes	0x1FFF F800 - 0x1FFF F80F	16
Flash memory interface	FLASH_ACR	0x4002 2000 - 0x4002 2003	4
	FLASH_KEYR	0x4002 2004 - 0x4002 2007	4
	FLASH_OPTKEYR	0x4002 2008 - 0x4002 200B	4
	FLASH_SR	0x4002 200C - 0x4002 200F	4
	FLASH_CR	0x4002 2010 - 0x4002 2013	

I am using STM 32 F 103 And it's a medium density controller as mentioned here there is not much to do in the setup, I am enabling the external crystal and setting the clock to run at max 72 megahertz save this to generate the code here is our main file. Let's include the library first, put the C file in source directory and header file in the include include the flash page dot h in the main. Let's take a look at the reference manual F 103 is a medium density device. As you can see, the main memory is divided into 128 pages. Each page is one kilobyte and have a range of addresses associated with it. Now, we are going to program this page you should always start as low in the memory as possible. I will tell you the reason for choosing this later in the code itself let's open the C file that we included. Flash write data will write the data to the memory it takes the stock page addresses the parameter and also appointed to 32 bit variable that you want to store. First of all, it will calculate how many 32 bit variables you want to write. Then it will calculate the number of pages needed to store the data. Flash page size varies according to the controller. In my case, it is 1024 Bytes like it said in the datasheet. After calculating the number of pages, it will erase that many pages starting from the staff page entered in the parameter. Now it will start writing data. Each work takes four bytes. So we have to increment the address by four you can also write in half word or double word but then the increment will also change. I have commented it out here and finally the flash will be locked again. To read the data, we just need to access the memory the data will be saved in this variable. Let's start now. I will write the data first.

The memory location that I copied from the datasheet I need to define this variable first. Here I am defining an array which can hold 232 bit variables and we will pass the address of this array to the flash right let's build this There is some warning, it's fine. Let's go ahead and debug the code here is the memory tab, let's enter the memory address that we want to observe you can see it's all clean here I also want to show you another memory address. This is the start of flash memory for f 103 controller. As you can see, it's not empty that's why I did not programs the start of flash memory it is already programmed to run this code that we are using right now, I will explain this in a while that what happens if we try to overwrite this part of the flash you can see it's occupied up to this address and therefore we should only program after this part that's why I chose the lowest part of the flash memory. Let's run this now we hit the breakpoint note that the memory location is empty right now. Now let's step over this and you can see the data being stored in the flash memory other than writing the 32 bit numbers we can also write some string to this memory we will write hello world in the flash memory let's build and debug this you can see right now the previous data is stored in the memory and as we run this function the data corresponding to hello world is stored in the flash memory I am creating another variable to store the data that is read from the memory this variable can hold four words we will read from the same memory address obviously I am putting our x data in the live expression we can see the data here.

Let's see if it is the same data our x data is in the integer format. So we need to select the same here and yes, we have the same data present in the memory and in our x data. Now I will show you what happens when we try to write from the beginning in the flash memory. I will try to write the same data that is hello world. Let's open the disassembly tab here. You can see the instructions have been stored in the same address that we want to program with hello world. Let's enter inside this function I will put another breakpoint at the Erase function. Let's center inside the Erase function. I am stepping over now just to show you guys where the problem occurs. Now once we call this function, the entire page will be raised and all the instructions will be raised along with it. And that's where the error occurs. As the instruction that was supposed to execute is not present in the memory you can see the memory details here. This entire page is erased the next instruction that was supposed to execute was present in that page and is not there anymore. That's why I advised in the beginning that we shouldn't write first few pages.

Next, I will show you how to use st link utility to see the memory details. See this the beginning of the flash memory is again occupied by the instructions. We will go to the address that we have programmed you can see the Hello World written to the location this is it guys.

EXAMPLE DUMMY CODE

In STM32 microcontrollers, the Flash memory can be programmed at the page level. Pages are typically larger than individual data bytes, and writing to a Flash page is more efficient than writing individual bytes.

Below is an example code that demonstrates how to write and read data to/from a Flash page in STM32 microcontrollers using the HAL (Hardware Abstraction Layer) libraries. In this example, we assume that you are using the STM32H7 series microcontroller, which has 512KB of Flash memory organized into 2KB pages.

```c
#include "main.h"
#include "flash.h"

#define FLASH_PAGE_TO_WRITE    32      // Page 32 (2KB) to write
#define FLASH_START_ADDR       0x08000000  // Start address of Flash memory

uint32_t page_data[FLASH_PAGE_SIZE/sizeof(uint32_t)];
// Buffer to hold data for Flash programming

void write_to_flash_page(uint32_t page, uint32_t* data, uint32_t data_size) {
  uint32_t page_address = FLASH_START_ADDR + (page * FLASH_PAGE_SIZE);
  uint32_t error;
```

```c
// Unlock the Flash memory
HAL_FLASH_Unlock();

// Erase the specified Flash page
FLASH_EraseInitTypeDef erase_init;
erase_init.TypeErase = FLASH_TYPEERASE_PAGES;
erase_init.Page = page;
erase_init.NbPages = 1;
erase_init.Banks = FLASH_BANK_1;
erase_init.VoltageRange = FLASH_VOLTAGE_RANGE_3;
HAL_FLASHEx_Erase(&erase_init, &error);

// Program data into the Flash page
for (uint32_t i = 0; i < data_size; i++) {
  if (HAL_FLASH_Program(FLASH_TYPEPROGRAM_WORD, page_address + (i * sizeof(uint32_t)), data[i]) != HAL_OK) {
    // Error occurred while programming the Flash
    // Handle the error here
    break;
  }
}

// Lock the Flash memory
```

```c
  HAL_FLASH_Lock();
}

void read_from_flash_page(uint32_t page,
uint32_t* data, uint32_t data_size) {
  uint32_t page_address = FLASH_START_ADDR +
(page * FLASH_PAGE_SIZE);

  // Read data from the Flash page
  for (uint32_t i = 0; i < data_size; i++) {
    data[i] = *(volatile uint32_t*)(page_address + (i
* sizeof(uint32_t)));
  }
}

int main(void) {
  // Initialize the HAL and other peripherals

  // Fill the data buffer with some sample data to
write to Flash
  for (uint32_t i = 0; i <
FLASH_PAGE_SIZE/sizeof(uint32_t); i++) {
    page_data[i] = i + 1;
  }

  // Write data to the Flash page
  write_to_flash_page(FLASH_PAGE_TO_WRITE,
page_data, FLASH_PAGE_SIZE/sizeof(uint32_t));
```

```
  // Clear the data buffer before reading from
Flash
  for (uint32_t i = 0; i <
FLASH_PAGE_SIZE/sizeof(uint32_t); i++) {
    page_data[i] = 0;
  }

  // Read data from the Flash page
  read_from_flash_page(FLASH_PAGE_TO_WRITE,
page_data, FLASH_PAGE_SIZE/sizeof(uint32_t));

  while (1) {
    // Your application code here
  }
}
```

In this example, we use the HAL_FLASH_Unlock and HAL_FLASH_Lock functions to unlock and lock the Flash memory for writing operations. The HAL_FLASHEx_Erase function is used to erase the specified page, and the HAL_FLASH_Program function is used to program the data into the Flash memory.

Please note that Flash programming is a critical operation, and you need to be careful while writing to the Flash memory. It is essential to follow the correct sequence and ensure proper error handling.

The Flash page size and page numbers can vary depending on the specific STM32 microcontroller you are using. Refer to the STM32 reference manual for your device to determine the correct Flash page size and layout.

Also, make sure to take proper precautions while erasing and programming the Flash memory, as incorrect usage can lead to the loss of your program and data. Always test the Flash programming code on a test board before using it in production systems.

STM32 SEND AND RECEIVE DATA TO PC WITHOUT UART USB COM PORT BLUEPILL

We will see how can we send and receive data from the computer without using UART I will use the USB to do so I have already made a project on it but that project only covers the sending part and this project will cover both the sending and the receiving parts. Let's start by creating the project in cube Id first I am using STM 32 F 103 C eight controller for this project. Give some name to the project and click Finish. Here is our cube MX I am selecting the external crystal for the clock first select serial wire here. Now in the USB select the device in the USB device settings select the classes communication device class leave everything to default here. I will just change this name to see if it shows up on the computer that's all here.

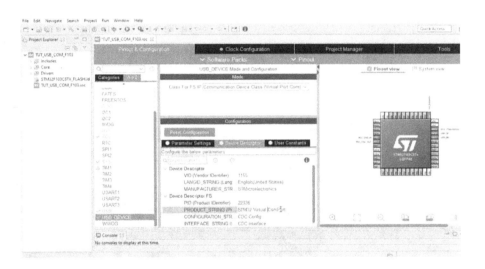

Now go to clock set up. I will set the clock manually. I have eight megahertz Crystal and I want the system to run at maximum frequency. Note here that USB clock is automatically set to 48 megahertz. That's all for the setup. Click Save to generate the project the functions used to send or receive data can be found in USB D CDC if dot c file but if you look into the header file, there is only a function available globally. And that is to transmit data, we will modify the receive function in a while here is the limit for the send and receive buffer you can change them if the data is quite big. Let's try to send some data to the computer first. This is the data I am going to send we also need to include USB d c d c f dot h as the function is available in that file include string dot h also now in the while loop, we will transmit the data. The first parameter is the buffer to send and second is the length of the data. Let's add some delay here build it and flashed to the board flushed successfully now before connecting the controller I am going to open the devices and now as I connected a new serial device gets detected.

It's not showing the name that I entered in the cube MX that might be due to drivers in Windows 10 It might show for you though. Anyway the device is connected to comm five and I will open a serial port there. You can choose any baud rate. It works for everything pretty much. You can see the data is being received by the computer every one second. So the transmit function is working properly. Now let's see how to receive data from the computer. As I mentioned, the function to receive data is not available globally. Lay So, here I am defining an array of 64 bytes to store the data into now, I am going to give a reference of this variable in the CTC if dot c file so that we can use it here in the CDC receive function, I am going to use mem copy to copy the data from the incoming buffer to our buffer.

Here the arguments are the buffer to copy into the buffer to copy from and the size of the data mem copy takes size t as the parameter so, we need to do the conversion here we are ready to receive the data now let's build it I should use the debugger here since I want to see the buffer I have added the buffer in the live expression let's run it now. As you can see the transmission is working all right and the controller is transmitting every second when I send some data to the controller, it gets saved in the buffer I will try transmitting something else you can see the new data but there is a small issue here and I will show that the data is again received successfully but now if I send this smaller data again you see the buffer still have the data from the previous transmission to handle this situation, I am going to clear the buffer before receiving any new data memset can be used for it. Also make sure you clear buff too. I have noticed that it also keeps the old data stored in it let's run the code again I will add the buffer again. This time you can see the buffer only contains the data we are sending.

You can later pass this buffer according to your requirement since it can be accessed from the main file itself. There shouldn't be any problem with that. This project can be useful if you are using blue pill or any discovery board. It can save you the hectic of connecting the T T L device for transferring data using U RT.

STM32 UART DMA AND IDLE LINE RECEIVE UNKNOWN LENGTH DATA

In the past I have covered few ways to handle the incoming data from the UART like the circular buffer or the ring buffer, even the methods were very effective, there was always some issue with different microcontrollers. It happens because there was some registers involved and they changed with different series of the MCU. So today, we will be looking at yet another method, which is not only easier to set up but completely based on the whole. So the same method will remain universal for all STM 32 devices. Cortex M seven processes needs a little changes due to memory restrictions, and I will show them in the end. So without wasting any more time. Let's start with cube ID, I am using a 446 R E. I will do my usual clock setup first. Now let's enable the URL to for the demonstration leave everything to default here.

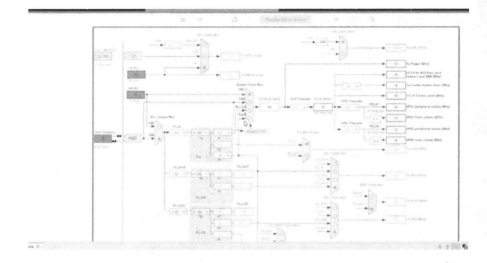

Go to DMA and add a receiver request. Make sure the mode is normal because this process will not work with the circular DMA data with his bytes as we transfer characters via the UART direction is peripheral to memory. Now go to n vi C and enable the global interrupt for the UART. This is it for the setup. Let's start the program I am going to use two buffers and these are their sizes in bytes off course create the buffers now RX buffer is where the DMA is going to copy the data and the main buffer is where the data will be finally stored. Now in the main function, we will call the UART receive function, the data will be stored in the RX buffer. And the size of data is the size of our x buffer. This function receives idle to DMA. Note that it's you are to e x. Here, it's mentioned that it will receive data till either the data is completely received or an idle event occurs. Idle event means when there is no incoming data for some amount of time. In that case, it will trigger the interrupt. The callback we are going to use is the RX event callback. Here the event can be anything, it could be idle event or the complete event but that's okay and we will handle the data in the same way for both of them. Inside the callback, we will check if the callback is called by the URL to I am putting this check so that you can use multiple URLs in the same function just make sure to check which you have called it this could be you out also it depends on if you are using you saw it or you aren't. If the data is incoming in the UART two, we will just copy the data to the main buffer. Now after the callback the DMA will stop and we must start it again the hall sets all the interrupts for the DMA by default and we will disable the half transfer complete interrupt this interrupt triggers when half the data has been transferred and we don't need it here.

So this is it. Let's build it now. Seems like I forgot to include the string File Build it again. And now we will debug. I have added the buffers in the live expression. Let's put a breakpoint here to understand the process. I will send 1234. First, we hit the breakpoint. Even though the receive size was set to 10, the interrupt gets triggered with just four values. This is because the line was idle after those four values. And that's what set the interrupt the idle line. Another interesting thing to note here is the value of the size variable. It's same as the number of characters we sent. So whenever the idle line triggers the interrupt, we will know how many characters actually got stored in the buffer. Now we will do the mem copy and copy the content in the main buffer. This time, I will send a single character, you can see the value of the size, it is one. Here, it starts writing in the RX buffer from the beginning again. And that's why we need a second buffer where we can store the data in the proper order. Not like this, of course, we will modify this code. But before that, let's see what happens if I try to send data greater than the RX buffer size. These are obviously more than 10 characters. This time the size is 10, so the remaining data is pretty much lost. To avoid this, use the largest size for the RX buffer, but not very large. I will demonstrate this in a while. Let's modify this code so that it can handle the incoming data in a proper manner. Here it is a big solution. Let me explain what's happening here. We need to keep track of the current position in the main buffer. Now let's assume we got some data. If the current position plus data size exceeds the buffer size, then we need to overlap from the start of the buffer. For example, if the buffer size is 20, and our current position is 15. Now if we get eight bytes of new data, the new position should be 23, which is exceeding the buffer size. Here we will first find how many bytes are remaining in the buffer, which in our case are five, we will copy these five bytes of data.

Now we have reached the end of the buffer. So we will start from the beginning update the position to zero and copy the remaining bytes, which in this case are three and finally we will update the position according to the current position. In another scenario, if the position plus the data does not exceed the buffer, we will simply copy the data into the main buffer and update the current position I have also included a test check function this can be used for quickly checking for a particular string in the incoming data keep this very small as it might disturb the receiving Let's build and run this let's see the working now. Since we have added a lot of stuff, this time things will be different here we have the 1234 in the main buffer. Now the P is saved in the next position keep checking the values of the old position and the new position. Now the new data is saved in the proper order and the positions are also updating as per the changes now if I send this data let's see what happens here the data is written till the end of the buffer and then it started from the beginning again. It's overlapping the old data. Let's see if this particular search thing works or not. I will just send some random data and put okay in the middle of it notice this variable this should set to one if the okay is found. You can see it's one since it found that okay in the middle if the data, you can use this to check for the strings, but not the large ones, you can implement the functions from ring buffer code here, and they will work all right, you might need to modify them a little. I will do that and update the code in few days. Keep checking the GitHub, the program works fine for small data. But how effective is it if the large data arrives in the UART? Let's test it, I am going to send a huge buffer. So let's modify the size RX buffer can accept 512 bytes at once, and the main buffer is two kilobytes. Here is the data I am going to send. This is a text file, which is 1.42 kilobytes 1459 bytes to be exact. Let's see if it can receive the file. Keep an eye on the physician variable. Let's send the file now. The new position is 1459, which was the size of the file. This means the entire file has been received. We can cross check the data. Here the file starts with this sentence. And that's exactly we have in the beginning of the buffer. The data is ending at 1459. So let's check that part. This is the end of the file. Here we have the same sentence in the end to so even the RX buffer was set to receive 512 Bytes the entire data was received successfully. This is because the transfers take place in chunks and we can receive one chunk of data processes and get ready to receive the next chunk. There is enough time in between two chunks so that we can process this data. So the things works just fine and we are able to receive the receive unknown length data from the UART. Soon I will make a project about file transfer using the UART where we can save the file in the SD card or the USB by using the UART and STM 32. This is it for the project.

The next part will focus on the Cortex M seven series MCU. In the Cortex M seven series, we need to make few changes in our memory location. I am using the H 745. And I have the same code here that I used in F 446. I would recommend that you watch my previous project on memory management first, the link is in the description if we see the memory details, here, the RX buffer is of the location 2.4 million a C. Like I mentioned in the previous project also that in my case, this location is in the XE RAM. So no issues for me as the DMA do have the access to this RAM. But in some cases, this location will be in the dtcm Ram and there you have the issue as the DMA can't access it. So if you have the controller whose main ram is dtcm, I would suggest that you move the buffer to some other location like SRAM one or two. It's explained in that memory management project. So watch it. I have it in the SRAM, so I will go ahead with the next step. Go to the cube MX and the Cortex M seven tap. Here we will modify the MPU configuration. Just follow it for this project. I will surely make another project to explain it in the details. Select this background region privileged access and MPU disabled during hard fault. Now enable the memory region. Enter the address of the RX buffer. Keep in mind that there is some alignment parameter also. So if it doesn't work for you put the buffer at the start of any SRAM and then try with that address. I will explain about MPU region size and all other things In few other projects, next we have to choose the region size. And since the RX buffer is set to receive 512 bytes, we will choose 512 bytes or more here in the access permission, Select All Access permitted and disable all the permissions. So this region is not cacheable not shareable or Buffer Abul that's all let's test it now. I will send the same file again it received the file successfully. The size is also exact, we can cross check the data in the beginning and end of the file. Now if we send the file again, the main buffer will be overlapped. You might be wondering how the main buffer is able to work here, since we haven't configured it in the MPU. Well, that's because we are performing mem copy while copying data between our x buffer and main buffer. And like I mentioned in the previous project, the CPU have access to all the Rams so it can freely copy the data around the DMA was the problem and since the DMA is copying the data from the peripheral into the RX buffer, we need to modify the region for the RX buffer.

Let me quickly show you what happens if we don't configure the MPU. I will set a breakpoint in the callback function so we did hit the breakpoint means the interrupt is working just fine. But if we see the RX buffer, there is nothing in it. This means that the data did arrived in the UART DATA register but it didn't got copied in the RX buffer. This happens due to the cacheable region and we will discuss it in another project. If we send the data again the interrupt is working the positions are updating but there is nothing in the RX buffer. So properly configure the MPU to avoid this, this is it for this project.

EXAMPLE DUMMY CODE

To send and receive data between an STM32 microcontroller (specifically, the STM32 Blue Pill) and a PC without using a UART or USB COM port, we can use the Virtual COM Port (VCP) feature provided by STM32's USB Peripheral. The USB VCP allows you to establish a serial communication link between the STM32 and a PC using the USB interface.

In this example, we will use the STM32CubeIDE and the HAL (Hardware Abstraction Layer) libraries to configure the USB VCP on the STM32 Blue Pill.

Set up STM32CubeIDE project with USB CDC VCP: Create a new STM32 project in STM32CubeIDE for your STM32 microcontroller (e.g., STM32F103C8T6 - Blue Pill).
Enable USB device and CDC class in the Middleware USB Device stack configuration. Enable "VCP" under the Class For FS IP in the Middleware USB Device stack configuration. Generate the code and make sure the USB configuration is correct.

Implement USB CDC VCP Transmit and Receive functions:

Now, you can use the following example code to demonstrate sending and receiving data over the USB CDC VCP.

C

```c
#include "main.h"
#include "usbd_cdc_if.h"

uint8_t rx_buffer[64];
uint8_t tx_buffer[] = "Hello from STM32 Blue Pill!\r\n";

int main(void) {
  // Initialize the HAL and USB
  MX_USB_DEVICE_Init();

  while (1) {
    // Check if there is data available from the PC
    if (CDC_Receive_FS(rx_buffer, sizeof(rx_buffer)) == USBD_OK) {
      // Process the received data here
      // For example, you can print the received data to the terminal
      CDC_Transmit_FS(rx_buffer, strlen((const char*)rx_buffer));
    }
```

```
  // Your application code here
  // For this example, we send a message to the
PC every 1 second
  HAL_Delay(1000);
  CDC_Transmit_FS(tx_buffer, sizeof(tx_buffer) -
1);
  }
}
```

This code utilizes the usbd_cdc_if.h and usbd_cdc_if.c files provided by STM32CubeIDE's USB CDC middleware. The CDC_Receive_FS function checks if there is any data received from the PC. If data is received, it is stored in the rx_buffer. The received data is then transmitted back to the PC using the CDC_Transmit_FS function.

Please note that you need to configure the USB descriptors correctly in the USB Device stack configuration to match your USB settings and requirements. Additionally, you need to ensure that the USB driver (VCP driver) is installed on the PC to establish the virtual serial communication.

With this setup, when you connect the STM32 Blue Pill to your PC using a USB cable, it will appear as a virtual COM port, and you can use a serial terminal program (e.g., PuTTY, Tera Term, etc.) on your PC to send and receive data to/from the STM32.

Keep in mind that this example assumes that the USB CDC VCP feature is supported by your STM32 microcontroller and is properly set up in the STM32CubeIDE project. The exact implementation and configuration might vary depending on the specific STM32 microcontroller and the USB peripheral available on it. Always refer to the STM32 reference manual and USB CDC documentation for your device for specific details and implementation guidance.

STM32 UART RING BUFFER USING DMA AND IDLE LINE

Today we will see how to use the UART ring buffer using the DMA. I have already made a project about the ring buffer, but that one was using some registers and hence the things were different for different microcontrollers. So this project will cover a universal method for the same and the process will be same for all the microcontrollers that support sidel line interrupt. Here I have already published the code few days ago and today I will just demonstrate the usage. In the end of the project, I will show one practical application where I will use the ESP 8266 To turn on the LED on the controller. I have covered it already if you remember the web server project few months ago. So let's start the cube ID and create a new project. I am using STM 32 F 446 r e controller give some name to the project and click finish here is our cube MX let's start with the clock configuration. I am using external high speed crystal for the clock. Type in the crystal frequency here I have eight megahertz crystal on board select H S E for external crystal select PC LK and type in the frequency you want to run the controller at All right, now we will configure the UART I am using u r two for the demonstration you can check the steps listed in the readme file. First we need to enable the UART interrupt then we will configure the DMA in the normal mode enable the receive DMA and keep the mode as normal. Also note that the data with this byte as that's the standard for the UART communication. That's all for the setup. Now click Save to generate the project I have the three files here that are provided in the GitHub let's copy the source and the head of the files into our project.

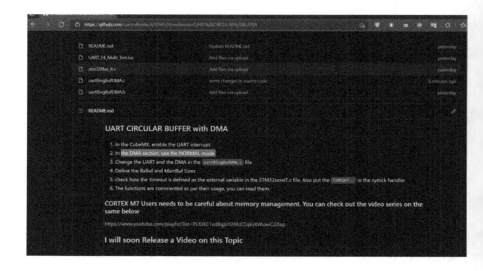

The next step is to change the UART and DMA according to your setup, you need to change them here if you are not using the UART two you can find the definition in the main file Next we need to change the buffer sizes as per the project requirement. Here I am going to perform some small tests so these small buffers are okay. Later when I will interface the ESP I will increase these sizes the next step is to define the timeout in the interrupt file the third downloaded file is for the reference and here you can see the timeout is defined as the external variable. Let's do the same in our interrupt file so we also need to decrease the timeout in the SysTick handler. This is it for the setup. Let's build it once to check for any errors and we are good to go now Now, let's take a look at the functions available to us. The first one is to initialize the ring buffer, this function resets everything. And other than that it also initializes the DMA idle line reception. The next is to reset the ring buffer. The next function is to check the string, it's checks if the particular string is present in the buffer or not. If the string is found, it will return one or else zero. The next one is a very important function. It waits for a particular string in the RX buffer. By default, it is set to look for the okay and if you want to change it, you can change it in the RX event handler. Here is the RX event handler. And you can see the check is being done for the Okay. This particular step is helpful during the interfacing of the devices such as ESP or any GPS GSM devices. These devices send some particular string in the end like Okay, so we can quickly check it without any additional function needed for it. This function uses timeout and if the okay isn't found in the required time, it will return zero. The next function is wait for it waits for a particular string to arrive in the incoming buffer. If the string is found, it will return one or else if the timeout occurs, it will return zero. The next function is copy up to and it copies the incoming data into our buffer up to the particular string has arrived. It will return one if the entered string is successfully copied. The next in line is get after it copies the entered number of characters after the particular string has arrived in the incoming data. It will also return one after the characters have been copied or else zero in case of the timeout The next one is get data from buffer. This is the same function from the previous ring buffer code. It copies the data between the two particular strings and save it into the provided buffer that's all the functions we have now let's see the main function here we will initialize the ring buffer. Now let's test all the functions one by one. We will start with these confirmed if these confirmed function does not return one within five seconds we will call the error handler I am giving some delay here so that I can set the breakpoint we also need to include the header file here let's test this part first. I am going to use the Hercules for the serial monitor I am sending random data along with okay in the middle let's set the breakpoints to see which one will it hit we reached here that means the function did returned one as it detected that okay we sent in the middle if I send this string which does not have okay, it will simply timeout and return zero we can check the main buffer and here you can see the data we sent is present in the buffer. But since there was no okay within the data, it returns zero after the timeout. Let's test another function now. The next in line is wait for So here we will wait for let's say hello. And if it doesn't arrive within six seconds, the timeout will occur this time I am going to send this string. To make this test even better, I have added this hell right here and the Hello comes afterwards. Also this data size is more than what the RX buffer can receive in a single go. So it's perfect for testing the circular buffer also. We hit the delay breakpoint, that means it did detected the hello and returned one. Next time test it again. But this time I am not going to send the entire hello and as expected, after six seconds, the timeout occurred and it returned zero you can see the data in the main buffer the next one is copy up to since this one copies the data into the buffer. Here I need to define a buffer first we will copy up to the hello we will copy it into the buffer and the timeout will again be six seconds I will send the same string and here it got the breakpoint it means that the string got copied successfully. If we check the buffer, we can see the string up to Hello got copied into the buffer. Let's test it again and this time I am not sending the hello this time the timeout occurred if we check the buffer it basically copied all the data we sent I have mentioned this in the description that it will copy irrespective of if the desired string arrives or not. So we should use it only if we are sure about the string that it will come in the incoming data. The next one is get after here I want to get four characters after hello and I want to save them in the buffer the four characters after Hello should be a B, C and D so we hit the breakpoint and in the buffer we have the four characters as expected. So this is it for the testing part. I hope you understood how to use these functions. The next half of this project will cover the practical application where I will interface the ESP eight to six six using these functions only. Let me delete the DMA setup from the UART two as I won't be using this one. ESP is connected with the UART one so I am enabling the DMA here that's all for the configuration. Now click Save to generate the project. I have these files here. They are same as the web server project I did few months ago. I have modified them a little so as to fit with the new ring buffer. Let me copy these in my project. I will leave the link to these files in the description J Just in case someone needs them I think I copied them the other way around All right, let's take a quick look at the source file. Here we have two parts defined just like how it used to be this function sends the data to the ESP and this one here is another UART used for the logs in the ESP in it, I am initializing the ring buffer first, then send the 80 command and notice here that I am using these confirmed function. This is because the ESP sends okay after receiving the 80 command Same goes for the CW mode command also then here I am using the wait for command after connecting to the network just go through this you will understand the functions used I got some errors here. This is because I haven't modified the ring buffer file I am not using u r two anymore so I need to modify these also I am increasing the sizes of the buffers. Alright it's fine now. Let's include the ESP header file and I will write the ESP functions here. Initialize the ESP with the SSID and password for the connections you can just do a Google search the connections remains pretty much the same just change the TX and RX pins as per your setup.

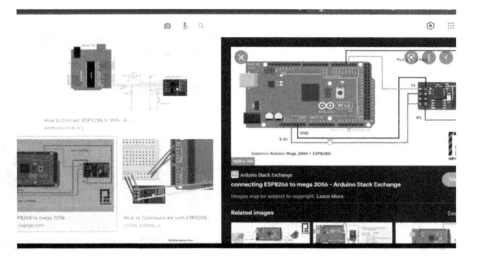

Here we can use a loop and if it fails, it will try again itself inside the ESP in it, I am not using the reset command. So I am going to put it here inside the while loop, we will call server start and it will handle the rest on its own. All right, let's test it now. This serial console will be used for the logs like here it failed at the at command so it will try again okay, it finally passed the at command. It fails a lot of time while connecting with the SSID maybe because I am using a hotspot from the phone. But when it finally connects, it's pretty stable. Let me reset this once it finally connected here we got the IP address. Now let's connect to it. This is the web page just like the last time the LEDs off right now. And if I click this button, it will turn on. We can turn on the LED and the button will change. So the web server code works with the new ring buffer also, you can use this ring buffer to interface other devices,

415

which are based on UART. I will probably add more functions to this library depending on the requirement.

EXAMPLE DUMMY CODE

Implementing a UART ring buffer using DMA and the idle line interrupt on STM32 microcontrollers can be a bit complex. It requires setting up the UART peripheral, configuring the DMA, handling the idle line interrupt, and managing the ring buffer to ensure data is transmitted and received efficiently.

Below is a simplified example code that demonstrates how to set up a UART with DMA for both transmit and receive, as well as how to handle the idle line interrupt to manage the ring buffer. For simplicity, we will use the STM32CubeIDE and the HAL (Hardware Abstraction Layer) libraries.

Set up STM32CubeIDE project with UART and DMA:
Create a new STM32 project in STM32CubeIDE for your STM32 microcontroller.
Enable the USART/UART peripheral and DMA in the STM32CubeMX configuration.

Configure the UART for your desired baud rate, word length, stop bits, and other settings. Enable the UART global interrupt and DMA receive complete interrupt.

Implement the UART with DMA and idle line interrupt:
Below is the simplified example code to demonstrate UART with DMA and idle line interrupt for the ring buffer.

```
#include "main.h"
#include "usart.h"

#define RX_BUFFER_SIZE 64

uint8_t rx_buffer[RX_BUFFER_SIZE];
volatile uint16_t rx_data_length = 0;

void
HAL_UART_IdleCallback(UART_HandleTypeDef
*huart) {
  if (huart == &huart2) {
    // Idle line interrupt occurred on UART2
(change to your UART if needed)
    // Calculate the number of received bytes in
the DMA buffer
    rx_data_length = RX_BUFFER_SIZE -
```

```c
    __HAL_DMA_GET_COUNTER(&hdma_usart2_rx);

    // Process the received data here (copy from
DMA buffer to your ring buffer)
    // For example, copy to your circular buffer or
queue

    // Restart the DMA for the next reception
    HAL_UART_Receive_DMA(&huart2, rx_buffer,
RX_BUFFER_SIZE);
  }
}

int main(void) {
  // Initialize the HAL and UART
  HAL_Init();
  MX_USART2_UART_Init();

  // Start the UART DMA receive
  HAL_UART_Receive_DMA(&huart2, rx_buffer,
RX_BUFFER_SIZE);

  while (1) {
    // Your application code here
  }
}
```

In this example, the idle line interrupt is used to

determine when data reception is completed. When the idle line is detected, the idle line interrupt triggers, and we calculate the number of received bytes in the DMA buffer. The DMA buffer stores the received data from the UART. After processing the received data (copying to your circular buffer or queue), the DMA is restarted for the next reception.

Note: The actual implementation of the circular buffer or queue is not shown in this simplified example. You would need to implement those data structures based on your specific application needs.

Remember to handle any other required UART interrupts (e.g., transmit complete, errors) and error conditions that may arise in your specific application.

Also, consider that this example does not include flow control, error handling, or other advanced features that you might need in a real-world application. Always refer to the STM32 reference manual and the HAL library documentation for your specific STM32 microcontroller to ensure proper implementation and usage of the UART, DMA, and interrupts.

STM32 USB CDC HOST AND DEVICE COMMUNICATE USING USB

And today we will see how to use communication class in USB. I will show the working of both host and device for the host I am using discovery of 411 microcontroller and STM 32 F 103 for the device. Let's start by creating a project for the host first like I mentioned I am using discovery F 411 for the host give some name here and click Finish I will clear the pinouts first I am selecting the external crystal for the clock in the USB OTG setup set the mode as host only and also enable the V bus post is responsible to give the power to the device and that's why we need the V bus to do so. You can see two pins for the USB and one for the V bus got selected here. This here is the schematics for this board. As you can see the buses connected to this IC here which can be controlled from the PC zero pin. When we pull up PCs zero to low the Enable pin gets activated and so does the voltage to the V bus.

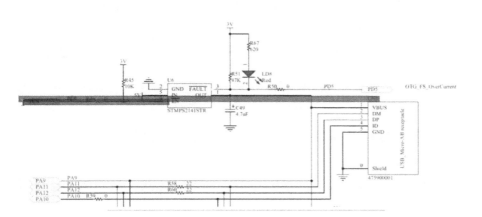

So I will set the PCs zero to low here now go to USB host and select the class as the communication host class. Click yes if there is a prompt you can see the V boss automatically took the PCs zero as the solution now let's go to the clock setup. It's already configured here so I don't need to do anything click Save to generate the project open the USB host dot c file here we have different states for the USB and we need to use them in our project I will copy this and the USB handle in the main file make sure you define them as the external variable let's include the USB C D C dot h file as we need to use some of the functions from there you can browse the file like this here we have maximum limit for the receive buffer and then we have all these functions that we will be using in our project. I am going to define a smaller buffer size since I am only expecting a small data from the device we have some more variables here.

These are the transfer and the receive buffers. I have defined and CDC type def here to switch between different states for the CDC. Actually we won't need the sense state I will send when the host is idle here is the CDC handler, it will switch between different CDC states if the state is idle, it will stop the CDC then copy the string into the transfer buffer and then transmit the data. Here the value will keep changing with every transmit. If the data transmission is successful, the status will change to receive and the variable will increment in the receive state post will receive the data from the device and store it in the RX buffer. Here the data size is the size of the RX buffer but it will only copy the amount the device is sending. Now, we will wait for a second and switch the stake to idle for the next transfer in the while loop, we will first check if the USB is ready for communication and if it is then call the CDC handle for processing the requests. That's all for the most part. Now let's create another project for the CDC device. I am using STM 32 F 103 C eight controller for the device give some name to the project and click Finish. First of all I am selecting external crystal for the clock select this and serial wire debug now select the USB device and you can see the two pins got selected here and in the settings select communication device class and leave everything to default let's configure the clock now it has already configured it I will just push it to the max Anyway that's all for the setup click Save to generate the project here we will write our code in the USB d c d c f dot c file first of all we have to deal with the line coding as you can see there are seven bytes involved here let's create a buffer to store these seven bytes. Now follow me. CDC receive will be called whenever the host sends the data and in the receive function, we will transmit the same data back to the host. I have defined a new length function because this function takes 16 bit integer whereas we have the pointer to a 32 bit integer. Let's build this now. No errors here.

So flash it to the board The flashing is dumb. Now let's go back to the host code and V bucket. I am going to put a breakpoint here in the transmit function. Also I have added the RX buffer to the live expression. Before starting it, let's take a look at the connection. Here you can see there is a USB connected between the host and the device. Also, the device is not powered from anywhere else as the host will be responsible to do so. That's basically all for the connection. Let's run it now. It hit the breakpoint. That means the USB is ready for the communication now. It hit again and now we have received the data from the device the value in the data is incrementing as well. Let's remove the breakpoint and let it run freely. Seems like it got stuck. Let's reset it and run again it's working pretty fine now. There seems to be some extra characters along with the data. I don't know where they are coming from.

STM32 USB MSC DEVICE USING RAM_SD CARD

We will see how to use USB mass storage class with all without using SD card. Let's start by creating the project in cube ID. I am using STM 32 F 407 Zed II give some name to the project and click finish here is our cube MX first of all, I am enabling the external crystal for the clock. Now go to USB OTG Fs and select Device only. In the USB device, select the mass storage class you can change the device descriptor here. In this first half I am going to show how to use mass storage without SD card and that's why I am not selecting SD i o go to the clock configuration now I have eight megahertz Crystal and I want the system to run at full 168 megahertz note that this 48 megahertz clock is also selected this is basically the clock for USB click Save to generate the project open USB D storage if dot c file.

This is the file where we are going to make all our changes let me first build this project as you can see here, the device have 123 kilobytes of free RAM and I am going to use this RAM as the storage Let's start then change the storage block number two twice the amount of RAM that you are going to use I want to use 100 kilobytes of this ram now create a buffer which can hold this 100 kilobytes of data storage block size is 512 and that's make this buffer 100 kilobytes in size next in the storage read function, we will copy the data from our assigned buffer into the buff. Same thing in the storage write function but this time copying will be the other way around. Let's build and debug this code let's run this as you can see there is no external drive here. Now I will connect the USB to the

STM 32 It's asking to format the disk so let's do that. You can see here the size is 100 kilobytes This is our mass storage disk of 100 kilobytes we can create a file write data and save it. Now I will remove the USB and connect it back and you can see the file is still available. But this is not always true. Sometimes it asked me to format the disk again. I am still working on how to solve this issue. Also see here that the RAM is almost full as we are using it as mass storage. Now I will show you how to use SD card as a mass storage. Let's go back to the cube MX leave USB configuration and select SDI oh four bit mode. As you can see here, these are the pins used for SD i o this is how the pins are connected to the module this is the timer diagram for STM 32 F four.

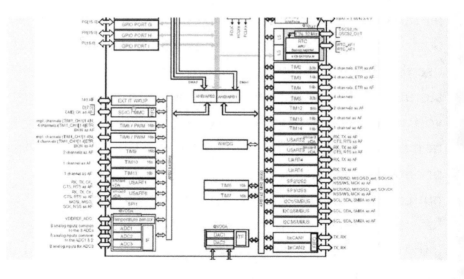

As you can see, the SD I O is connected to the APB two clock and the APB two is running at 84 megahertz. Now if you remembered the USB full speed clock is 12 megahertz so we need to bring SDI o to the same range as mentioned here, SDI o CK is equal to the SDI o clock divided by divide factor plus two APD clock is 84 megahertz so we need to divided by seven for the SD I O to become 12 therefore the divide factor will be five that's all for the setup now save to generate the project. Delete the USB D storage if dot c file and copy this USB storage file at the same position this file contains the functions needed for SD card to work I am commenting out the RAM related functions this function we'll get the size of the SD card this will be used to read the SD card and this one will be used to write the SD card let's build this notes that the round is free now again you can see there is no external storage right now. When I connect the USB the SD card is detected as the mass storage device. The card is one gigabyte in size these are some contents I was testing with initially I will copy this folder now. Let's see how much time it takes You can see this is only 2.3 megabytes folder I have removed the USB connection when connected back, you can see the files are still present. This sums up everything for this project. You can use the mass storage with or without SD card. speed is slow right now, but I will work on it. Maybe DMA can make it a bit faster.